THE THOUGHT OF KARL MARX

*the text of this book is printed
on 100% recycled paper*

Books by David McLellan
The Thought of Karl Marx
Marx Before Marxism

Edited and translated
The Grundrisse, by Karl Marx

THE THOUGHT
OF KARL MARX

An Introduction

DAVID McLELLAN

HARPER TORCHBOOKS
Harper & Row, Publishers
New York, Hagerstown, San Francisco, London

THE THOUGHT OF KARL MARX. Copyright © 1971 by David McLellan. All
rights reserved. Printed in the United States of America. No part of this
book may be used or reproduced in any manner whatsoever without written
permission except in the case of brief quotations embodied in critical articles
and reviews. For information address Harper & Row, Publishers, Inc.,
10 East 53rd Street, New York, N.Y.10022.

First HARPER TORCHBOOK edition published 1974

ISBN: 0-06-131839-6

78 79 80 81 82   10 9 8 7 6 5 4 3

*To all my students,
past and present*

Contents

PART TWO

Preface

THERE are several books designed to serve as introductions to Marx's thought. Books of selections cannot fulfil this function by themselves as selections need to be placed within a context and cannot be read continuously with much profit. Most commentaries, on the other hand, quote too little from Marx's writings and treat his ideas as a static system with little reference to any change or development in his ideas. When some of Marx's works are cited, the reader who has not much previous knowledge of Marx does not know what sort of a work is being quoted from, nor the circumstances under which it was written. It is therefore the aim of this book to provide the elementary groundwork essential for an understanding of Marx's thought by giving, in the first half, a straight descriptive account of Marx's writings in chronological order with a small amount of biographical detail; in the second half, a synoptic approach is adopted with an exposition of certain themes central to Marx's thought and relevant selections from his writings attached to each chapter. In reproducing these selections I have corrected existing translations where necessary and made my own where none existed previously. I have tried to include passages from some of the lesser known and untranslated writings of Marx – for example the drafts for the *Civil War in France* or Marx's remarks on Bakunin's *Statism and Anarchy* – as too many selections simply reproduce the material available in the Moscow *Selected Works* edition. As the book is merely an introduction, and thus necessarily superficial, I have added detailed lists of further reading rigorously restricted to books in English.

D. M.

Littlecroft,
Chilham,
Kent
January 1971

PART ONE

CHAPTER ONE

A. WRITINGS

Letter to his Father (1837)
Doctoral Thesis (1838–41)
Articles for the 'Rheinische Zeitung' (1842)
Critique of Hegel's Philosophy of Right (1843)

B. BIOGRAPHY

MARX was born in Trier in the Rhineland province of Prussia in 1818, as the third of eight children and the eldest son. His ancestors on both sides had for generations been rabbis. His father was a fairly prosperous lawyer, a man much influenced by the Enlightenment, a liberal and a patriot who had had himself baptised when his post was threatened by the anti-Jewish laws that followed the fall of Napoleon and the annexation of the Rhineland to Prussia. In 1830 Marx entered the High School in Trier where he stayed five years. In the school-leaving examination of 1835 he wrote, in suitably idealistic terms:

> When we have chosen the vocation in which we can contribute most to humanity, burdens cannot bend us because they are sacrifices for all. Then we experience no meagre, limited, egotistic joy, but our happiness belongs to millions, our deeds live on quietly but eternally effective, and glowing tears of noble men will fall on our ashes.[1]

The following year he attended the University of Bonn as a student in the Faculty of Law. Here he wrote poems feverishly, spent more money than any other student (according to his father), went in for duelling and was even imprisoned for 'disturbing the peace of the night with drunken noise'. After a year he transferred to Berlin, a university still under the domination of

[1] *Writings of the Young Marx on Philosophy and Society*, ed. L. Easton and K. Guddat (New York, 1967) p. 39.

Hegel's philosophy, where he remained until 1841. Here he turned over a new leaf and, as he said himself later, 'entirely avoided the society of his friends'. He signed on for all the lectures and, though he progressively withdrew from official university teaching, constantly worked himself to the point of exhaustion. In the summer of 1835 he had become secretly engaged to Jenny von Westphalen, the daughter of one of the most prestigious families in Trier and the Marx's next-door neighbours, an event which spurred him to fresh poetic efforts. During his first year, so he informed his father, as well as poetry he wrote a complex classification of legal concepts three hundred pages long, a new basic system of metaphysics, a comic novel, a tragic play, was converted to Hegelianism, and wrote a philosophical dialogue. Although Marx had thought of going in for law professionally, he came under the influence of a group of radical intellectuals at Berlin University and changed his chosen career to university teaching. He hoped to get a job at Bonn through the good offices of Bruno Bauer, a lecturer in theology who, because of his radical New Testament criticism, had been transferred there from Berlin. With a view to his academic career, Marx began a dry doctoral thesis on 'The Difference between the Natural Philosophies of Democritus and Epicurus'. It was submitted to the University of Jena and earned Marx the degree of Doctor of Philosophy.

In the summer of 1841 Marx went to Bonn. Bauer, however, was dismissed from his teaching post for unorthodox views, and Marx turned instead to journalism. The first few months of 1842 he spent at Trier and wrote his first article for the *Deutsche Jahrbücher*, a journal edited by Arnold Ruge, to whom Marx had been recommended by Karl Köppen, the closest of Marx's Berlin friends. In April Marx moved back to Bonn and began to write regularly for the *Rheinische Zeitung*, a recently-founded daily paper: its finance came from liberal Rhenish industrialists who saw in it a vehicle for the promotion of free trade, but the moving spirit in its foundation was Moses Hess, the first German Communist. Marx already made a strong impression on his contemporaries, as the following extract from a letter of Hess to a friend shows:

The greatest, perhaps the only, genuine philosopher now alive, who will soon attract the eyes of all Germany, Dr Marx will give medieval religion and politics their *coup de grâce*. He combines the deepest philosophical seriousness with the most biting wit. Imagine Rousseau, Voltaire, Holbach, Lessing, Heine and Hegel, fused into one person – fused, I say, not juxtaposed – and you have Dr Marx.[1]

Marx began his collaboration with the *Rheinische Zeitung* with an article on the freedom of the Press and a reply to a rival paper's attack on the *Rheinische Zeitung* for publishing novel opinions on philosophy and religion. Marx spent July and August in Trier, but, his father having died in 1838, he became more and more estranged from his family. In October Marx took over the editorship of the *Rheinische Zeitung* and published articles adopting a neutral position vis-à-vis communism, attacking the laws forbidding the collection of lumber by the poor and exposing the misery of the Moselle wine-growers. In March the paper was suppressed following an attack on Russian absolutism and Marx wrote to Ruge, with whom he planned to edit a radical journal in Zürich: 'As soon as the contract is completed, I will go to Kreuznach and get married.'

Paris was decided on as the base for the new journal, which was to be called – anticipating collaboration from the French socialists – *Deutsch-Französische Jahrbücher*. In June Marx married Jenny von Westphalen after their seven-year engagement and settled in his mother-in-law's house until October. Here he read widely on the history of the French Revolution and wrote a long critique of Hegel's political philosophy. In October he left for Paris with Jenny, who was three months pregnant, to take up his post as editor of the *Deutsch-Französische Jahrbücher*.

C. Commentary

Marx's writings up to the end of 1843 show a development through successive stages of idealism – romantic and then Hegelian – to liberal rationalism and his first critique of Hegel, where many of the key theories in Marx's thought occur for the first time.

[1] M. Hess, *Briefwechsel*, ed. E. Silberner (The Hague, 1959) p. 80.

The first documents of Marx that survive are his school-leaving essays of 1835. Some commentators have thought that they saw the germs of historical materialism in such remarks as 'our social relations, to some extent, have already begun to form before we are in a position to determine them'; but the essays only exhibit the simple youthful idealism proclaiming that 'man's nature makes it possible for him to reach his fulfilment only by working for the perfection and welfare of his society'.[1]

Much more interesting is Marx's *Letter to his Father*, written in November 1837, which gives an account of his intellectual development during his first year at Berlin. His main concern on arrival was lyrical poetry in an extremely idealistic vein, of which he offered the following self-criticism:

> I attacked the present, feeling was expressed without moderation or form, nothing was natural, everything built of moonshine; I believed in a complete opposition between what is and what ought to be and rhetorical reflections occupied the place of poetic thoughts though there was perhaps also a certain warmth of emotion and desire for exuberance. These are the characteristics of all the poems of the first three volumes that Jenny received from me.[2]

He also attempted a philosophy of law in which his main problem was the conflict – peculiar to idealism – between what is and what ought to be. Marx abandoned the project when he discovered that his idealism, inspired by Kant and Fichte, however internally coherent, had no connection with any actual law. So he returned to pure philosophy and wrote a new metaphysics which he equally rejected as futile. However, during convalescence from an illness brought on by overwork, he 'got to know Hegel from beginning to end and most of his disciples as well' and, although previously he 'had read fragments of Hegel's philosophy, but did not care for its grotesque and rocky melody', Marx found in Hegel the solution to his previous problems of the gap between the ideal and the real. 'I left behind the idealism which, by the way, I had nourished with that of Kant and Fichte, and came to seek the idea in the real itself. If the Gods had before dwelt above the earth they had now become its centre.' This reluctant conversion was reinforced by

[1] *Writings of the Young Marx*, p. 39.
[2] K. Marx, *Early Texts*, ed. D. McLellan (Oxford, 1971) pp. 2 f.

discussions with radical Young Hegelian friends at the university in which, he said, 'I attached myself ever more closely to the current philosophy that I had thought to escape'.[1]

For the next two years Marx was working on his doctoral thesis. This he dedicated to his father-in-law, Baron von Westphalen, who admired the French socialist Saint-Simon and was for Marx 'the living proof that idealism is no figment of the imagination but the true reality'. The body of the thesis compared the theories of Democritus and Epicurus on the movement of atoms. Marx criticised Democritus' strict determinism and came out in favour of Epicurus' position of freedom of man's consciousness to change his surroundings.

Although the thesis itself is of no great interest, the preface, preparatory studies and notes are more personal. In the preface Marx explained that his thesis was only a preliminary to a longer work that would deal with the whole cycle of Epicurean, Stoic and Sceptic philosophy in their relation to Greek thought as a whole. Hegel, continued Marx, had given an accurate account of the systems in the history of philosophy but, 'gigantic thinker' though he was, had neither entered into detail nor realised their importance in the history of Greek philosophy. Marx explained that he had added an appendix on Plutarch's attack on Epicurus, since he wished to defend Epicurus' view of the radical opposition between philosophy and religion. This was a matter of concern to all the Young Hegelians (as the radical disciples of Hegel were called), as Hegel had claimed that philosophy and religion had different forms but the same content, whereas the Young Hegelians considered religion as essentially irrational and saw the loosening of the Church's grip on the Prussian state as a precondition of any progress. Marx echoed this sentiment by proclaiming: 'philosophy makes no secret of it. Prometheus' confession "in a word, I detest all the Gods", is its own confession, its own slogan against all Gods in heaven and earth who do not recognise man's self-consciousness as the highest divinity.'[2]

The preparatory notes indicate the reasons for Marx's choosing this subject. Bruno Bauer, as a New Testament critic, was interested in Greek philosophy and, more importantly, Marx saw a parallel between Greek philosophy after the 'total' philosophy of Aristotle and his own situation as a post-Hegelian philosopher.

[1] Ibid. p. 8.   [2] Ibid. p. 13.

'Like Prometheus', he wrote, 'who stole fire from heaven and began to build houses and settle on the earth so philosophy which has evolved so as to impinge on the world, turns itself against the world that it finds. So now with the Hegelian philosophy.'[1]

Marx expands his views on the task of a post-Hegelian philosophy in a note appended to the thesis where he explains that the philosopher has to go beyond Hegel by employing Hegel's essential principles:

> It is conceivable that a philosopher should be guilty of this or that inconsistency because of this or that compromise; he may himself be conscious of it. But what he is not conscious of is that in the last analysis this apparent compromise is made possible by the deficiency of his principles or an inadequate grasp of them. So if a philosopher really has compromised it is the job of his followers to use the inner core of his thought to illuminate his own superficial expressions of it. In this way, what is a progress in conscience is also a progress in knowledge. This does not involve putting the conscience of a philosopher under suspicion, but rather construing the essential characteristics of his views, giving them a definite form and meaning, and thus at the same time going beyond them.[2]

Philosophy had now, according to Marx, to become practical:

> It is a psychological law that once the theoretical intellect has achieved freedom within itself it turns into practical energy and, emerging from the shadow kingdom of Amenthes at will, directs itself against the exterior reality of the world. . . . But the praxis of philosophy is itself theoretical. It is the sort of critique that measures individual existing things by their essence and particular realities by the idea. But this immediate realisation of philosophy is fraught with contradictions in its innermost essence and it is its essence that appears in the phenomena and imprints its seal on them.[3]

In a further note, Marx compares the revolutionary thought of the young Schelling with Schelling's recent lectures, and in particular attacks the proofs for the existence of God as empty tautologies. 'For example', he wrote, 'the ontological proof really

[1] K. Marx, *Early Texts*, ed. D. McLellan (Oxford 1971) p. 19.
[2] Ibid. p. 14.   [3] Ibid. p. 15.

merely amounts to this: what I really imagine is for me a real imagination. Anyone who brought a nomad God to the ancient Greeks would have the proof for the non-existence of this God for he did not exist for the Greeks: what a particular land is for particular foreign Gods, the land of reason is for God in general, an area in which his existence ceases.' Marx considered that, in reality, these proofs were nothing but 'proofs for the existence of an essentially human self-consciousness and logical explications of it'.[1]

These preparatory studies and notes were never published, nor was the thesis expanded, as Marx had intended. The impossibility of combining an academic career and his journalistic commitments drew his attention elsewhere. Thus his remarks are fragmentary and obscure; but they have an importance as they show Marx first grappling with problems of the philosophy of Hegel, problems that were to preoccupy him for the rest of his life.

During the year he spent in journalism, Marx wrote seven major articles. Here he seldom made his own ideas explicit, since he gave his articles the form of critical exegesis by exposing the absurdities in his opponents' ideas. For this he used any weapon to hand, usually combining a radical Hegelianism with the simple rationalism of the Enlightenment.

Marx's first article, written for Ruge's *Jahrbücher*, but rejected by the censorship and only published a year later, was entitled 'Comments on the Latest Prussian Censorship Instruction'. Marx exposed the inconsistencies of the new censorship regulations that were supposed to relax the prevailing ones. But since they forbade attacks on the Christian religion and offences against 'discipline, morals and outward loyalty', Marx considered that the 'censorship must reject the intellectual heroes of the morality – Kant, Fichte, Spinoza, for example – as irreligious and violating discipline, morals and exterior respectability. And these moralists start from a contradiction in principle between morality and religion, for morality is based on the autonomy of the human mind whereas religion is based on its heteronomy.'[2] Further, the new regulations were inimical to good law inasmuch as they were to punish 'tendencies' and 'intentions' instead of acts. For Marx, this was to create a society in which one organ thought of itself as the only possessor of reason and morality at the state level, whereas 'in an ethical state the view of the state is subordinated

[1] Ibid. p. 18.   [2] Ibid. pp. 29 f.

to its members, even if they oppose an organ of the state or the government'.[1] Marx was thus beginning to draw liberal democratic conclusions from Hegel's political philosophy.

Marx's first article for the *Rheinische Zeitung* was consecrated to the debates in the Rhenish Parliament and particularly to the 'Debates on Freedom of the Press and the Publication of Parliamentary Debates'. Marx found that the 'characteristic outlook of each class' was 'nowhere more clearly expressed than in these debates'. The speakers did not regard freedom as a natural gift to all rational men; for them it was 'an individual characteristic of certain persons and classes'. Such an attitude was incapable of drawing up any laws to govern the Press. For 'laws are positive, bright and generous norms, in which freedom has attained an expression that is impersonal, theoretical and independent of the arbitrariness of individuals'. Thus even proposed 'concessions' were inadequate, and Marx quoted Voltaire: 'these words, "liberties", "privileges" presuppose a state of subjection. Liberties are exemptions from a general servitude.'[2]

In an article on 'The Historical School of Law', Marx attacked some of his old teachers, and particularly Karl von Savigny, who had just become Minister of Justice. The Historical School held that historical existence was the prime justification of any law. Marx showed how such a view was both contradictory and tended to conserve existing political irrationalities.

Marx argued more specifically for the separation of Church and State in his reply to 'The Leading Article of the *Kölnische Zeitung*'. The editor of the *Kölnische Zeitung* had taken objection to Marx's views on censorship and advocated the suppression of philosophical and religious discussion in newspapers, claiming that it was the decline of religion that was the ruin of the ancient world. Marx thought the contrary: 'it was not the ruin of the ancient religions that entailed the fall of the states of antiquity but the fall of the states of antiquity that entailed the ruin of the ancient religions'.[3] The ideal of a Christian state was incompatible with rational freedom, a freedom which Marx at the end of his article described, in a very Hegelian manner:

> But if the previous professors of constitutional law have
> constructed the state from instincts either of ambition or

[1] *Writings of the Young Marx*, p. 80.
[2] *Early Texts*, p. 36.   [3] Ibid. p. 38.

sociability or even from reason, but from the individual's reason and not social reason, the profounder conception of modern philosophy deduces the state from the idea of the all. It considers the state to be the organism in which juridical, moral and political liberties must be realised and in which each citizen, by obeying the laws of the state, only obeys the natural laws of his own reason, human reason.[1]

In October 1842 Marx was forced for the first time to comment on socialist ideas. For the *Augsburger Zeitung* accused the *Rheinische Zeitung* of 'flirting with communism'. Marx's reply was ambivalent:

> the *Rheinische Zeitung* does not even concede theoretical validity to communist ideas in their present form, let alone desires their practical realisation, which it anyway finds impossible, and will subject these ideas to a fundamental criticism. If she had aims and capacities beyond well-polished phrases the *Augsburger* would have perceived that books like those of Leroux and Considérant and above all the acute work of Proudhon cannot be criticised by superficial and transitory fancies but only after consistent and probing study ... we are firmly convinced that the true danger does not lie in the practical attempt to carry out communist ideas but in their theoretical development; for practical attempts, even by the masses, can be answered with a cannon as soon as they become dangerous, but ideas that have overcome our intellect and conquered our conviction, ideas to which reason has riveted our conscience, are chains from which one cannot break loose without breaking one's heart; they are demons that one can only overcome by submitting to them.[2]

In his final articles for the *Rheinische Zeitung* Marx dealt with the 'Proceedings of the Rhenish Parliament on Thefts of Wood' and 'The Poverty of the Moselle Wine-growers'. These subjects, he stated later, 'provided the first occasions for occupying myself with economic questions'.[3] It was here that Marx realised how closely the laws were formed by the interests of the ruling class – in this case the forest owners. Marx concluded his article by

[1] Ibid. p. 42.   [2] Ibid. pp. 47 f.
[3] K. Marx, F. Engels, *Selected Works* (Moscow, 1962) I 362. (Hereafter referred to as *MESW*.)

comparing an independent observer's impression that wood was the Rhinelander's fetish with the belief of the Cuban savages that gold was the fetish of the Spaniards.

The article on the Moselle district went into great detail to substantiate the *Rheinische Zeitung*'s alarmist view of the poverty there. Marx laid great stress on the importance of economic conditions as a determinant of political action:

> In the investigation of political conditions one is too easily tempted to overlook the objective nature of the relationships and to explain everything from the will of the persons acting. There are relationships, however, which determine the actions of private persons as well as those of individual authorities, and which are as independent as are the movements in breathing. Taking this objective standpoint from the outset, one will not presuppose an exclusively good or bad will on either side. Rather, one will observe relationships in which only persons appear to act at first.[1]

When the suppression of the *Rheinische Zeitung* became imminent, Marx seized the opportunity to resign and, as he put it, 'to withdraw from the public stage into the study'.[2] The result of the month that Marx spent at Kreuznach was a 150-page-long critical commentary on Hegel's *Philosophy of Right* in which Marx's views on democracy, class and the abolition of the state began to take form.

Marx's fundamental criticism of Hegel was that, as in religion men had made God the Creator and man dependent on him, so Hegel started from the Idea of the State and made everything else – the family and various social groups – dependent on this Idea. Marx said:

> The Idea is thoroughly subjectivised. The actual relationship of family and civil society to the state is grasped as their inner imaginary activity. Family and civil society are the presuppositions of the state; they are really the active forms. But in speculation this is reversed. As the Idea is subjectivised, the actual subjects – civil society, family, etc. – become unactual objective moments of the Idea, meaning something else.[3]

[1] *Writings of the Young Marx*, pp. 144 f.
[2] *MESW* i 362. [3] *Early Texts*, p. 62.

Marx was inspired in this approach to Hegel by a fellow Young Hegelian, Ludwig Feuerbach. Feuerbach had declared that God was merely a projection of desires that man found himself powerless to realise and thus that man was the true 'subject' and God the 'predicate'. Feuerbach had recently applied this analysis to Hegel's metaphysics and now Marx applied it to Hegel's political philosophy, by stating:

It is important that Hegel always converts the Idea into the subject and the particular actual subject . . . into the predicate. But the development always takes place on the side of the predicate.[1]

The later sections of Marx's manuscript applied this general analysis to three particular issues that Hegel discussed – those of democracy, bureaucracy and suffrage.

In his comments on democracy Marx outlined a position that was humanist, since man was viewed as the basic factor in society; libertarian, in that man was considered to be a free subject; socialist, in that man was said to be a communal being; and finally Marx went beyond republicanism by predicting the abolition of the state. He said:

Hegel proceeds from the state and makes man into the state subjectivised. Democracy proceeds from man and makes the state into man objectivised. Just as religion does not create man, but man creates religion, so the constitution does not create the people, but the people create the constitution. . . . Democracy is the essence of every constitution, socialised man as a particular constitution. . . . Recently the French have conceived of this in such a way that the political state disappears in true democracy. This is true insofar as the political state as such, as constitution, no longer applies to the whole.[2]

Hegel had claimed that bureaucracy performed a mediating function between the state and different social groups. Marx, however, considered that bureaucracy encouraged the political divisions that were essential to its own existence and thus pursued its own ends to the detriment of the community at large.

The purposes of the state [he wrote] are changed into the purposes of bureaus and vice versa. Bureaucracy is a circle no

[1] *Writings of the Young Marx*, p. 159.   [2] *Early Texts*, pp. 65 f.

one can leave. Its hierarchy is a hierarchy of information. The top entrusts the lower circles with an insight into details, while the lower circles entrust the top with an insight into what is universal, and thus they mutually deceive each other.[1]

Hegel had made much of the competitive nature of entry into the bureaucracy, but for Marx

> . . . what counts in the genuine state is not the chance of any citizen to devote himself to the universal class as something special, but the capacity of the universal class to be actually universal, that is, to be the class of every citizen.[2]

Towards the end of his manuscript Marx explained how he thought the divisions in society could be overcome: the solution was to be found in universal suffrage.

> It is not a question whether civil society should exercise legislative power through deputies or through all as individuals. Rather it is a question of the extent and greatest possible universalisation of voting, of active as well as passive suffrage. This is the real bone of contention of political reform, in France as well as in England.[3]

Marx went on to describe, in his involved language, how universal suffrage would bring about the reform of civil society by bringing back to it the social essence of man as a communal being that had been stolen from him and transferred to the sphere of constitutions that had no effect on his real life:

> Only in unlimited voting, active as well as passive, does civil society actually rise to an abstraction of itself, to political existence as its true universal and essential existence. But the realisation of this abstraction is also the transcendence of the abstraction. By making its political existence actual as its true existence, civil society also makes its civil existence unessential in contrast to its political existence. And with the one thing separated, the other, its opposite falls. Within the abstract, political state, the reform of voting is the dissolution of civil society.[4]

---

[1] *Early Texts*, p. 69.   [2] *Writings of the Young Marx*, p. 190.
[3] Ibid. p. 201.   [4] Ibid. p. 202.

Engels stated that Marxism was composed of three elements: German idealist philosophy, French socialism and English economic theory. With his Feuerbachian critique of Hegel's political philosophy, Marx had largely assimilated the first element; the last two elements he obtained in Paris.

BIBLIOGRAPHY

TRANSLATIONS

Letter to Father, Doctoral Thesis, Newspaper articles
Excerpts in:
K. Marx, *Writings of the Young Marx on Philosophy and Society*, ed. L. Easton and K. Guddat (New York, 1967).
K. Marx, *The Early Texts*, ed. D. McLellan (Oxford, 1971).

Doctoral Thesis
D. Livergood, *Marx's Philosophy of Action* (The Hague, 1967).
H. Mins, 'Marx's Doctoral Dissertation', *Science and Society* (winter 1948).

Critique of Hegel's Philosophy of Right
K. Marx, *Critique of Hegel's Philosophy of Right*, ed. J. O'Malley (Cambridge, 1970).

COMMENTARIES

H. Adams, *Karl Marx in his Earlier Writings*, 2nd ed. (London, 1965).
S. Avineri, *The Social and Political Thought of Karl Marx* (Cambridge, 1968).
S. Avineri, 'The Hegelian Origins of Marx's Political Thought', *Review of Metaphysics* (Sept 1967).
C. Bailey, 'Karl Marx on Greek Atomism', *The Classical Quarterly* (1928).
L. Dupré, *The Philosophical Foundations of Marxism* (New York, 1966).
R. Garaudy, *Karl Marx: The Evolution of his Thought* (London, 1967).
W. Johnston, 'Marx's Verse of 1836–37', *Journal of the History of Ideas* (Apr 1967).
E. Kamenka, *The Ethical Foundations of Marxism* (London, 1962).
D. McLellan, *The Young Hegelians and Karl Marx* (London, 1969).
D. McLellan, *Marx before Marxism* (New York, 1970).
J. O'Malley, 'Methodology in Karl Marx', *Review of Politics* (1970).
R. Tucker, *Philosophy and Myth in Karl Marx* (Cambridge, 1961).

CHAPTER TWO

A. WRITINGS

A Correspondence of 1843 (1843)
On the Jewish Question (1843–4)
Towards a Critique of Hegel's Philosophy of Right: Introduction
   (1844)
Economic and Philosophical Manuscripts (1844)
Critical Notes on 'The King of Prussia and Social Reform' (1844)

B. BIOGRAPHY

MARX arrived in Paris in October 1843 and settled in the Quartier Latin, sharing a house – as an experiment in community living – with his co-editor Ruge, Herwegh and other German exiles. The first and last number of their *Deutsch-Französische Jahrbücher* was published in February 1844. Of the two essays of Marx's included in it, he had brought *On the Jewish Question* with him to Paris and had written *Towards a Critique of Hegel's Philosophy of Right: Introduction* when he got there. Marx was still reading material on the French Revolution and his friends gathered that he proposed to write a history of the Convention. At the same time he established contact with the 'League of the Just', a secret communist organisation founded in 1836, and attended workers' meetings. Marx's growing communist tendencies led to a break with Ruge, who saw nothing in communism but a desire to degrade everyone to the level of workman.

While in Paris, Marx began to pay more attention to the English economists Smith and Ricardo, reading them in French translation. Ruge described, in a letter of May 1844, Marx's feverish mode of study:

Marx has a peculiar nature, very fitted for study and writing, but a total loss as far as journalism is concerned. He reads an enormous amount; he works with uncommon intensity and has a critical talent that sometimes degenerates into a wanton dialectic, but he finishes nothing, is always breaking off and plunging afresh into an endless sea of books.[1]

The *Deutsch-Französische Jahrbücher* ceased publication after its first number: its editors were in violent disagreement; the French socialists, shocked by its advocacy of violence and atheism, refused collaboration; and the confiscation of many copies of the journal in Germany increased already pressing financial difficulties. Meanwhile Marx conceived the plan of writing a series of monographs dealing critically with law, ethics, politics, etc., and began to draw together material for the first of these. This, known as the *Economic and Philosophical Manuscripts* or *Paris Manuscripts*, contained extracts from the English economists, a description of humanist communism as an alternative to contemporary alienated society, and a critique of Hegel's *Phenomenology of Spirit*. In addition, Marx spent a lot of his time with the poets Heine and Herwegh, and sat up the whole night through discussing the Hegelian dialectic with Proudhon, the leading French socialist, and Bakunin, the exiled Russian anarchist.

In July Marx made public his break with Ruge by publishing in *Vorwärts*, a weekly paper for German workers in Paris, an attack on Ruge's view of the impossibility of revolution in Germany. In September Engels returned to the Continent after working in his father's factory in Manchester. He and Marx had met before when Marx was editor of the *Rheinische Zeitung* but Marx had received him coldly. Now, however, after fourteen days' almost continuous discussion, they found that their ideas were so similar that they decided immediately to collaborate on a book.

C. Commentary

A Correspondence of 1843, an exchange of letters among forthcoming contributors to the journal, published as the first item in the *Deutsch-Französische Jahrbücher*, shows how Marx's ideas

---

[1] A. Ruge, *Briefwechsel* etc., ed. P. Nerrlich (Berlin, 1886) I 343.

were developing. Already in his letter of May 1843 he hinted at the inevitable clash that the economic situation would produce:

> But the system of profit and commerce, of property and human exploitation leads much quicker than increase of population to a rift inside contemporary society that the old society is incapable of healing, because it never heals or creates, only exists and enjoys. The existence of a suffering humanity which thinks and a thinking humanity which is oppressed must of necessity be disagreeable and unacceptable for the animal world of philistines who neither act nor think but merely enjoy.
>
> On our side the old world must be brought right out into the light of day and the new one given a positive form. The longer that events allow thinking humanity time to recollect itself and suffering humanity time to assemble itself the more perfect will be the birth of the product that the present carries in its womb.[1]

In a further letter in September Marx defined what he conceived to be the policy of the journal: a 'reckless criticism of all that exists'; participation in the political struggle for a truly democratic state; and a reform of men's attitudes, not through socialist or communist dogma, but through 'the analysis of mystical consciousness that is not clear to itself, whether it appears in religious or political form'.[2]

Marx began this programme of 'reckless criticism' with a review essay of two of Bruno Bauer's writings on the Jewish question. Marx was criticising here, through Bauer, his own idealistic political ideas in his articles for the *Rheinische Zeitung*.

The general theme of Marx's essay was to contrast political emancipation, which liberated man as little as religion, with human emancipation which could only be achieved through the disappearance of the state and of money.

Bauer's answer to the Jews who demanded religious emancipation was that this was impossible without political emancipation. For in order to cease discriminating against Jews, the state must cease being Christian. But for Marx this answer did not go far enough: Bauer had only subjected the Christian state to his criticism, not the state as such; thus he had not been able to see the link between political emancipation and human emancipation.

[1] *Early Texts*, p. 79.   [2] Ibid. p. 82.

Plainly, abolition of religion from the political sphere was not the answer, for the United States of America, where this had been achieved, was yet notorious for its religiosity.

But since the existence of religion is the existence of a defect, the source of this defect can only be sought in the nature of the state itself. Religion for us no longer has the force of a basis for secular deficiencies but only that of a phenomenon. We do not change secular questions into theological ones. We change theological questions into secular ones. History has for long enough been resolved into superstition: we now resolve superstition into history. The question of the relationship of political emancipation to religion becomes for us a question of the relationship of political emancipation to human emancipation.[1]

The limitations of political emancipation were shown by the fact that the state could free itself from religion without its citizens being freed. Indeed, the existence of religion was thereby presupposed, as was the existence of private property by its abolition as a qualification for voting. This kind of problem arose because man was split into a dual personality: the communal, social aspect of his nature only existed, in an unreal form, at the level of constitutions and talk of 'citizenship', whereas in his real everyday life he was an isolated individual involved in the economic war of all against all.

Man has a life both in the political community, where he is valued as a communal being, and in civil society where he is active as a private individual, treats other men as means, degrades himself to a means and becomes the plaything of alien powers.[2]

Marx then discussed Bauer's view that neither Jews nor Christians could claim the universal rights of man, since they proclaimed themselves to be particular and exclusive sorts of human beings. Marx, however, rejected the whole notion of the rights of man in a discussion that contains his most accessible criticism of classical liberal principles. He began by quoting the American Declaration of the Rights of Man to show that these rights were not only compatible with religion but actually guaranteed its free exercise. For Marx the rights of man were the

[1] Ibid. p. 91.   [2] Ibid. p. 94.

rights of the atomised, mutually hostile individuals of civil society.
Quoting the French Revolutionary Constitution of 1793, he said:

> The right of man to freedom is not based on the union of man
> with man, but on the separation of man from man. It is the right
> to this separation, the right of the limited individual who is
> limited to himself. . . . The right of man to property is the right
> to enjoy his possessions and dispose of the same arbitrarily,
> without regard for other men, independently from society, the
> right of selfishness. It is the former individual freedom together
> with its latter application that forms the basis of civil society.
> It leads man to see in other men not the realisation but the
> limitation of his own freedom.[1]

Marx continued with a contrast between the Middle Ages
whose feudal society included at least some communal aspects and
the post-1789 society which considered the realm of needs, labour,
private interest and private right as its neutral basis. Marx ended
the first of his reviews with the following sketch of his own solution
to the problem:

> Political emancipation is the reduction of man, on the one
> hand to a member of civil society, an egoistic and independent
> individual, on the other hand to a citizen, a moral person.
> The actual individual man must take the abstract citizen
> back into himself and, as an individual man in his empirical
> life, in his individual work and individual relationships, become
> a species-being; man must recognise his own forces as social
> forces, organise them and thus no longer separate social forces
> from himself in the form of political forces. Only when this has
> been achieved will human emancipation be completed.[2]

In his review of Bauer's second article, Marx discussed Bauer's
view that, in order to achieve emancipation, the Jew would also
have to emancipate himself from Christianity which was one step
nearer emancipation than Judaism. Once again Marx reversed
Bauer's theological formulation of the question and asked: what
specific *social* elements need to be overcome in order to abolish
Judaism? Playing on the double meaning of Judaism, which in
German meant also 'commerce', Marx discovered the roots of

[1] *Early Texts*, p. 103.   [2] Ibid. p. 108.

Judaism in the commercial spirit and particularly in the importance ascribed to money. This led him to adumbrate for the first
time the theory of alienated labour that was to be so central to
his thought.

Money is the universal, self-constituted value of all things. It
has therefore robbed the whole world, human as well as natural,
of its own values. Money is the alienated essence of man's work
and being, this alien essence dominates him and he adores it.

Marx continued:

Under the domination of egoistic need man can only become
practical, only create practical objects by putting his products
and his activity under the domination of an alien entity and
lending them the significance of an alien entity – money.[1]

In his analysis of Bauer's views Marx had already moved from
the sphere of politics to the one he was henceforth to regard as
fundamental – that of economics. But though he proclaimed the
goal of full human emancipation, he had yet to identify the means
to achieve it. That was the task of his next article.

Marx's second article for the *Deutsch-Französische Jahrbücher*
was one of the most scintillating pieces that he ever wrote. It was
intended as an introduction to the unpublished *Critique of Hegel's
Philosophy of Right* which he hoped to write up for publication.
Beginning with his famous epigrams on religion, Marx posed the
problem of the backwardness of Germany in all but the philosophical field, and finished with the *dénouement* – a proletarian
revolution.

Religious alienation was to Marx a problem that he had
already got beyond, and his first few sentences summed up what
was already past history:

As far as Germany is concerned, the criticism of religion is
essentially complete, and the criticism of religion is the
presupposition of all criticism.

The foundation of irreligious criticism is this: man makes
religion, religion does not make man. But man is no abstract
being squatting outside the world. Man is the world of man,
the state, society. This state, this society, produces religion's

[1] Ibid. p. 114.

inverted attitude to the world, because they are an inverted
world themselves. Thus the struggle against religion is indirectly the struggle against that world whose spiritual aroma is
religion . . . .

Religion is the sigh of the oppressed creature, the feeling of a
heartless world and the soul of soulless circumstances. It is the
opium of the people. . . . The first task of philosophy, which is
in the service of history, once the holy form of human self-
alienation has been discovered, is to discover self-alienation in
its unholy forms. The criticism of heaven is thus transformed
into the criticism of earth, the criticism of religion into the
criticism of law, and the criticism of theology into the criticism
of politics.[1]

This 'criticism of politics' was highly appropriate, according to
Marx, for Germany was, by French standards, still pre-1789.
The duty of political commentators was to proclaim this fact until
it became unbearable:

The point is not to allow the Germans a moment of self-deceit
or resignation. We must make the actual oppression even more
oppressive by making them conscious of it, and the insult even
more insulting by publicising it.[2]

The one hope for Germany lay in her political philosophy, which
was very progressive; the Germans had *thought* what other nations
had *done*. So to criticise this philosophy and progress beyond it
would show, at least theoretically, what the future of society was
to be. But, to have any effect, philosophy needed a practical
counterpart. So Marx put the question:

Can Germany attain to a *praxis* that will be equal to her
principles, i.e. can she attain to revolution that will not only
raise her to the official level of modern peoples, but to the
human level that is the immediate future of these peoples?[3]

Marx's answer shows his radical humanist tendencies:

The weapon of criticism cannot, of course, supplant the
criticism of weapons, material force must be overthrown by
material force. But theory, too, will become material force as
soon as it seizes the masses. Theory is capable of seizing the
masses as soon as its proofs are *ad hominem* and its proofs are

[1] *Early Texts*, pp. 115 f.   [2] Ibid. p. 118.   [3] Ibid. p. 122.

ad hominem as soon as it is radical. To be radical is to grasp the matter by the root. But for man the root is man himself. The manifest proof of the radicalism of German theory and its practical energy is that it starts from the decisive and positive abolition of religion. The criticism of religion ends with the doctrine that man is the highest being for man, that is, with the categorical imperative to overthrow all circumstances in which man is humiliated, enslaved, abandoned and despised.[1]

The difficulty obviously lay in finding 'a passive element, a material basis' necessary to revolution. Marx considered that a partial revolution, a revolution which left 'the pillars of the house still standing' was impossible in Germany. For the essence of partial revolution – Marx was thinking particularly of 1789 – was that a particular class found itself able to identify itself with the aims and desires of society as a whole. But in supine Germany no class seemed to be in a position to realise this. So Marx put the question: 'So where is the real possibility of a German emancipation?' And he answered, almost in the form of a manifesto:

In the formation of a class with radical chains, a class in civil society that is not a class of civil society, of a social group that is the dissolution of all social groups, of a sphere that has a universal character because of its universal sufferings and lays claim to no particular right, because it is the object of no particular injustice but of injustice in general. This class can no longer lay claim to a historical status, but only to a human one. It is, finally, a sphere that cannot emancipate itself without emancipating itself from all other spheres of society and thereby emancipating these other spheres themselves. In a word, it is the complete loss of humanity and thus can only recover itself by a complete redemption of humanity. This dissolution of society, as a particular class, is the proletariat. . . .

As philosophy finds in the proletariat its material weapons so the proletariat finds in philosophy its intellectual weapons and as soon as the lightning of thought has struck deep into the virgin soil of the people, the emancipation of the Germans into men will be completed.[2]

Having become clear as to the vehicle of revolution, Marx once more 'withdrew into the study' and applied himself to the study

[1] Ibid. pp. 122 f.   [2] Ibid. pp. 127 f.

of economics and philosophy, the result of which was the *Paris Manuscripts*. These contain three main sections: the first is on the alienation of labour, the second on private property and communism, and the third is a critique of Hegel's dialectic.

The section on alienated labour is preceded by extracts or paraphrases on capital, wages and rent from the books that Marx was reading at the time, largely under the inspiration of Engels's essay *Outlines of a Critique of Political Economy* published in the *Deutsch-Französische Jahrbücher*. Marx summed up his conclusions from his reading as follows:

> Using the very words of political economy we have demonstrated that the worker is degraded to the most miserable sort of commodity; that the misery of the worker is in inverse proportion to the power and size of his production; that the necessary result of competition is the accumulation of capital in a few hands, and thus a more terrible restoration of monopoly; and that finally the distinction between capitalist and landlord, and that between peasant and industrial worker disappears and the whole of society must fall apart into the two classes of the property owners and the propertyless workers.[1]

Marx goes on to analyse the phenomenon that he considered to be at the root of the capitalist system and that he called alienated labour. Alienated labour had four aspects to it. Firstly, the worker was related to the product of his labour as to an alien object; it stood over and above him, opposed to him with a power independent of the producer. Secondly, the worker became alienated from himself in the very act of production; for the worker did not view his work as part of his real life and did not feel at home in it. Thirdly, man's 'species-life', his social essence, was taken away from him in his work which did not represent the harmonious efforts of man as a 'species-being'. Fourthly, man found himself alienated from other men. Marx then spelled out the relationship of alienated labour to private property:

> We have, of course, obtained the concept of externalised labour (externalised life) from political economy as the result of the movement of private property. But it is evident from the analysis of this concept, that although private property appears to be the ground and reason for externalised labour, it is rather a

[1] *Early Texts*, p. 133.

consequence of it, just as the gods are originally not the cause but the effect of the aberration of the human mind, although later this relationship reverses itself.[1]

This analysis represented the negative side of Marx's views: the positive side is contained in notes on James Mill that Marx wrote about the same time. After describing the mutual deception and pillage of capitalism, he outlined, in philosophical and almost lyrical tones, his conception of the truly human society:

> Supposing that we had produced in a human manner; each of us would in his production have doubly affirmed himself and his fellow men. I would have: (1) objectified in my production my individuality and its peculiarity and thus both in my activity enjoyed an individual expression of my life and also in looking at the object have had the individual pleasure of realising that my personality was objective, visible to the senses and thus a power raised beyond all doubt. (2) In your enjoyment or use of my product I would have had the direct enjoyment of realising that I had both satisfied a human need by my work and also objectified the human essence and therefore fashioned for another human being the object that met his need. (3) I would have been for you the mediator between you and the species and thus been acknowledged and felt by you as a completion of your own essence and a necessary part of yourself and have thus realised that I am confirmed both in your thought and in your love. (4) In my expression of my life I would have fashioned your expression of your life, and thus in my own activity have realised my own essence, my human, my communal essence.[2]

In the second main section of the *Manuscripts*, Marx describes his solution to the problem of alienation – communism. This communism, according to Marx, was the outcome of the ideas of the French socialists Proudhon, Fourier and Saint-Simon, and itself had stages: the first Marx called 'crude communism' in which 'the domination of material property is so great that it wishes to destroy everything that cannot be possessed by everybody as private property'.[3] It was the negation of all culture and civilisation, and, typically, intended to replace marriage by the community of women. The second stage of communism either still

---

[1] Ibid. p. 146.　　[2] Ibid. p. 202.　　[3] Ibid. p. 146.

wished to conserve the state, whether a despotic or a democratic one, or at least was still obsessed by the notion of private property. Marx's description of the third and final stage of communism was almost mystical in tone:

... communism as the positive abolition of private property and thus of human self-alienation and therefore the real reappropriation of the human essence by and for man. This is communism as the complete and conscious return of man conserving all the riches of previous development for man himself as a social, i.e. human being. Communism as completed naturalism is humanism and as completed humanism is naturalism. It is the genuine solution of the antagonism between man and nature and between man and man. It is the true solution of the struggle between existence and essence, between objectification and self-affirmation, between freedom and necessity, between individual and species. It is the solution to the riddle of history and knows itself to be this solution.[1]

Marx then expanded on the characteristics of true communism: in it, society produced man and was produced by him; man's proper relationship to nature was restored, he dominated it and thus achieved 'the fulfilled naturalism of man and humanism of nature'; this enabled man to lay hold on his essence in a complete, and no longer in a one-sided manner; finally this process would be able to be studied by a single science, a fusion of the natural and the human sciences. Marx ended this section with an unsatisfactory attempt to rebut Aristotle's proof of the existence of God, which he broke off by declaring that atheism had become as irrelevant for socialist man as the denial of private property had for a communist.

The third and final section was devoted to a critique of Hegel's dialectic as found in his most famous work, the *Phenomenology of Spirit*. Marx began by paying tribute to the achievements of Feuerbach, particularly in having shown that Hegel's philosophy was no more than a rationalised theology, and having discovered the true materialist approach by starting from the social relationship of man to man. Marx's attitude to Hegel was ambivalent:

The greatness of Hegel's *Phenomenology* and its final product, the dialectic of negativity as the moving and creating principle,

[1] *Early Texts*, p. 148.

is on the one hand that Hegel conceives of the self-creation of man as a process, objectification as loss of the object, as externalisation and the transcendence of this externalisation. This means, therefore, that he grasps the nature of labour and understands objective man, true, because real, man as the result of his own labour.[1]

But on the other hand this whole dialectic was viewed from an idealist standpoint: 'The appropriation of man's objectified and alienated faculties, is thus first only an appropriation that occurs in the mind, in pure thought, i.e. in abstraction.'[2] Marx, however, started from the 'real man of flesh and blood, standing on the solid round earth and breathing in and out all the powers of nature'[3] and defined his position as a consistent naturalism or humanism that avoided both idealism and materialism. The rest of the section contains an obscure and involved justification of his basic criticism of Hegel – that Hegel had mistakenly identified alienation with objectification (the existence of material objects) and thus thought that it could be overcome simply in the mind.

In his anti-Ruge article of July 1844, Marx continued his remarks on the political state made in his *On the Jewish Question*. What was needed was not political revolt but social revolution, for any worth-while conception of democracy had to go beyond the political state.

> Revolution in general [wrote Marx] – the overthrow of the existing power and dissolution of previous relationships – is a political act. Socialism cannot be realised without a revolution. But when its organising activity begins, when its peculiar aims, its soul comes forward, then socialism casts aside its political cloak.[4]

BIBLIOGRAPHY

TRANSLATIONS

A Correspondence of 1843

Writings of the Young Marx on Philosophy and Society, ed. L. Easton and K. Guddat (New York, 1967).
K. Marx, *The Early Texts*, ed. D. McLellan (Oxford, 1971).

[1] Ibid. p. 164.   [2] Ibid. p. 163.   [3] Ibid. p. 167.   [4] Ibid. p. 221.

On the Jewish Question

K. Marx, *A World without Jews*, ed. D. Runes (New York, 1959).
K. Marx, *Early Writings*, ed. T. Bottomore (London, 1963).
Writings of the Young Marx on Philosophy and Society, ed. L. Easton and K. Guddat (New York, 1967).
K. Marx, *The Early Texts*, ed. D. McLellan (Oxford, 1971).

Towards a Critique of Hegel's Philosophy of Right: Introduction

K. Marx and F. Engels, *On Religion* (Moscow, n.d.).
K. Marx, *Early Writings*, ed. T. Bottomore (London, 1963).
Writings of the Young Marx on Philosophy and Society, ed. L. Easton and K. Guddat (New York, 1967).
K. Marx, *The Early Texts*, ed. D. McLellan (Oxford, 1971).

Economic and Philosophical Manuscripts

K. Marx, *Economic and Philosophical Manuscripts*, trans. M. Milligan (London, 1959).
K. Marx, *Early Writings*, ed. T. Bottomore (London, 1963).
Writings of the Young Marx on Philosophy and Society, ed. L. Easton and K. Guddat (New York, 1967).
K. Marx, *The Early Texts*, ed. D. McLellan (Oxford, 1971).

Critical Notes on 'The King of Prussia and Social Reform'

Writings of the Young Marx on Philosophy and Society, ed. L. Easton and K. Guddat (New York, 1967).
K. Marx, *The Early Texts*, ed. D. McLellan (Oxford, 1971).

COMMENTARIES

H. Adams, *Karl Marx in his Earlier Writings*, 2nd ed. (London, 1965).
L. Althusser, *For Marx* (London, 1970).
S. Avineri, 'Marx and Jewish Emancipation', *Journal of the History of Ideas* (1964).
S. Avineri, *The Social and Political Thought of Karl Marx* (Cambridge, 1968).
T. Bottomore, introduction to K. Marx, *Early Writings* (London, 1963).
L. Dupré, *The Philosophical Foundations of Marxism* (New York, 1966).
E. Fromm, *Marx's Concept of Man* (New York, 1961).
R. Garaudy, *Karl Marx: The Evolution of his Thought* (London, 1967).
E. Kamenka, *The Ethical Foundations of Marxism* (London, 1962).
H. Lefebvre, *Dialectical Materialism* (London, 1969).
D. McLellan, *The Young Hegelians and Karl Marx* (London, 1969).
D. McLellan, *Marx before Marxism* (New York, 1970).
D. Struik, introduction to *Economic and Philosophical Manuscripts* (London, 1959).
R. Tucker, *Philosophy and Myth in Karl Marx* (Cambridge, 1961).

CHAPTER THREE

A. Writings

The Holy Family (1844–5)
Theses on Feuerbach (1845)
The German Ideology (1846)
Letter to Annenkov (1846)
The Poverty of Philosophy (1847)

B. Biography

IN January 1845 the French Government, under pressure from Prussia, issued an order expelling the leading collaborators of *Vorwärts*, and Marx left Paris for Brussels the following month. Before he left, he had completed his first joint work with Engels, entitled *The Holy Family*, by which was meant Marx's former colleagues Bruno Bauer and his friends. Marx had also signed a contract with a Darmstadt publisher for a book on *Politics and Economics*.

Engels organised a collection among their mutual friends to defray the financial expenses that his deportation caused Marx. He settled in Brussels, where he remained for the next three years and renewed his studies in economics. In the summer of 1845 Engels came to Brussels and there began the period of continuous co-operation between the two that ended only with Marx's death. They began by undertaking a trip to England to study conditions there; in London they met exiled members of the League of the Just, including Wilhelm Weitling. In October, following the birth of his second daughter Laura, Marx applied for permission to emigrate to the United States, but took no further steps, though he renounced his Prussian citizenship at the end of the year. During the last three months of 1845, Marx and Engels were occupied in writing *The German Ideology*, another long tract directed against Feuerbach, Bauer, Stirner, etc.

Early in 1846 Marx and Engels took the opportunity of their recent visit to London to found a network of communist correspondence committees to keep German, French and English socialists informed about each other's ideas and activities. In March there was a violent argument in the Brussels committee between Marx and Weitling, then on a visit to Belgium. Marx opposed Weitling's appeals to the workers for an immediate revolutionary insurrection, saying, according to Weitling, that 'the bourgeoisie must first come to the helm'.[1] The committee decided in favour of Marx. In May Proudhon was invited to represent Paris on the network. Proudhon's reply was friendly but contained the words: 'Let us not set ourselves up as the masters of a new intolerance, let us not rise up as the apostles of a new religion, even though the religion be one of logic or reason.'[2] The Darmstadt publisher was pressing Marx for the manuscript he had promised, but his work on this was interrupted by news from Engels in Paris of Proudhon's new book on economics. Marx outlined his first reactions in December in his *Letter to Annenkov*, a Russian *émigré* interested in socialism.

Early in 1847 Marx wrote *The Poverty of Philosophy*, a reply to Proudhon's book which had been subtitled *The Philosophy of Poverty*. The League of the Just in London invited Marx and Engels to join them in an enlarged Communist League. The first congress of the League was held in London in June: Engels attended, though Marx was prevented by lack of money. Marx continued writing articles for the German Press and speaking at propaganda meetings in Brussels.

C. COMMENTARY

1. *The Holy Family*

The book contains much sarcastic, and often turgid, polemic that is of little permanent interest. This is particularly so of the long sections dealing with the comments of Bauer's followers on the novel of Eugène Sue, *The Mysteries of Paris*. These comments endeavoured to show, in a Hegelian manner, that Sue's novel

[1] Cf. Hess, *Briefwechsel*, p. 151.
[2] Quoted in P. Haubtmann, *Marx et Proudhon* (Paris, 1957) p. 57.

contained the key to the 'mysteries' of modern society. Marx criticised at great length both this vapourising interpretation and also the moralising tone of the novelist himself. The three sections of real interest in the book are Marx's replies to Bauer's attacks on Proudhon, on the role of the masses in history, and on materialism.

(i) Marx praised Proudhon as the first thinker to have questioned the existence of private property and to have demonstrated the inhuman results it had for society. Marx then summarised his own view of the relationship between private property and the proletariat:

> The propertied class and the class of the proletariat represent the same human self-alienation. But the former feels comfortable and confirmed in this self-alienation, knowing that this alienation is its own power and possessing in it the semblance of a human existence. The latter feels itself ruined in this alienation and sees in it its impotence and the actuality of an inhuman existence. . . . The proletariat executes the sentence that private property inflicts on itself by creating the proletariat just as it carries out the verdict that wage-labour pronounces on itself by creating wealth for others and misery for itself. When the proletariat triumphs, it does not thereby become the absolute side of society because it triumphs only by transcending itself and its opposite. Then the proletariat and its determining antithesis, private property, disappear.[1]

In answer to the criticism that socialist writers, by attributing this historic role to the proletariat, seemed to consider them as gods, Marx continued:

> It is not a question of what this or that proletarian or even the whole proletariat momentarily imagines to be the aim. It is a question of what the proletariat is and what it consequently is historically compelled to do. Its aim and historical action is prescribed, irrevocably and obviously, in its own situation in life as well as in the entire organisation of contemporary civil society.[2]

(ii) Bauer wished to oppose his philosophy to the mass of the people and considered the operative force in society to be ideas

---

[1] *Writings of the Young Marx*, pp. 367 f.   [2] Ibid. p. 368.

or even history itself personified. Marx's view was the opposite: 'History . . . does not use man to realise its own ends, as though it were a particular person: it is merely the activity of man pursuing his own objectives.'[1] Or again: 'Ideas never lead beyond the established situation, they only lead beyond the ideas of the established situation. Ideas can accomplish absolutely nothing. To become real, ideas require men who apply a practical force.'[2] For Bauer, the ideas of an intellectual élite were threatened by popular contact and he believed that the ideas of the French Revolution had been corrupted by the enthusiasm of the masses. For Marx, on the other hand, these ideas had not sufficiently penetrated the masses and the bourgeoisie had been able to turn the French Revolution to its own profit. Bauer made much of the 'human rights' embodied in the French Revolution. But Marx, pursuing the theme of his *On the Jewish Question*, declared that it was only a ruthless egoism that had been really emancipated.

(iii) Marx also disagreed with Bauer on the significance of French materialism. Bauer held that the materialist movement in France was a direct descendant of Spinoza's metaphysical monism. Marx wished to emphasise the anti-metaphysical humanist aspects of French materialists such as Helvétius and Holbach. He traced the influence of the materialist doctrine of the eighteenth-century social philosophers in socialism and communism:

If man forms all his knowledge, perception, etc., from the world of sense and experience in the world of sense, then it follows that the empirical world must be so arranged that he experiences and gets used to what is truly human in it, that he experiences himself as a man. If enlightened interest is the principle of all morality, it follows that man's private interests should coincide with human interests. If man is unfree in the material-istic sense – that is, free not through the negative capacity to avoid this or that but through the positive power to assert his true individuality – crime must not be punished in the individual but the anti-social sources of crime must be destroyed to give everyone social scope for the essential assertion of his vitality. If man is formed by circumstances, then his circumstances must be made human. If man is by nature social, then he

[1] K. Marx, F. Engels, *The Holy Family* (Moscow, 1956) p. 125.
[2] Ibid. p. 160.

develops his true nature only in society and the power of his nature must be measured not by the power of the single individual but by the power of society.[1]

The Holy Family was little read at the time of its publication and was certainly not one of Marx's major works. But several of the themes of what was to become 'the materialistic conception of history' appeared there for the first time and Marx, re-reading the book after twelve years, was able to comment: 'I was pleasantly surprised to find that we do not need to be ashamed of our work, although the cult of Feuerbach strikes me as very amusing.'[2]

2. *Theses on Feuerbach*

In the spring of 1845 Marx subjected his 'cult of Feuerbach' to a critical examination and wrote the eleven theses that form the link between *The Holy Family* and *The German Ideology*. The first thesis contained the essence of Marx's criticism of Feuerbach's materialism: 'The chief defect of all previous materialism (including Feuerbach's) is that the object, actuality, sensuousness is conceived only in the form of the object or perception, but not as sensuous human activity, practice, not subjectively.' In the second thesis, Marx outlined his doctrine of the unity of theory and practice: 'The question whether human thinking can reach objective truth is not a question of theory but a practical question. In practice man must prove the truth, that is, actuality and power, this-sideness of his thinking. The dispute about the actuality or non-actuality of thinking – thinking isolated from practice – is a purely scholastic question.' And in the third Marx pointed out the deficiencies of the French materialists: 'The materialist doctrine concerning the change of circumstances and education forgets that circumstances are changed by men and that the educator must himself be educated. Hence this doctrine must divide society into two parts – one of which towers above.' The following theses elaborated Marx's rejection of the 'static' attitude of Feuerbach to religion, and the final thesis read: 'The philosophers have only interpreted the world in various ways; the point is, to change it.'[3]

[1] *Writings of the Young Marx*, pp. 394 f.
[2] K. Marx, F. Engels, *Werke* (Berlin, 1956 ff.) xxxi 290. (Hereafter referred to as *MEW*.) [3] *Writings of the Young Marx*, pp. 400 ff.

3. *The German Ideology*

The aim of this work, as Marx wrote later, was 'to settle accounts with our erstwhile philosophical conscience'.[1] The book contains three main sections: one on Feuerbach, one on Max Stirner and one on the 'true socialists'. Of these, the first is by far the most important.

Marx and Engels began by making fun of the philosophical pretensions of the Young Hegelians which they described as 'the putrescence of the absolute spirit'.[2] The main body of the section is then divided into three parts: a general statement of the historical and materialist approach in contrast to that of the Young Hegelians; a historical analysis employing this method; and an account of the present state of society and its immediate future – a communist revolution.

Marx and Engels began by stating their general position, which deserves lengthy quotation as it is the first concise statement of historical materialism:

> The premises from which we start are not arbitrary; they are no dogmas but rather actual premises from which abstraction can be made only in imagination. They are the real individuals, their actions, and their material conditions of life, those which they find existing as well as those which they produce through their actions.
>
> The first premise of all human history, of course, is the existence of living human individuals. The first fact to be established, then, is the physical organisation of these individuals and their consequent relationship to the rest of nature. Of course, we cannot discuss here the physical nature of man or the natural conditions in which man finds himself – geological, oro-hydrographical, climatic, and others. He begins to distinguish himself from the animal the moment he begins to produce his means of subsistence, a step required by his physical organisation. By producing food, man indirectly produces his material life itself.
>
> The way in which man produces his food depends first of all

---

[1] *MESW*, i 364.
[2] K. Marx, F. Engels, *The German Ideology*, 2nd ed. (Moscow, 1968) p. 27.

on the nature of the means of subsistence that he finds and has to reproduce. This mode of production must not be viewed simply as reproduction of the physical existence of individuals. Rather it is a definite form of their activity, a definite way of expressing their life, a definite *mode of life*. As individuals express their life, so they are. What they are, therefore, coincides with what they produce, and how they produce. The nature of individuals thus depends on the material conditions which determine their production.[1]

They went on to state that 'how far the productive forces of a nation are developed is shown most evidently by the degree to which the division of labour has been developed'.[2] They showed how the division of labour led to the separation of town and country and then to the separation of industrial from commercial labour and so on. Next they summarised the different stages of ownership that had corresponded to the stages in the division of labour: tribal ownership, communal and state ownership, feudal or estate ownership. Marx and Engels summarised their conclusions so far as follows:

The fact is, then, that definite individuals who are productively active in a specific way enter into these definite social and political relations. The social structure and the state continually evolve out of the life-process of definite individuals, but individuals not as they may appear in their own or other people's imagination but rather as they really are, that is, as they work, produce materially, and act under definite material limitations, presuppositions, and conditions independent of their will.[3]

They then reiterated their general approach, stating that 'consciousness does not determine life, but life determines consciousness', and showed how the division of labour, leading to private property, created social inequality, class struggle and the erection of political structures:

Out of this very contradiction between the interest of the individual and that of the community the latter takes an independent form as the State, separated from the real interests

---

[1] *Writings of the Young Marx*, p. 408.
[2] Ibid. p. 410.   [3] Ibid. p. 413.

of individual and community, and at the same time as an illusory communal life, but always based on the real bonds present in every family and every tribal conglomeration such as flesh and blood, language, division of labour on a larger scale, and other interests, and particularly based, as we intend to show later, on the classes already determined by the division of labour, classes which form in any such mass of people and of which one dominates all the others. It follows from this that all struggles within the State, the struggle between democracy, aristocracy and monarchy, the struggle for franchise, etc., etc., are nothing but the illusory forms in which the real struggles of different classes are carried out among one another.'[1]

Marx and Engels then turned to the imminence of a communist revolution. 'Things have come to the point', they wrote, 'where individuals must appropriate the existing totality of productive forces not merely to achieve self-activity but to secure their very existence.'[2] The coming revolution would be a total one at least as far as the instruments of production were concerned: 'in all appropriations up to now a mass of individuals remained subservient to a single instrument of production. In the appropriation by the proletarians, a mass of instruments of production must be subservient to each individual and the property of all. The only way for individuals to control modern universal interaction is to make it subject to the control of all.'[3] The transition to communism was inevitable: 'Communism is not for us a state of affairs still to be established, not an ideal to which reality will have to adjust. We call communism the real movement which abolishes the present state of affairs.'[4] Marx and Engels did not say much about the organisation of the future communist society, though they did emphasise the abolition of the division of labour: 'In communist society, however, where nobody has an exclusive area of activity and each can train himself in any branch he wishes, society regulates the general production, making it possible for me to do one thing today and another tomorrow, to hunt in the morning, fish in the afternoon, breed cattle in the evening, criticise after dinner, just as I like without ever becoming a hunter, a fisherman, a herdsman, or a critic.'[5]

[1] *Writings of the Young Marx*, p. 425. [2] Ibid. p. 467.
[3] Ibid. pp. 467 f.   [4] Ibid. p. 426.   [5] Ibid. pp. 424 f.

The remainder of the book is of far less interest. There is an extended and wearisome attack on Max Stirner's book *The Ego and his Own*. Stirner was an anarchist who preached that the fundamental and sole reality was the Self which must reject all ideologies and systems. There is also a concluding section on the 'true socialists' – Moses Hess and his disciples – who, inspired by Feuerbach, turned socialism into an ethical ideal, whereas for Marx it was an economic reality.

4. *The Poverty of Philosophy*

In December 1846, Marx, who had received Proudhon's new book on economics, wrote a first appraisal of it in a letter to the Russian journalist Annenkov. Marx here insisted that social organisation and political ideology corresponded to the development of the productive forces which were outside the control of men:

> Are men free to choose this or that form of society for themselves? By no means. Assume a particular state of development in the productive forces of man and you will get a particular form of commerce and consumption. Assume particular stages of development in production, commerce and consumption and you will have a corresponding social constitution, a corresponding organisation of the family, of orders or of classes, in a word, a corresponding civil society.[1]

Marx took up and elaborated the ideas of his letter in a full-scale reply to Proudhon published in the summer of 1847. This book was the first published statement of what came to be known as historical materialism (Marx and Engels had been unable to find a publisher for *The German Ideology*). Lassalle, the prominent German socialist leader of the 1860s, said of the book that in the first half Marx showed himself to be a Ricardo turned socialist, and in the second part a Hegel turned economist.

Ricardo had shown that the exchange of commodities in capitalist society was based on the amount of labour time contained in them; and Proudhon proposed that the value of commodities should be so 'constituted' that the product of one producer should be exchangeable with that of another containing the same labour time. The reform of society would be achieved if all its

[1] K. Marx, *The Poverty of Philosophy* (Moscow, n.d.) p. 180.

members became workers exchanging similar qualities of labour. Marx, however, considered it a bourgeois illusion to suppose that class contradictions could be abolished by a blue-print based on some imaginary ideal of harmony and equality. Money could not become a vehicle for Proudhon's proposed exchange of equal values for it was merely a social relation and thus reflected a given mode of production. The correct balance between supply and demand was impossible under contemporary conditions, for large-scale industry was compelled to produce in steadily increasing quantities without waiting for demand, which resulted in recurrent crises.

In the second part of his book, Marx dealt with what he considered to be Proudhon's 'pseudo-Hegelianism'. Proudhon claimed to be giving an account of the evolution of economic ideas in theses and antitheses in order to develop them into a reconciling synthesis.[1] Marx criticised Proudhon for not realising that economic categories were only the theoretical expressions of social relations of production.

> Proudhon the economist [he wrote] has clearly understood that men make cloth, linen and silk stuffs in definite relations of production. But what he has not understood is that these definite social relations are just as much produced by men as are the cloth, the linen, etc. Social relations are intimately bound up with productive forces. In acquiring new productive forces men change their mode of production, and in changing their mode of production, their manner of making a living, they change all their social relations. The windmill gives you society with the feudal lord; the steam mill, society with the industrial capitalist.
>
> The same men who establish social relations in conformity with their material productivity also produce principles, ideas, and categories conforming to their social relations.
>
> Hence these ideas, these categories are no more eternal than the relations which they express. They are historical and transitory products.

[1] It is worth while pointing out, in view of the very widespread misconception that Marx presented his view of history in terms of thesis, antithesis and synthesis, that this is the only place where he talks in such language and his purpose is to refute its use by Proudhon.

There is a continual movement of growth in productive force,
of destruction in social relations, and of formation in ideas;
there is nothing immutable but the abstraction of the movement – *mors immortalis*.[1]

Marx went on to criticise Proudhon's unhistorical views on the
division of labour, machinery, monopoly and land. Finally Marx
rejected Proudhon's disapproval of strikes and unions. For him
they were indispensable instruments of a revolution both social
and political: 'Do not say that social movement excludes political
movement. There is never a political movement which is not at the
same time social. It is only in an order of things in which there
are no more classes, and class antagonisms, that *social evolutions*
will cease to be *political revolutions*'.[2]

The Poverty of Philosophy was Marx's first comprehensive
statement on economics and he recommended it, together with the
Communist Manifesto, as an introduction to *Capital*.

BIBLIOGRAPHY

TRANSLATIONS

The Holy Family

K. Marx and F. Engels, *The Holy Family* (Moscow, 1956).
Writings of the Young Marx on Philosophy and Society, ed. L. Easton and
K. Guddat (New York, 1967) (excerpts).

Theses on Feuerbach

Writings of the Young Marx on Philosophy and Society, ed. L. Easton and
K. Guddat (New York, 1967).
K. Marx, *Selected Writings in Sociology and Social Philosophy*, ed. T.
Bottomore and M. Rubel (London, 1956).

The German Ideology

K. Marx and F. Engels, *The German Ideology*, 2nd ed. (Moscow, 1968).
K. Marx and F. Engels, *The German Ideology,* ed. with further
selections and an introduction by C. Arthur (New York and London, 1971).

[1] *Writings of the Young Marx*, pp. 480 f.
[2] *The Poverty of Philosophy*, p. 175.

Writings of the Young Marx on Philosophy and Society, ed. L. Easton and
   K. Guddat (New York, 1967) (excerpts).

The Poverty of Philosophy

K. Marx, *The Poverty of Philosophy* (Moscow, n.d.).

Writings of the Young Marx on Philosophy and Society, ed. L. Easton and
   K. Guddat (New York, 1967) (excerpts).

COMMENTARIES

C. Cohen, 'Bourgeois and Proletarians', *Journal of the History of Ideas*
   (1968).

O. Hammen, 'The Young Marx, Reconsidered', *Journal of the History of
   Ideas* (1970).

N. Rothenstreich, *Basic Problems of Marx's Philosophy* (Indianapolis and
   New York, 1965).

Also the books quoted in the reading list for Part II, Chapter 2.

CHAPTER FOUR

A. WRITINGS

The Communist Manifesto (1848)
Wage Labour and Capital (1849)
Addresses of the Central Committee to the Communist League
(1850)

B. BIOGRAPHY

IN November 1847 Marx did manage to attend, together with
Engels, the second annual congress of the Communist League.
The League was intended to be open and democratic (as opposed
to its predecessor the League of the Just). Thus the League
decided to issue a manifesto to make plain to all the true nature
of the 'spectre' that was supposed to be 'haunting Europe'. The
job was entrusted to Marx and Engels. Both the Central
Committee in London and Moses Hess in Paris had already
produced a draft; and Engels capped these with a *Basic Principles
of Communism*, drawn up in the form of questions and answers,
on which the final version leaned quite heavily. In fact, this
version was nearly not published at all: Marx was so busy with
his other activities that it was only an ultimatum from the Central
Committee that persuaded him to write. The *Communist Manifesto*
was sent to London at the end of January and published there in
February. Although it became later the most read document of
communist literature, it made virtually no impression when first
published.

By the time the *Manifesto* was out, Marx was in revolutionary
Paris. Sparked by a blaze of riots in Italian cities, there was a
powerful rising in Paris on 22 February. The middle-class
National Guard turned against King Louis-Philippe, who was
force to abdicate, and a new provisional government of liberal
tendencies with a more radical socialist wing was formed. Marx
was immediately invited back to Paris by the government, an

invitation that he accepted the more readily as the Belgian Government had just issued him with an expulsion order for contravening his undertaking not to engage in political journalism. On arrival in Paris Marx opposed the quixotic idea of the German workers there to form a legion to liberate Germany: their task, he said, was to remain in Paris and support the revolution there.

In March the revolution reached Germany. There were riots in Berlin and the Prussian King Frederick William IV decided to make concessions. He declared himself in favour of a federal German Reich to replace the existing federation, with an elected Parliament and freedom of the Press. He formed a liberal government under Camphausen and an Assembly was elected to draw up the proposed new constitution, a task that dragged on all through the summer. On the outbreak of disturbances in Germany, Marx and others from the Communist League went to Cologne where Marx started in June a radical newspaper entitled *Neue Rheinische Zeitung*, of which he was editor-in-chief. In all, he wrote about eighty articles for the paper and travelled widely, in August to Berlin where he met Bakunin, and in September to Vienna.

However, the summer of 1848 brought the first reaction of counter-revolution. In June a virtually spontaneous popular rising in Paris, put down with much bloodshed by the army and the National Guard, drove the Parliamentary government into the arms of the reaction. In Germany the Assembly had forfeited popular support and Frederick William IV was once more firmly in control. Marx was expelled by the government, and the *Neue Rheinische Zeitung*, its last number printed in red, ceased to appear. Marx went to Paris, but the French Government would only let him stay in France on condition that he went to stay in Morbihan, a marshy district of Brittany. He decided instead to leave for London. Lassalle, a fellow socialist, started a collection among friends in the Rhineland to finance his trip and Marx left in August. He was followed in September by his wife and their three children.

C. COMMENTARY

The *Communist Manifesto* has four sections. The first section gives a history of society as class society since the Middle Ages and ends with a prophecy of the victory of the proletariat over the present ruling class, the bourgeoisie. The second section describes the position of communists inside the proletarian class, rejects bourgeois objections to communism and then characterises the communist revolution, the measures to be taken by the victorious proletariat and the nature of the future communist society. The third section contains an extended criticism of other types of socialism, reactionary, petty-bourgeois and utopian. The final section contains a short description of communist tactics towards other opposition parties and finishes with an appeal to proletarian unity.

The opening words characterise the approach of Marx and Engels to history:

> The history of all hitherto existing society is the history of class struggles.
>
> Freeman and slave, patrician and plebeian, lord and serf, guild-master and journeyman, in a word, oppressor and oppressed, stood in constant opposition to one another, carried on an uninterrupted, now hidden, now open fight, a fight that each time ended, either in a revolutionary re-constitution of society at large, or in the common ruin of the contending classes.[1]

The present age, they continued, was unique in that class antagonisms had been so simplified that there were now two hostile camps facing each other: bourgeoisie and proletariat. The bourgeoisie, from its origins in feudal society, helped by the discovery of America, the development of a world market and modern industry, had everywhere imposed the domination of its class and its ideas. Historically, the bourgeoisie had been a most revolutionary class: 'it has accomplished wonders far surpassing Egyptian pyramids, Roman aqueducts and Gothic cathedrals; it has conducted expeditions that put in the shade all former Exoduses of nations and crusades'.[2] But this progress had to continue: the bourgeoisie could not exist without constantly revolutionising the means of production. And just as the bourgeoisie had caused the downfall of feudal society, so now they were preparing their own downfall 'like the sorcerer who is no longer able to control the powers of the nether world whom he has called up by his spells'.[3] For the bourgeoisie had not only forged

[1] *MESW* i 34.   [2] Ibid. 37.   [3] Ibid. 39.

the weapons of their destruction; they had also called into existence the men to wield those weapons, the proletariat.

Marx and Engels then described the revolutionary nature of the proletariat. Workers had become mere appendages of machines. In proportion as the use of machinery and division of labour increased, so the wages of the workers got less in spite of the longer hours they worked. The lower middle class was forced down into the proletariat:

> the lower strata of the middle class – the small tradespeople, shopkeepers, and retired tradesmen generally, the handicraftsmen and peasants – all these sink gradually into the proletariat, partly because their diminutive capital does not suffice for the scale on which Modern Industry is carried on, and is swamped in the competition with the large capitalists, partly because their specialised skill is rendered worthless by new methods of production. Thus the proletariat is recruited from all classes of the population.[1]

The proletariat itself went through several stages: at first their principal aim was to restore the vanished status of workmen in the Middle Ages; with increase of numbers they began to form trade unions; finally the class struggle became a political struggle. As the struggle neared its decisive hour, a process of dissolution set in within the ruling class, and a small section, of bourgeois ideologists in particular, went over to the proletariat. No other class in society could fulfil the revolutionary role of the proletariat: the lower middle class were in fact reactionary in that they tried to roll back the wheel of history; and the '"dangerous class", the social scum, that passively rotting mass thrown off by the lower layers of society',[2] was ripe for bribery by reactionary intrigue. Marx and Engels summed up this section with the words:

> The advance of industry, whose involuntary promoter is the bourgeoisie, replaces the isolation of the labourers, due to competition, by their revolutionary combination, due to association. The development of Modern Industry, therefore, cuts from under its feet the very foundation on which the bourgeoisie produces and appropriates products. What the bourgeoisie, therefore, produces, above all, is its own grave-diggers. Its fall and the victory of the proletariat are equally inevitable.[3]

[1] *MESW* i 41.   [2] Ibid. 44.   [3] Ibid. 45.

In the second section Marx and Engels raised the question of the relationship of the communists to the proletarians as a whole. The communists were not opposed to other working-class parties; their interests were those of the proletariat as a whole. Their distinction from other working-class groups was twofold: they were international, and they understood the significance of the proletarian movement. Their ideas were not invented or discovered; they merely expressed actual relations springing from an existing class struggle and could be summed up in a single sentence: abolition of private property.

Marx and Engels then dealt with objections.

The first was that communists desired to abolish 'the right of personally acquiring property as the fruit of a man's own labour'.[1] They replied that the property of the petty artisan and small farmer was being abolished anyway by the power of capital; the proletariat did not have any property; and capital, being a collective product and the result of the united action of all members of society, should be owned collectively. Private property was bourgeois property and all arguments against its abolition were bourgeois arguments.

Similarly, the abolition of the family meant the abolition of the bourgeois family whose counterpart was the practical absence of family life among proletarians and public prostitution.

The real point about the so-called 'community of women' was to do away with the status of women as mere instruments of production. The present system was merely public and private prostitution.

It was also said that the communists wished to abolish countries and nationality. But working men had no country. Modern industry was abolishing the differences between nations and, with the disappearance of class antagonisms, the hostility of one nation to another would also end.

Ideological objections to communism were not worthy of serious consideration:

Does it require intuition to comprehend that man's ideas, views and conceptions, in one word, man's consciousness, changes with every change in the conditions of his material existence, in his social relations and in his social life?

[1] Ibid. 47.

What else does the history of ideas prove, than that intellectual production changes its character in proportion as material production is changed? The ruling ideas of each age have ever been the ideas of its ruling class.[1]

Having dealt with these objections, Marx and Engels gave a brief sketch of the measures that would be taken by the proletariat once it was raised to the level of ruling class:

The proletariat will use its political supremacy to wrest, by degrees, all capital from the bourgeoisie, to centralise all instruments of production in the hands of the State, i.e. of the proletariat organised as the ruling class; and to increase the total of productive forces as rapidly as possible.[2]

There followed a programme including the abolition of landed property and inheritance, income tax, centralisation of credit and communications, state ownership of factories, and free education. They concluded:

When, in the course of development, class distinctions have disappeared, and all production has been concentrated in the hands of a vast association of the whole nation, the public power will lose its political character. Political power, properly so called, is merely the organised power of one class for oppressing another. If the proletariat during its contest with the bourgeoisie is compelled, by the force of circumstances, to organise itself as a class, if, by means of a revolution, it makes itself the ruling class, and, as such, sweeps away by force the old condition of production, then it will, along with these conditions, have swept away the conditions for the existence of class antagonisms and of classes generally, and will thereby have abolished its own supremacy as a class.

In place of the old bourgeois society, with its classes and class antagonisms, we shall have an association, in which the free development of each is the condition for the free development of all.[3]

The third section of the *Communist Manifesto* contained criticism of three types of socialism: reactionary, bourgeois, and utopian. The first was a feudal socialism preached by the aristo-

[1] *MESW* i 52.   [2] Ibid. 53.   [3] Ibid. 54.

cracy to revenge themselves on the bourgeoisie who had supplanted them as the ruling class. Hand in hand with feudal socialism was Christian socialism which Marx dismissed as only 'the holy water with which the priest consecrates the heart-burnings of the aristocrat'.[1] The second type – petty-bourgeois socialism – was chiefly represented by the French economist Sismondi. This school had well analysed the contradictions inherent in modern methods of production; but in its positive proposals it was reactionary, wishing to restore corporate guilds in manufacture and patriarchal relations in agriculture.

The third party among those whom Marx and Engels called reactionary socialists were the German or 'true' socialists. These were the German philosophers, mainly followers of Feuerbach, who had emasculated French socialism by turning it into a metaphysical system. This was inevitable in a backward country like Germany where the philosophers did not represent the struggle of one class with another, and thus claimed to represent:

> . . . not true requirements, but the requirements of Truth; not the interests of the proletariat, but the interests of Human Nature, of Man in general, who belongs to no class, has no reality, who exists only in the misty realm of philosophical fantasy.[2]

The second section in the review of socialist and communist literature, devoted to bourgeois socialism, was short. Proudhon was the main representative of this tendency and Marx had already devoted considerable space to examining his theories. Here he confined himself to observing that:

> the Socialistic bourgeois want all the advantages of modern social conditions without the struggles and dangers necessarily resulting therefrom. They desire the existing state of society minus its revolutionary and disintegrating elements. They wish for a bourgeoisie without a proletariat.[3]

Thus the reforms advocated in no respect affected the relations between capital and labour, but at least lessened the cost, and simplified the administrative work, of bourgeois government.

The final school discussed is the 'critical-Utopian' school represented by such writers as Saint-Simon, Fourier and Owen.

---

[1] Ibid. 56.   [2] Ibid. 58.   [3] Ibid. 60.

They originated during the early, undeveloped period of the struggle between the bourgeoisie and the proletariat. The writers appreciated class antagonisms but the proletariat was still insufficiently developed to appear as a vehicle for the solution. Hence they wished to attain their ends by peaceful means and small-scale experiments, rejecting political, and in particular revolutionary, action. Their utopias, constructed at a time when the proletariat was still underdeveloped, 'correspond with the first instinctive yearnings of that class for a general reconstruction of society'.[1] But at the same time these utopians also contained a critical element: since they attacked every principle of existing society, they were full of valuable materials for the enlightenment of the working class. But as the modern class struggle developed and took shape, these utopias lost all practical value or theoretical justification. Thus 'although the originators of these systems were, in many respects, revolutionary, their disciples have, in every case, formed mere reactionary sects'.[2]

The fourth and final section of the *Manifesto* dealt with the attitude of communists to various opposition parties: in France they supported the social democrats, in Switzerland the radicals, in Poland the peasant revolutionaries, in Germany the bourgeoisie. Nevertheless in Germany they never ceased to instil into the working class the clearest possible recognition of the hostility between bourgeoisie and proletariat. The communists directed their attention chiefly to Germany, which was on the eve of a bourgeois revolution. The *Manifesto* ended:

> The Communists disdain to conceal their views and aims. They openly declare that their ends can be attained only by the forcible overthrow of all existing social conditions. Let the ruling classes tremble at a Communistic revolution. The Proletarians have nothing to lose but their chains. They have a world to win.

WORKING MEN OF ALL COUNTRIES, UNITE![3]

Marx published in the *Neue Rheinische Zeitung* a version of the lectures he had delivered to workmen in Brussels under the title *Wage Labour and Capital*. Here Marx expanded on the harmful effects on wages of the growth of productive capital, stated clearly for the first time his doctrine of the relative

[1] *MESW* I 62. [2] Ibid. 63. [3] Ibid. 65.

pauperisation of the proletariat, and sketched the idea of the reserve army of workers that was to appear forcibly in *Capital*.

The line pursued by the *Neue Rheinische Zeitung* under the editorship of Marx was opposed to the federalism advocated by many German radicals. German unity could be achieved through a 'revolutionary war' against Russia. After the success of the counter-revolution Marx declared: 'there is only one means of shortening the lethal death agony of the old society and the bloody birth of the new, only one means – revolutionary terrorism.'

How this was to be carried out was the burden of Marx and Engels's *Address to the Communist League*, written in March 1850, defining the tactics to be followed in the future struggles of the proletariat. What had to be achieved was an independent political organisation of the proletariat and the creation of a workers' party with both public and secret sections; they advocated the re-establishment of revolutionary workers' governments in the shape of town councils, clubs and armed committees. The next wave of revolutions would bring the petty-bourgeoisie to power.

> The revolutionary workers will co-operate with the petty bourgeois democrats against the faction whose overthrow they both desire, but it will oppose them in all points where its own interests arise.[1]

After the limited demands of the petty-bourgeoisie had been achieved, there would be an open divergence between the two parties:

> while the democratic petty bourgeois wish to bring the revolution to a conclusion as quickly as possible, and with the achievement, at most, of the above demands, it is our interest and our task to make the revolution permanent, until all more or less possessing classes have been forced out of their position of dominance, until the proletariat has conquered state power, and the association of proletarians, not only in one country but in all the dominant countries of the world, has advanced so far that competition among the proletarians of these countries has ceased and that at least the decisive productive forces are concentrated in the hands of the proletarians.[2]

[1] Ibid. 109.   [2] Ibid. 110.

There might well be a long struggle in front of the proletariat, but an independent organisation was the first condition of its success. The *Address* ended:

> But they themselves must do the utmost for their final victory, by clarifying their minds as to what their class interests are, by taking up their position as an independent party as soon as possible and by not allowing themselves to be seduced for a single moment by the hypocritical phrases of the democratic petty bourgeois into refraining from the independent organisation of the party of the proletariat. Their battle cry must be: The Revolution in Permanence.[1]

The *Address* certainly contains views that seem quite close to those of Blanqui, and it has been argued that Marx adopted a Blanquist attitude during the first half of 1850. However, there is no necessity to adopt this view as Marx's approach here is quite consistent with his previous and subsequent views.[2]

BIBLIOGRAPHY

TRANSLATIONS

The Communist Manifesto
K. Marx, F. Engels, *Selected Works* (Moscow, 1962) vol. i.
The Communist Manifesto, ed. A. J. P. Taylor (Harmondsworth, 1969).
The Communist Manifesto, ed. H. Laski (London, 1961).

Wage Labour and Capital
K. Marx, F. Engels, *Selected Works* (Moscow, 1962) vol. i.

Address of the Central Committee to the Communist League
K. Marx, F. Engels, *Selected Works* (Moscow, 1962) vol. i.

COMMENTARIES

S. Avineri, *The Social and Political Thought of Karl Marx* (Cambridge, 1968).
H. Draper, 'Marx and the Dictatorship of the Proletariat', *Cahiers de l'ISEA* (1962).
H. Laski, introduction to *The Communist Manifesto* (London, 1961).

[1] *MESW* i 117.
[2] See particularly on this question the books by Wolfe and Avineri quoted in the Bibliography.

B. Nicolaievsky, 'Towards a History of the Communist League', *International Review of Social History* (1956).

D. Struik (ed.), *The Birth of the Communist Manifesto* (New York, 1971).

A. J. P. Taylor, introduction to *The Communist Manifesto* (Harmondsworth, 1969).

Y. Wagner and M. Strauss, 'The Programme of the Communist Manifesto and its Theoretical Implications', *Political Studies* (Dec 1969).

B. Wolfe, *Marxism: 100 Years in the Life of a Doctrine* (London, 1967).

CHAPTER FIVE

A. Writings

The Class Struggles in France (1850)
The Eighteenth Brumaire of Louis Bonaparte (1852)

B. Biography

IMMEDIATELY after the arrival of the Marx family in England, their fourth child, Guido, was born. They were evicted from their lodging-house in Camberwell in 1850 for inability to pay the rent, found refuge for a week in a German hotel in Leicester Square and then moved into two small rooms in Dean Street, Soho, where they stayed for the next six years.

Marx attempted to continue his journalistic activities by founding a monthly entitled *Neue Rheinische Zeitung-Revue* which, edited in London, would be sold in Germany. The three essays in which Marx reconsidered the significance of the 1848 revolution, subsequently published under the title of *The Class Struggles in France*, originally appeared in the *Revue*. Marx was also occupied by political activities and in particular a regrouping of the Communist League. The *Address* quoted in the previous chapter was a part of this effort. In April a meeting was arranged with the followers of the French revolutionary leader Blanqui and a World Association of Revolutionary Communists was formed, the first article of whose statutes read: 'The aim of the Association is the overthrow of all privileged classes and their subjection to the dictatorship of the proletariat, in which a permanent revolution will be maintained until the realisation of communism which will be the final form that the organisation of the human family takes.'[1]

By the autumn, however, a split developed in the Communist

[1] *MEW* vii 553.

League. One faction advocated immediate revolutionary action virtually irrespective of circumstances; whereas Marx, who had taken up his economic studies again, considered that there was no possibility of a successful revolution in the comparatively prosperous economic climate of the early 1850s. In a speech to the Central Committee Marx characterised the differences between the two positions: 'while we tell the workers: "You have to endure and go through fifteen, twenty, fifty years of civil war in order to change the circumstances, in order to make yourselves fit for power" – instead of that, you say: "we must come to power immediately, or otherwise we may just as well go to sleep". In the same way as the word "People" has been used by the Democrats as a mere phrase, so the word "Proletariat" is being used now . . . .'[1] Faced with the prospect of defeat on this issue, Marx managed to get the headquarters of the Communist League transferred to Cologne – which meant its virtual dissolution. November saw the last number of the *Neue Rheinische Zeitung-Revue*, which gave up publication owing to lack of finance and lack of readers. Engels, seeing no scope for further activity in London, left for Manchester where he took up a position in his father's firm which he retained until 1869.

During the first few months of 1851 Marx gave up his active life and read an immense amount in the British Museum. The young German refugee Pieper, who sometimes acted as Marx's secretary, wrote: 'Marx lives a very retiring life, his only friends are J. S. Mill and Lloyd, and when you visit him you get economic categories instead of compliments.'[2] The Marx family lived almost perpetually on the verge of starvation; Guido died in 1850, and their fifth child, Franziska, born in 1851, died the following year. A further complication was the birth to Helene Demuth, the Marx's maidservant, of Frederick, Marx's illegitimate son, who survived until well on into the twentieth century. Marx's private studies in 1851 were interrupted by two events apart from his household worries. Firstly, some members of the Communist League in Germany had been arrested, certain documents, including Marx's *Address* of 1850, had been discovered, and a political trial was being prepared with great publicity. Marx spent much of his time collecting evidence to refute the prosecution's allegations, many of which were based on pure forgeries. Secondly,

[1] Ibid. VIII 598.   [2] Ibid. XXVII 169.

Charles Dana, editor of the *New York Daily Tribune*, a radical paper with a very large circulation, asked Marx to become its European correspondent. Marx agreed and for the next few years his only regular source of income was his weekly articles for the *Tribune*, many of which were in fact written by Engels.

Meanwhile in France Louis Napoleon Bonaparte, nephew of the former Emperor, who had been elected President of the Republic by an immense majority at the end of 1848, secured by a *coup d'état* in December 1851 the extension of his presidency for another ten years; one year later he was to formalise his auto-cratic powers by proclaiming the Second Empire. Marx analysed the socio-economic background to this *coup d'état* in a series of articles for a New York journal entitled *The Revolution*. He called the series *The Eighteenth Brumaire of Louis Bonaparte*, an allusion to the seizure of power by Napoleon the First.

C. Commentary

Almost immediately on arrival in London Marx undertook a historical and sociological study of the 1848 revolution to analyse the reasons for the provisional defeat of the French proletariat and the lessons to be drawn for future revolution. It was above all French history (always Marx's preferred reading subject) that inspired his reflections on the political significance of the class struggle. These reflections gave rise to three main works: *The Class Struggles in France*, *The Eighteenth Brumaire of Louis Bonaparte*, discussed below, and *The Civil War in France*, discussed in Part I, Chapter 8.

Of *The Class Struggles in France* Engels said that it was 'Marx's first attempt to explain a section of contemporary history by means of his materialist conception, on the basis of the given economic situation'.[1] But it is more than this: it is also a political pamphlet. Marx's opening words immediately show his attitude towards the recent victory of reaction:

> With the exception of only a few chapters, every more important part of the annals of the revolution from 1848 to 1849 carries the heading: *Defeat of the revolution!*

[1] *MESW* i 118.

What succumbed in these defeats was not the revolution. It was the pre-revolutionary traditional appendages, results of social relationships which had not yet come to the point of sharp class antagonisms – persons, illusions, conceptions, projects from which the revolutionary party before the February Revolution was not free, from which it could be freed not by the *victory of February*, but only by a series of *defeats*.

In a word: the revolution made progress, forged ahead, not by its immediate tragicomic achievements, but on the contrary by the creation of a powerful, united counter-revolution, by the creation of an opponent in combat with whom, only, the party of overthrow ripened into a really revolutionary party.[1]

The first of the four sections begins with an analysis of the class structure in France under the July monarchy, and particularly the clash of the finance aristocracy and the industrial bourgeoisie. According to Marx, since the July revolution of 1830 the real power behind the throne had been the finance aristocracy of bankers, stock-exchange brokers and large landed proprietors. The easy suppression of sporadic workers' revolts and the exclusion of the petty-bourgeoisie and peasants from any share in political power meant that the only real opposition was the industrial bourgeoisie. The result was that the July Monarchy was nothing but a joint-stock company with the state continually kept on the verge of bankruptcy so that the finance aristocracy could speculate on its debts to the ruin of the small investor.

This general discontent, Marx goes on, erupted into revolution owing to the potato blight and crop failures of 1845 and 1846 and the general commercial and industrial crisis in England. This second factor in particular meant that the bourgeoisie were thrown back exclusively on their own home markets, and the consequent competition and ruin of large numbers gave ample encouragement to revolution. The provisional government, set up after the February barricades,

necessarily mirrored in its composition the different parties which shared in the victory. It could not be anything but a *compromise between the different classes*, which together had overturned the July throne, but whose interests were mutually antagonistic. . . .[2]

[1] Ibid. 139.   [2] Ibid. 144.

Inside this provisional government any hope that the workers' representatives might have real power proved illusory. Although verbal, and even organisational, concessions were made, they remained entirely peripheral:

> In common with the bourgeoisie the workers had made the February Revolution, and *alongside* the bourgeoisie they sought to secure the advancement of their interest, just as they had installed a worker in the Provisional Government itself alongside the bourgeois majority. *Organise labour!* But wage labour, that is the existing, the bourgeois organisation of labour. Without it there is no capital, no bourgeoisie, no bourgeois society. *A Special Ministry of Labour!* But the Ministries of Finance, of Trade, of Public Works — are not these the *bourgeois* Ministries of Labour? And *alongside* these a *proletarian* Ministry of Labour had to be a ministry of impotence, a ministry of pious wishes, a Luxembourg Commission. Just as the workers thought they would be able to emancipate themselves side by side with the bourgeoisie, so they thought they would be able to consummate a proletarian revolution within the national walls of France, side by side with the remaining bourgeois nations. But French relations of production are conditioned by the foreign trade of France, by her position on the world market and the laws thereof; how was France to break them without a European revolutionary war, which would strike back at the despot of the world market, England?[1]

Even inside France the economic conditions were far from ripe for a proletarian revolution, although a very temporary success in Paris might be possible; for the power of the finance aristocracy had not allowed the industrial bourgeoisie to shape the means of production. This meant that the proletariat had yet to achieve an extensive national existence, that the last vestiges of feudal society had not yet disappeared and that French industry was still essentially insular. Therefore the task of the provisional government could not be the revolutionary transformation of the world, but only the adaptation of itself to the relations of bourgeois society. This adaptation was nearest in the government's financial measures: instead of letting the Bank of France go bankrupt, and thus destroying the finance aristocracy, they

[1] *MESW* i 147 f.

bought the confidence of the capitalists by taxing the peasants. And because the promises that had been made to the workers would have proved too expensive to maintain the all-important system of credit, the only solution was to play off one part of the proletariat against the other, and the government bought the *Lumpenproletariat* by recruiting them into the specially formed Mobile Guard.

The May elections ended the ambivalent position of the provisional government by returning an Assembly that created a bourgeois republic and nothing more. The desperate workers' insurrection in June was hopeless from the start:

> The Paris proletariat was *forced* into the June insurrection by the bourgeoisie. This sufficed to mark its doom. Its immediate, avowed needs did not drive it to engage in a fight for the forcible overthrow of the bourgeoisie, nor was it equal to this task. The *Moniteur* had to inform it officially that the time was past when the republic saw any occasion to bow and scrape to its illusions, and only its defeat convinced it of the truth that the slightest improvement in its position remains a *utopia within* the bourgeois republic, a utopia that becomes a crime as soon as it wants to become a reality. In place of its demands, exuberant in form, but petty and even bourgeois still in content, the concession of which it wanted to wring from the February republic, there appeared the bold slogan of revolutionary struggle: *Overthrow of the bourgeoisie!* Dictatorship of the working class![1]

But the proletariat were not the only group to differ in June 1848: having helped to strike down the workers, the petty-bourgeoisie saw with horror that they had delivered themselves into the hands of their creditors. Meanwhile the new constitution promulgated in the autumn could provide no lasting solution, hamstrung as it was by the contradiction between the political power still given to the lower classes and the social power reserved to the bourgeoisie:

> The classes whose social slavery the constitution is to perpetuate, proletariat, peasantry, petty bourgeoisie, it puts in possession of political power through universal suffrage. And from the class whose old social power it sanctions, the bourgeoisie, it withdraws the political guarantees of this power.

[1] Ibid. 162.

It forces the political rule of the bourgeoisie into democratic conditions, which at every moment help the hostile classes to victory and jeopardise the very foundations of bourgeois society. From the ones it demands that they should not go forward from political to social emancipation; from the others that they should not go back from social to political restoration.[1]

The overwhelming victory of Louis Napoleon in the presidential election in December represented, according to Marx, a peasant insurrection against the republic of the rich. For Napoleon was the only man who 'had exhaustively represented the interests and the imagination of the peasant class, newly created in 1789'.[2] But Napoleon was attractive to other classes also. To the proletariat his election meant the dismissal of bourgeois republicanism and revenge for their June defeat; to the petty-bourgeoisie, it meant the rule of the debtor over the creditor; and to the grand bourgeoisie Napoleon presented an opportunity of ridding themselves of the alliance into which they had been forced with potentially progressive elements. Marx concluded that thus 'the most simple-minded man in France acquired the most multifarious significance. Just because he was nothing, he could signify everything, save himself.'[3]

Marx then described the manœuvring of the Assembly and Bonaparte during the first half of 1849, leading up to the attempt by the more radical section of the Assembly to censure Bonaparte by appealing to the constitution. When it appeared that Bonaparte and the royalist majority of the Assembly were the only authentic interpreters of the constitution, the democratic petty-bourgeoisie took to the streets, but their revolt was crushed. Marx then asked why the industrial bourgeoisie did not play, in 1848–9, the progressive part that they played in England. His answer was:

In England – and the largest French manufacturers are petty bourgeois compared with their English rivals – we really find the manufacturers, a Cobden, a Bright, at the head of the crusade against the bank and the stock-exchange aristocracy. Why not in France? In England industry predominates; in France, agriculture. In England industry requires free trade; in France protective tariffs, national monopoly alongside of the other monopolies. French industry does not dominate

---

[1] *MESW* i 172.   [2] Ibid. 173.   [3] Ibid. 174.

French production; the French industrialists, therefore, do not dominate the French bourgeoisie. In order to secure the advancement of their interests as against the remaining factions of the bourgeoisie, they cannot, like the English, take the lead of the movement and simultaneously push their class interests to the fore; they must follow in the train of the revolution, and serve interests which are opposed to the collective interests of their class. In February they had misunderstood their position; February sharpened their wits. And who is more directly threatened by the workers than the employer, the industrial capitalist? The manufacturer, therefore, of necessity became in France the most fanatical member of the party of Order. The reduction of his *profit* by finance, *what is that compared with the* abolition of profit by the proletariat?[1]

Marx went on to analyse the party of opposition, the so-called party of social-democracy, and found it no less a coalition of interests than the party of order. In particular Marx was concerned to mark the difference between petty-bourgeois socialism, which demanded credit institutions, progressive taxes, limits on inheritance, etc., and revolutionary socialism. The former was a doctrinaire socialism that was a theoretical expression of the proletariat only so long as the proletariat had not developed into a free historical movement of its own:

While this *utopian, doctrinaire socialism*, which subordinates the total movement to one of its moments, which puts in place of common, social production the brainwork of individual pedants and, above all, in fantasy does away with the revolutionary struggle of the classes and its requirements by small conjurers' tricks or great sentimentality; while this doctrinaire socialism, which at bottom only idealises present society, takes a picture of it without shadows and wants to achieve its ideal athwart the realities of present society; while the proletariat surrenders this socialism to the petty bourgeoisie; while the struggle of the different socialist leaders among themselves sets forth each of the so-called systems as a pretentious adherence to one of the transit points of the social revolution as against another – the *proletariat* rallies more and more round *revolutionary socialism*, round *communism*, for which the bourgeoisie

[1] Ibid. 211.

has itself invented the name of *Blanqui*. This socialism is the *declaration of the permanence of the revolution*, the *class dictatorship* of the proletariat as the necessary transit point to the *abolition of class distinctions generally*, to the abolition of all the relations of production on which they rest, to the abolition of all the social relations that correspond to these relations of production, to the revolutionising of all the ideas that result from these social relations.[1]

In the autumn of 1850, after the split in the Communist League, Marx added a fourth article to his previous three, more quiescent in tone. This concluded the series of articles with comments on the forthcoming revolution. This could not take place for some time, for France was entering a period of prosperity following, as was the rule, that in England.

> With this general prosperity, in which the productive forces of bourgeois society develop as luxuriantly as is at all possible within bourgeois relationships, there can be no talk of a real revolution. Such a revolution is only possible in the periods when *both* these *factors*, the *modern* productive *forces* and the *bourgeois productive forms*, come *in collision* with each other. The various quarrels in which the representatives of the individual factions of the Continental party of Order now indulge and mutually compromise themselves, far from providing the occasion for new revolutions are, on the contrary, possible only because the basis of the relationships is momentarily so secure and, what the reaction does not know, so *bourgeois*. From it all attempts of the reaction to hold up bourgeois development will rebound just as certainly as all moral indignation and all enthusiastic proclamations of the democrats. *A new revolution is possible only in consequence of a new crisis. It is, however, just as certain as this crisis.*[2]

Marx's second essay on contemporary French politics, entitled *The Eighteenth Brumaire of Louis Bonaparte*, is his most brilliant political pamphlet. The title is an allusion to the date of Napoleon Bonaparte's *coup d'état* in 1796, and Marx is concerned to examine the socio-political circumstances of Louis Napoleon's imitation *coup* in December 1851. In a preface to a second edition

[1] *MESW* I 222 f.　　　　　[2] Ibid. 231

of his essay, Marx compared his own approach to that of two other well-known works on the same subject by Victor Hugo and Proudhon: Hugo confined himself to bitter and witty invective while Proudhon, seeking to represent the *coup d'état* as the result of antecedent historical development, ended up with a historical apologia for its hero. 'I, on the contrary,' wrote Marx, 'demonstrate how the class struggle in France created circumstances and relationships that made it possible for a grotesque mediocrity to play a hero's part.'[1]

Marx began his demonstration by referring to the remark of Hegel that all facts and personages of great importance in world history occurred twice and added that the first time was tragedy and the second, farce. So it was with the two Bonapartes. He continued:

> Men make their own history, but they do not make it just as they please; they do not make it under circumstances chosen by themselves, but under circumstances directly encountered, given and transmitted from the past. The tradition of all the dead generations weighs like a nightmare on the brain of the living. And just when they seem engaged in revolutionising themselves and things, in creating something that has never yet existed, precisely in such periods of revolutionary crisis they anxiously conjure up the spirits of the past to their service and borrow from them names, battle cries and costumes in order to present the new scene of world history in this time-honoured disguise and this borrowed language.[2]

Marx then applied these considerations to the 1848 revolution and drew a distinction between eighteenth-century bourgeois revolutions whose very speed and brilliance made them short-lived and nineteenth-century proletarian revolutions which possessed a slow thoroughness born of constant interruption and self-criticism. Turning to the recent *coup d'état*, Marx found the excuse that the nation was taken unawares unacceptable:

> A nation and a woman are not forgiven the unguarded hour in which the first adventurer that came along could violate them. The riddle is not solved by such turns of speech, but merely formulated differently. It remains to be explained how a

[1] Ibid. 244. [2] Ibid. 247.

nation of thirty-six millions can be surprised and delivered unresisting into captivity by three swindlers.[1]

Marx then summarised the period dealt with in his *Class Struggles*. The success of Bonaparte was due to his having organised the *Lumpenproletariat* of Paris under the cover of a 'benevolent society' and put himself at their head. However, this immediate force had to be set against the long-term factors in Bonaparte's favour. The first of these was the old finance aristocracy who 'celebrated every victory of the President over its ostensible representatives as a victory of order'. And the reason for this was evident:

> If in every epoch the stability of the state power signified Moses and the prophets to the entire money market and to the priests of this money market, why not all the more so today, when every deluge threatens to sweep away the old states, and the old state debts with them?[2]

The industrial bourgeoisie, too, saw in Napoleon the man who could put an end to recent disorders. For this class, 'the struggle to maintain its public interests, its own class interests, its political power, only troubled and upset it, as it was a disturbance of private business'.[3] When trade was good, the commercial bourgeoisie raged against political squabbles for fear that trade might be upset; when trade was bad, they blamed it on the instability of the political situation. In 1851 France had indeed passed through a minor trade crisis and this, coupled with constant political ferment, had led the commercial bourgeoisie to cry 'Rather an end with terror than terror without end'[4] – a cry well understood by Bonaparte.

Marx devoted the last part of his article to a closer examination of the class basis of Bonaparte's power. To Marx this seemed to be non-existent: 'The struggle seems to be settled in such a way that all classes, equally impotent and equally remote, fall on their knees before the rifle butt.'[5] The explanation was that, having perfected parliamentary power only to withdraw it, the revolution had now to perfect the executive power in order then to destroy it. Marx outlined the history of this bureaucracy:

[1] *MESW* I 252. [2] Ibid. 318. [3] Ibid. 319.
[4] Ibid. 324. [5] Ibid. 332.

This executive power with its enormous bureaucratic and military organisation, with its ingenious state machinery, embracing wide strata, with a host of officials numbering half a million, besides an army of another half million, this appalling parasitic body, which enmeshes the body of French society like a net and chokes all its pores, sprang up in the days of the absolute monarchy, with the decay of the feudal system, which it helped to hasten.[1]

During and after the revolution of 1789 the bureaucracy had prepared the class rule of the bourgeoisie; under Louis Philippe and the parliamentary republic it had still been the instrument of the ruling class; under the second Bonaparte 'the state seems to have made itself completely independent'.[2] Marx then immediately qualified this by saying: 'and yet the state power is not suspended in mid-air. Bonaparte represents a class, and the most numerous class of French society at that, the small-holding peasants.'[3] The identity of interest of these peasants did not create a community since they were physically so scattered. Thus:

They cannot represent themselves, they must be represented. Their representative must at the same time appear as their master, as an authority over them, as an unlimited governmental power that protects them against the other classes and sends them rain and sunshine from above. The political influence of the small-holding peasants, therefore, find its final expression in the executive power subordinating society to itself.[4]

But the peasants on whom Napoleon relied were burdened by a mortgage debt whose interest was equal to the annual interest on the entire British national debt. And there were also taxes:

Taxes are the source of life for the bureaucracy, the army, the priests and the court, in short, for the whole apparatus of the executive power. Strong government and heavy taxes are identical. By its very nature, small-holding property forms a suitable basis for an all-powerful and innumerable bureaucracy. It creates a uniform level of relationships and persons over the whole surface of the land. Hence it also permits of uniform action from a supreme centre on all points of this uniform mass.[5]

[1] Ibid. 332.   [2] Ibid. 333.   [3] Ibid.
[4] Ibid. 334.   [5] Ibid. 338.

Finally the army had degenerated from the flower of the peasant youth into 'the swamp flower of the peasant Lumpenproletariat'.[1] Thus, according to Marx, the three key ideas of Napoleon I – independent small-holdings for peasants, taxes to support strong central administration, and a large army drawn from the peasants – had found their ultimate degeneration under Louis Napoleon. However, centralisation had been acquired and that would be an important feature of the future society:

> The demolition of the state machine will not endanger centralisation. Bureaucracy is only the low and brutal form of a centralisation that is still afflicted with its opposite, with feudalism. When he is disappointed in the Napoleonic Restoration, the French peasant will part with his belief in his small holding, the entire state edifice erected on this small holding will fall to the ground and the proletarian revolution will obtain that chorus without which its solo song becomes a swan song in all peasant countries.[2]

It is possibly significant that this passage, with its emphasis on centralisation as a progressive factor, was omitted in the second edition of the *Eighteenth Brumaire* in 1869.

BIBLIOGRAPHY

TRANSLATIONS

The Class Struggles in France
K. Marx, F. Engels, *Selected Works* (Moscow, 1962) vol. i.
The Eighteenth Brumaire of Louis Bonaparte
K. Marx, F. Engels, *Selected Works* (Moscow, 1962) vol. i.

COMMENTARIES

F. Mehring, *Karl Marx: The Story of his Life* (London, 1936).
I. Zeitlin, *Marxism: A Re-examination* (New York, 1967).

[1] *MESW* i 339.   [2] Ibid. 340.

CHAPTER SIX

A. Writings

Revelations Concerning the Cologne Communist Trial (1853)
Articles in the 'New York Daily Tribune' (1852–62)
Outlines of the Critique of Political Economy (1857–8)
(German title: *Grundrisse der Kritik der politischen Ökonomie*)
Critique of Political Economy (1859)

B. Biography

MARX's 'sleepless night of exile' began in earnest in 1853. The early 1850s marked the lowest point in the fortunes of the Marx family. In 1852 his daughter Franziska had died and Marx wrote to Engels: 'My wife is ill, little Jenny is ill, Lenchen has a sort of nervous fever. I could not and cannot call the doctor as I have no money for medicine. For 8–10 days I have fed the family on bread and potatoes and it is still questionable whether I can get any together today.'[1] In 1855 Marx received the hardest blow of his life when his eight-year-old son Edgar died. Months later, Marx wrote to Lassalle: 'The death of my child has deeply shaken both my heart and my brain and I feel the loss just as freshly as on the first day.'[2] In 1856 the situation was improved financially by an inheritance from Jenny's mother, which enabled them to move from the flat in Dean Street to a rented house in Maitland Park Road, on the northern outskirts of the then built-up area of London.

Marx's only regular source of income in these years came from the articles that he contributed once or twice weekly to the *New York Daily Tribune*, a radical paper with the largest circulation in America. Some of these articles, particularly those that

[1] *MEW* xxviii 128.   [2] Ibid. 617.

dealt with military matters, were written by Engels. At first they
dealt with British politics, but Marx soon widened their scope to
take in Europe and all aspects of the international scene. The
articles were vividly written and one of the most popular features
of the paper. Marx, however, regarded his journalism principally
as a distraction from his main work: 'the continual journalistic
muck annoys me. It takes up a lot of time, disperses my energies
and in the end is nothing. However independent one wishes to be
one is always bound to the paper and the public, particularly if
one receives cash payments, as I do. Purely scientific work is
something quite different.'[1]

Throughout this period, Marx indulged in no political activities.
At the end of 1852, the Communist League was dissolved following
the arrest of the leaders of its German section, which effectively
meant the end of its activities. When they were brought to trial,
Marx spent much time collecting evidence to show that the
League was merely a secret propaganda society and not actively
plotting the overthrow of existing governments. When the accused
were convicted in spite of this evidence, Marx published it under
the title *Revelations Concerning the Cologne Communist Trial*.

As early as 1851 Marx had announced the imminent publication
of a work, in several volumes, on *Economics*. But he found great
difficulty in drafting his material in a form fit for publication,
and also the political implications of the Cologne trial made
publishers wary of accepting such a work. By 1852 Marx had
given up his efforts to find a publisher and neglected his economic
studies for the next three years. The economic crisis of 1857,
however, moved him to fresh enthusiasm and by the autumn he
wrote to Engels: 'I am forced to kill the day with professional
work. I have only the night left for real work and even then I am
interrupted by illness . . . I have no news to give as I am living a
hermit's life.'[2] 'I am working madly through the nights on a
synthesis of my economic studies, so that I at least have the main
principles clear before the deluge.'[3] The resulting work was 'the
result of fifteen years research, thus the best period of my life'.[4]
But Marx was once again unable to draft the seven hundred very
discursive pages that he had compiled and only managed to
publish a few 'preliminary chapters' in 1859, with a general
Preface, under the title *Critique of Political Economy*. As ten

[1] *MEW* xxviii 592.   [2] Ibid. xxix.   [3] Ibid. 225.   [4] Ibid. 554.

years previously, Marx was interrupted by domestic troubles and refugee politics and had temporarily to abandon his economic studies.

C. Commentary

From 1857 to 1859, in many ways the most productive period of Marx's life, he wrote four pieces, each of a very different character: a *General Introduction* to his proposed six-volume *Economics*, a draft subsequently given the title *Outlines of a Critique of Political Economy*, a *Preface*, and the first few chapters of a work entitled *Towards a Critique of Political Economy*.

1. *General Introduction*

This was intended to introduce the *Outlines* or *Grundrisse* but was left unpublished 'because on closer reflection any anticipation of results still to be proved appears to me to be disturbing'.[1]

In the first of its three sections, entitled 'Production in General', Marx defined the subject of his inquiry as 'the socially determined production of individuals'.[2] He rejected the starting-point of Smith, Ricardo and Rousseau who began with isolated individuals outside society: 'production by isolated individuals outside society . . . is as great an absurdity as the idea of the development of language without individuals living together and talking to one another'.[3] Marx then pointed out that it was important to try to isolate the general factors common to all production in order not to ignore the essential differences between epochs. Modern economists like J. S. Mill were guilty of this ignorance when they tried to portray modern bourgeois relations of production as immutable laws of society. Marx cited two examples: thinkers like Mill tended to jump from the tautology that there was no such thing as production without property to presupposing a particular form of property – *private* property – as basic, whereas history pointed to common property as being basic. Secondly, there was a tendency to suppose that the legal system under which contemporary production took place was based on eternal principles

[1] *MESW* I 361.
[2] *Marx's Grundrisse*, ed. D. McLellan (New York, 1971) p. 16.
[3] Ibid. p. 18.

without realising that 'every form of production creates its own
legal relations'.[1] Marx summed up his first section with the
words: 'all the stages of production have certain determinations
in common which we generalise in thought; but the so-called
general conditions of production are nothing but abstract
conceptions which do not go to make up any real stage in the
history of production'.[2]

The second section bore the title 'The General Relation of
Production to Distribution, Exchange, and Consumption'. Here
Marx was concerned to refute the view that the four economic
activities of production, distribution, exchange and consumption
could be treated in isolation from each other. Marx began by
claiming that production was, in a sense, identical to consumption
in that one talked of productive consumption and consumptive
production; that each was in fact a means of bringing the other
about; and further that each involved the forms of existence of its
counterpart. Marx similarly denied that distribution formed an
independent sphere standing side by side with, and outside of,
production. This could not be maintained, since 'to the single
individual, distribution naturally appears as a law established by
society determining his position in the sphere of production,
within which he produces, and thus antedating production'.[3]
Conquering peoples or revolutions also seemed, by their distribution of property, to antedate and determine production. Similarly
with exchange, which seemed to Marx to be a constituent part of
production. 'The result we arrive at', Marx concluded, 'is not that
production, distribution, exchange and consumption are identical,
but that they are all members of one entity, different aspects of
one unit.'[4]

The third section is entitled 'The Method of Political Economy'
and is exceedingly abstract. Marx wished to establish that the
correct method of discussing economics was to start from simple
abstract concepts like value or labour and build up from these to
the larger entities of empirical observation like population or
classes. The reverse was characteristic of the seventeenth century;
but the thinkers of the following century had followed what was
'manifestly the scientifically correct method'.[5]

Marx then took money and labour as examples of the simple

---

[1] *Marx's Grundrisse*, p. 21.   [2] Ibid. p. 22.
[3] Ibid. p. 29.   [4] Ibid. p. 33.   [5] Ibid. p. 34.

abstract concepts with which he wished to start his analysis. He claimed that both these only attained their full complexity in bourgeois society and thus only someone thinking in the context of bourgeois society could hope fully to understand pre-capitalist economics, just as 'the anatomy of the human beings is the key to the anatomy of the ape'.[1] Marx continued: 'it would be thus impractical and wrong to arrange the economic categories in the order in which they were the determining factors in the course of history. Their order of sequence is rather determined by the relation which they bear to one another in modern bourgeois society.'[1] Marx then outlined the tentative plan of his *Economics* in five sections and concluded with a discussion of why Greek art was so much appreciated in the nineteenth century when the socio-economic background which produced it was so different.

2. *Outlines (Grundrisse) of a Critique of Political Economy*

The two sections into which the *Grundrisse* is divided are entitled 'On Money' and 'On Capital', and the very few other sub-headings also give the impression of a strictly economic treatise. However, the actual content is much broader than the title indicates. It is interesting that the *Grundrisse* begins, as do virtually all of Marx's major writings, as a critique of someone else's ideas: Marx was always happiest when he could work out his own views by attacking others. The *Grundrisse* opens with a few pages containing a critique of the reformist economists, Carey and Bastiat, brilliantly portrayed as incarnating respectively the vices (and virtues) of the mid-nineteenth-century Yankee and the disciples of Proudhon. After ten pages or so, however, Marx writes: 'It is impossible to pursue this nonsense further'; Carey and Bastiat are 'dropped' and Marx, having sharpened his tools on lesser minds, proceeds to carve out his own path. The jumbled nature of this manuscript of rough notes, the variety of subjects discussed, and the tremendous compression of the style make it difficult to give a satisfactory brief account of its contents and even more difficult to paraphrase it.

However, some things stand out at first glance. Firstly, there is the continuity of thought and style with the *1844 Manuscripts*, most noticeable in the influence of Hegel in both writings. If the *1844 Manuscripts* are Hegelian, then so is the *Grundrisse*, no

[1] Ibid.   [1] Ibid. p. 42.

more and no less. The concepts of alienation, objectification, appropriation, man's dialectical relationship to nature and his generic, or social, nature are all equally present in 1858. Early in the manuscript of the *Grundrisse* Marx offers the following comments on the economic ideas of his day, comments entirely reminiscent of his remarks on the 'reification' of money in 1844:

> The economists themselves say that men accord to the object [money] a trust that they would not accord to each other as persons. . . . Money can only possess a social property because individuals have alienated their own social relationships to a thing.[1]

Or later, and more generally:

> But if capital thus appears as the product of labour, the product of labour also appears as capital – no more as a simple product, not as exchangeable goods, but as *capital*; objectified labour becomes mastery, has command over living labour. It appears equally to be the result of labour, that its product appears as alien property, an independent mode of existence opposed to living labour, an equally autonomous value; that the product of labour, objectified labour, has acquired its own soul from living labour as an *alien* force. Considered from the standpoint of labour, labour thus appears to be active in the production process in such a way that it seems to reject its realisation in objective conditions as alien reality, and that it puts itself in the position of an unsubstantial labour capacity endowed only with needs against this reality which is estranged from it and which belongs, not to it, but to others; that it establishes its own reality not as an entity of its own, but merely as an entity for others, and thus also as a mere entity of others, or other entity, against itself.[2]

The most striking passage of the *Grundrisse* in this respect is the draft plan for Marx's *Economics* which is couched in language that might have come straight out of Hegel's *Logic*.

But there is also a striking difference. In 1844 Marx had read some classical economists but had not yet had time to integrate this knowledge into his critique of Hegel. As a result, the 1844

---

[1] K. Marx, *Grundrisse der Kritik der politischen Ökonomie* (Berlin, 1953) p. 78.   [2] *Marx's Grundrisse*, p. 100.

Manuscripts fall into two separate halves as illustrated by the title given them by their first editors: the *Economic and Philosophical Manuscripts*. By 1857–8 Marx has assimilated both Ricardo and Hegel (there are, interestingly, no references to Feuerbach in the *Grundrisse*), and he is in a position to make his own synthesis. He is, in Lassalle's words, 'a Hegel turned economist, a Ricardo turned socialist'.[1]

From the point of view of economics, the *Grundrisse* contains the first elaboration of Marx's mature theory. There are two key changes of emphasis. Firstly, instead of analysing the market mechanisms of *exchange*, as he had done earlier, Marx now starts from a consideration of *production*. Secondly, he now says that what the worker sells is not his *labour*, but his *labour power*. It is a combination of these two views that gives rise to the doctrine of surplus value. For, according to Marx, surplus value is not created by exchange but by the fact that the development of the means of production under capitalism enables the capitalist to enjoy the use value of the worker's labour power and with it to produce values that far exceed the mere exchange value of this labour power – which amounts only to food for the worker's subsistence. In fact, virtually all the elements of Marx's economic theory are elaborated in the *Grundrisse*. Since, however, these elements are dealt with at greater length in *Capital*, the *Grundrisse* is more interesting for the discussions that are not taken up again in the complete fragments of Marx's vast enterprise.

What, therefore, is new in Marx's picture of alienation in the *Grundrisse* is that it attempts to be firmly rooted in history. Capital, as well as being obviously an 'alienating' force, had fulfilled a very *positive* mission. Within a short space of time it had developed the productive forces enormously, had replaced natural needs by those historically created, and had given birth to a world market. It was thus the turning-point between the limitations of the past and the untold riches of the future:

> The universal nature of this production with its generality creates an alienation of the individual from himself and others, but also for the first time the general and universal nature of his relationships and capacities. At early stages of development the single individual appears to be more complete, since he has

[1] Lassalle to Marx, 12 May 1851.

not yet elaborated the wealth of his relationships, and has not established them as powers and autonomous social relationships that are opposed to himself. It is as ridiculous to wish to return to that primitive abundance as it is to believe in the necessity of its complete depletion. The bourgeois view has never got beyond opposition to this romantic outlook and thus will be accompanied by it, as a legitimate antithesis, right up to its blessed end.[1]

The ideas produced by capitalism were as transitory as capitalism itself: here Marx formulated his most succinct critique of 'classical' liberal principles. Pointing out that, although free competition may have been necessary at the beginning of capitalism, it was bound eventually to hamper its development, Marx alludes to

the absurdity of considering free competition as being the final development of human liberty; and the negation of free competition as being the negation of individual liberty and of social production founded on individual liberty. We are concerned only with free development on a limited foundation – that of the dominion of capital. This kind of individual liberty is thus at the same time the most complete suppression of all individual liberty and total subjugation of individuality to social conditions which take the form of material forces – and even of overpowering objects that are independent of the individuals relating to them. The development of what free competition is, is the only rational answer to the deification of it by the middle-class prophets, or its bedevilment by the socialists. If it is said that, within the limits of free competition, individuals by following their pure self-interest realise their social or rather their general interest this means merely that they exert pressure upon one another under the conditions of capitalist production and that collision between them can only again give rise to the conditions under which their interaction took place. Moreover, once the illusion that competition is the ostensible absolute form of free individuality disappears, this proves that the conditions of competition, i.e. production founded on capital, are already felt and thought of as a barrier, as indeed they already are and will increasingly become so. The assertion that free competition is the final form of the develop-

[1] *Marx's Grundrisse*, p. 71.

ment of productive forces, and thus of human freedom, means only that the domination of the middle class is the end of the world's history – of course quite a pleasant thought for yesterday's parvenus![1]

This richer historical content implies that the *Grundrisse*, while continuing the themes central to the *Paris Manuscripts*, treats them in a much 'maturer' way than was possible before Marx had achieved a synthesis of his ideas on philosophy and economics.

The key to the understanding of the ambivalent nature of capitalism – and the possibilities that it contained for an unalienated society – was the notion of *time*. 'All economics', said Marx, 'can be reduced in the last analysis to the economics of time.' The profits of capitalism were built on the creation of surplus work time, yet at the same time the wealth of capitalism emancipated man from manual labour and gave him increasing access to free time. Capital was itself a 'permanent revolution':

> Pursuing this tendency, capital has pushed beyond national boundaries and prejudices, beyond deification of nature and the inherited self-sufficient satisfaction of existing needs confined within well-defined bounds, and the reproduction of the traditional way of life.

> It is destructive of all this, and permanently revolutionary, tearing down all obstacles that impede the development of productive forces, the expansion of needs, the diversity of production and the exploitation and exchange of natural and intellectual forces.[2]

But, in Marx's eyes, these very characteristics of capitalism entailed its dissolution. Its wealth was based on the introduction of machinery followed (Marx's foresight here is extraordinary) by that of automation and this entailed an ever-growing contradiction between the decreasing role played by labour in the production of social wealth and the necessity for capital to appropriate surplus labour. Capital was thus both hugely creative and hugely wasteful:

> Capital is contradiction embodied in a process, since it makes an effort to reduce labour time to the minimum, while at the

[1] Ibid. p. 131.   [2] Ibid. pp. 94 f.

same time establishing labour time as the sole measurement and
source of wealth. Thus it diminishes *labour* time in its necessary
form, in order to increase its *superfluous* form; therefore it
increasingly establishes superfluous labour time as a condition
(a question of life and death) for necessary labour time.

On the one hand it calls into life all the forces of science and
nature, as well as those of social co-operation and commerce,
in order to create wealth which is relatively independent of the
labour time utilised. On the other hand, it attempts to measure
the vast social forces thus created in terms of labour time, and
imprisons them within the narrow limits that are required in
order to retain the value already created *as* value. Productive
forces and social relationships – the two different sides of the
development of social individuality – appear only as a means for
capital, and are for it only a measure to enable it to produce
from its own cramped foundation. But in fact they are the
material conditions that will shatter this foundation.[1]

Passages like this show clearly enough that such apparently
purely economic doctrines as the labour theory of value are not
economic doctrines in the sense that, say, Keynes or Schumpeter
understand them. The reading of Marx as an economist among
other economists is bound to falsify to some extent his thought.
For Marx, as he himself proclaimed as early as 1844, economics
and ethics were inextricably linked. The *Grundrisse* shows that
this is as true of his later writings as it is of the earlier.

In such a state of affairs there is danger that the forces guiding
human development will be taken over entirely by machines to
the exclusion of human beings:

Science thus appears, in the machine, as something alien and
exterior to the worker: and living labour is subsumed under
objectified labour which acts independently. The worker
appears to be superfluous insofar as his action is not determined by the needs of capital.[2]

---

[1] *Marx's Grundrisse*, pp. 142 f.

[2] Ibid. p. 135. In his correspondence with Engels, Marx says that he considers the primitive model of an automatic machine to be a clock. Marx got a
lot of his information on automatic spinning machinery (as well as other
aspects of factory life) from Engels, to whom he often turned for help in these

In the age of automation, science itself can become the biggest factor making for alienation:

> The worker's activity, limited to a mere abstraction, is determined and regulated on all sides by the movement of the machinery, not the other way round. The knowledge that obliges the inanimate parts of the machine, through their construction, to work appropriately as an automaton, does not exist in the consciousness of the worker, but acts through the machine upon him as an alien force, as the power of the machine itself.[1]

Yet this enormous expansion of the productive forces did not necessarily bring with it the alienation of the individual: it afforded the opportunity for society to become composed of 'social' or 'universal' individuals – beings very similar to the 'all-round' individuals of the *Paris Manuscripts*. This is how Marx describes the transition from individual to social production:

> Production based on exchange value therefore falls apart, and the immediate material productive process finds itself stripped of its impoverished, antagonistic form. Individuals are then in a position to develop freely. It is no longer a question of reducing the necessary labour time of society to a minimum. The counterpart of this reduction is that all members of society can develop their artistic, scientific, etc., education, thanks to the free time now available to all. . . .
>
> Bourgeois economists are so bogged down in their traditional ideas of the historical development of society in a single stage, that the necessity of the *objectification* of the social forces of labour seems to them inseparable from the necessity of its *alienation* in relation to living labour.
>
> But as living labour loses its *immediate*, individual character, whether subjective or entirely external, as individual activity becomes directly general or social the material elements of production lose this form of alienation. They are then produced

---

practical questions. He confessed to his friend: 'I understand the mathematical laws, but the simplest technical reality, where observation is necessary, is as difficult for me as for the greatest ignoramus . . .' (*MEW* xxx 320).

[1] *Marx's Grundrisse*, p. 133.

as property, as the organic social body in which individuals are reproduced as individuals, but as social individuals.

The conditions for their being such in the reproduction of their life, in their productive life process, can only be established by the historical economic process: both these conditions are objective and subjective conditions, which are only the two different forms of the same condition.[1]

It is noteworthy that here, and throughout the *Grundrisse*, the agent of the transformation – the revolutionary activity of the proletariat – is never alluded to.

The 'universal individual' – a notion that Marx returns to almost *ad nauseam* in the *Grundrisse* – is at the centre of Marx's vision of utopia; the millenarian strain is no less clear here than in the passage in the *Paris Manuscripts* on communism as 'the solution to the riddle of history'. The universal tendency inherent in capital, says Marx, creates

as a basis, a development of productive forces – of wealth in general – whose powers and tendencies are of a general nature, and at the same time a universal commerce, and thus world trade as a basis. The basis as the possibility of the universal development of individuals; the real development of individuals from this basis as the constant abolition of each limitation conceived of *as* a limitation and not as a sacred boundary. The universality of the individual not as thought or imagined, but as the universality of his real and ideal relationships. Man therefore becomes able to understand his own history as a *process* and to conceive of nature (involving also practical control over it) as his own real body. The process of development is itself established and understood as a prerequisite. But it is necessary also and above all that full development of the productive forces should have become a *condition of production*, not that determined *conditions of production* should be set up as a boundary beyond which productive forces cannot develop.[2]

Marx very rarely discussed the form of the future communist society – reasonably enough in his own terms, for he would have laid himself open to the charge of 'idealism', the spinning of ideas that had no foundation in reality. But certain passages in the

[1] *Marx's Grundrisse*, p. 151.   [2] Ibid. pp. 121 f.

Grundrisse give a better idea than the well-known accounts in the *Communist Manifesto* or the *Critique of the Gotha Programme* of what lay at the heart of Marx's vision. One of the central factors is time, since the development of the 'universal individual' depends above all on the free time that he has at his disposal. Time is of the essence in Marx's utopia:

> If we suppose communal production, the determination of time remains, of course, essential. The less time society requires in order to produce wheat, cattle, etc., the more time it gains for other forms of production, material or intellectual. As with a single individual, the universality of its development, its enjoyment and its activity depends on saving time. . . .
>
> On the basis of community production, the first economic law thus remains the economy of time, and the methodical distribution of working time between the various branches of production. This law becomes indeed of much greater importance. But all this differs basically from the measurement of exchange values (labour and the products of labour) by labour time. The work of individuals participating in the same branch of activity, and the different kinds of labour, are not only quantitatively but also qualitatively different. What is the precondition of a merely *quantitative* difference between things? The fact that their *quality* is the same. Thus units of labour can be measured quantitatively only if they are of equal and identical quality.[1]

This free time is due entirely to the extensive use of machinery. Whereas in the past machinery has been a power hostile to the worker, in the future its function can be radically altered:

> No special sagacity is required in order to understand that, beginning with free labour or wage-labour for example, which arose after the abolition of slavery, machines can only develop in opposition to living labour, as a hostile power and alien property, i.e. they must, as capital, oppose the worker.
>
> It is equally easy to see that machines do not cease to be agents of social production, once they become, for example, the property of associated workers. But in the first case, their means of distribution (the fact that they do not belong to the

[1] Ibid. pp. 75 f.

workers) is itself a condition of the means of production that is founded on wage-labour. In the second case, an altered means of distribution will derive from an altered new basis of production emerging from the historical process.[1]

Marx rejected Adam Smith's view of work as necessarily an imposition. But neither did he subscribe to Fourier's idea that work could become a sort of game. According to Marx, Smith's view is true of the labour

> which has not yet created the subjective and objective conditions (which it lost when it abandoned pastoral conditions) which make of it attractive labour and individual self-realisation. This does not mean that labour can be made merely a joke, or amusement, as Fourier naïvely expressed it in shop-girl terms. Really free labour, the composing of music for example, is at the same time damned serious and demands the greatest effort. The labour concerned with material production can only have this character if (1) it is of a social nature, (2) it has a scientific character and at the same time is general work, i.e. if it ceases to be achieved by human effort as a definite, trained natural force, and – no longer a merely natural, primitive force – becomes the activity of a subject controlling all the forces of nature in the production process.[2]

Marx envisages a time when production depends not on the amount of labour employed but on the general level of science and technology, when the measure of wealth is the enormous disproportion between the labour time employed and the size of the product, when 'man behaves as the supervisor and regulator of the process of production'. Then the true emancipation of mankind will take place:

> In this re-orientation what appears as the mainstay of production and wealth is neither the immediate labour performed by the worker, nor the time that he works – but the appropriation of his general productive force, his understanding of nature and the mastery of it as a special force; in a word, the development of the social individual.
> The theft of others' labour time upon which wealth depends

---

[1] *Marx's Grundrisse*, p. 152.   [2] Ibid. p. 124.

today seems to be a miserable basis compared with the newly-developed foundation that has been created by heavy industry itself.

As soon as labour, in its direct form, has ceased to be the main source of wealth, then labour time ceases, and must cease, to be its standard of measurement, and thus exchange value must cease to be the measurement of use-value. The surplus labour of the masses has ceased to be a condition for the development of wealth in general in the same way that the non-labour of the few has ceased to be a condition for the development of the powers of the human mind in general.[1]

Thus in the *Grundrisse* the nature of the vision that inspired Marx is at least sketched out: communal production in which the quality of work determined its value; the disappearance of money with that of exchange value; and an increase in free time affording opportunities for the universal development of the individual.

3. *Contribution to a Critique of Political Economy*

Marx opened the *Preface* to this work with a list of the six volumes which were to comprise his *Economics*: capital, landed property, wage-labour, state, foreign trade, world market. The 'total material' for these books, Marx wrote, 'lies before me in the form of monographs, which were written at widely separated periods, for self-clarification, not for publication, and whose coherent elaboration according to the plan indicated will be dependent on external circumstances'.[2]

There followed a short piece of intellectual autobiography in which Marx stressed the importance of his journalistic work for the *Rheinische Zeitung* in giving him an insight into the importance of 'material interests' and 'economic questions'. He then withdrew into his study to examine Hegel's political philosophy. The conclusion of this retreat was that

legal relations as well as forms of state are to be grasped neither from themselves nor from the so-called general development of the human mind, but rather have their roots in the material conditions of life, the sum total of which Hegel, following the example of the Englishmen and Frenchmen of the eighteenth

[1] Ibid. p. 142.   [2] *MESW* i 361.

century, combines under the name of 'civil society', that, however, the anatomy of civil society is to be sought in political economy'.[1]

Marx then, in a famous and often quoted passage, summed up the 'guiding thread' of his subsequent studies of political economy. This summary contained four main points:

(i) The sum total of relations of production – the way men organised their social production as well as the instruments they used – constituted the real basis of society on which there arose a legal and political superstructure and to which corresponded definite forms of social consciousness. Thus the way men produced their means of subsistence conditioned their whole social, political, and intellectual life.

(ii) At a certain stage in their evolution the forces of production would develop beyond the relations of production and these would act as a fetter. Such a stage inaugurated a period of social revolution.

(iii) These productive forces had to develop to the fullest extent possible under the existing relations of production before the old social order would perish.

(iv) It was possible to pick out the Asiatic, ancient, feudal and modern bourgeois modes of production as progressive epochs in the economic formation of society. These bourgeois relations of production were the last ones to create a divided society and with their end the prehistory of human society would be brought to a close.

Marx added a few more biographical details, described his views as 'the result of conscientious investigation lasting many years', and finished with a quotation from Dante against any intellectual compromise.

The text which followed this *Preface* was, according to Marx, only 'some preliminary chapters' – in fact, one on commodities and one on money. Since the roles of both commodities and money in the capitalist system were dealt with at greater length in *Capital*, an account of Marx's views here can be left to the next chapter.

[1] *MESW* i 362.

BIBLIOGRAPHY

TRANSLATIONS

K. Marx, *On Colonialism and Modernisation*, ed. S. Avineri (New York, 1968).

K. Marx, *The Cologne Communist Trial*, ed. with an introduction by R. Livingstone (New York and London, 1970).

Outlines of the Critique of Political Economy
Marx's Grundrisse, trans. D. McLellan (New York, 1971).

Preface to a Critique of Political Economy
K. Marx, F. Engels, *Selected Works* (Moscow, 1962) vol. i.

Critique of Political Economy

K. Marx, *Critique of Political Economy*, trans. Stone (Chicago, 1904).

K. Marx, *Critique of Political Economy,* ed. with an introduction by M. Dobb (New York and London, 1971).

COMMENTARIES

R. Daniels, 'Fate and Will in the Marxian Philosophy of History', *Journal of the History of Ideas* (1960).

D. McLellan, introduction to *Marx's Grundrisse* (New York, 1971).

S. Moore, 'Marx and the Origins of Dialectical Materialism', *Inquiry* (autumn 1971).

M. Nicolaus, 'The Unknown Marx', *New Left Review* (1968).

J. Plamenatz, *German Marxism and Russian Communism* (London, 1954).

A. Prinz, 'Background to Marx's Preface of 1859', *Journal of the History of Ideas* (1969).

CHAPTER SEVEN

A. WRITINGS

Herr Vogt (1860)
Theories of Surplus Value (1862–3)
Capital, vol. III (1865)
Wages, Prices and Profit (1865)
Results of the Immediate Process of Production (1865)
Capital, vol I (1867)
Capital, vol. II (1869–79)

B. BIOGRAPHY

MARX could not follow up his *Critique of Political Economy*, as he spent the whole of 1860 answering attacks on himself and his 'party' launched by Karl Vogt. His only financial resources were still the articles that he was writing – in decreasing numbers – for the *New York Herald Tribune*. Charles Dana, the editor, wrote supporting Marx in the Vogt affair: 'You are not only one of the most highly valued, but one of the best paid contributors to the journal.' His only qualification was that Marx had 'manifested too great an anxiety for the unity and independence of Germany'. The beginning of the Civil War meant that Marx stopped writing for the paper completely. In 1861 he went to Holland where he persuaded his uncle to give him an advance on his mother's estate, then continued to Germany where he discussed with Lassalle the prospect of recovering his Prussian citizenship and their founding a newspaper together in Berlin. Both projects failed.

Also in 1861 Marx returned to his 'third chapter' and wrote in typical vein to Lassalle in April of the following year: 'As far as my book is concerned, it will not be ready for two months. In order to avoid starvation during the last year I have had to do the most contemptible sort of jobs and have often not been able to write a line of the stuff for months on end. In addition it is characteristic of me that, if I see something that I completed four weeks or so ago, I find it unsatisfactory and rework it completely. In any case, the book doesn't lose anything in the process'. In the same year Marx informed Engels of the repercussions of this on their family life: 'My wife tells me every day that she wishes she were in the grave with the children and really I cannot hold it against her; for the humiliations, torments and fears that we have to endure are in fact indescribable.' These troubles were also the cause of Marx's only serious quarrel with Engels, who considered Marx's reaction to the death of Mary Burns, his wife in all but name, to have been insensitive in the extreme. Marx pleaded financial worry and friendship was restored. Marx's depression was increased by the phenomenal success that Lassalle was having in organising the German workers. Marx considered that Lassalle adopted too conciliatory an attitude towards Bismarck and this difference of opinion led to a breach when Lassalle visited Marx in London in 1862 which lasted until the death of Lassalle in 1864.

In 1864 Marx's financial position improved dramatically: the death of his mother gave him £400 and he was left twice that sum in the will of his friend Wilhelm Wolff. The Marx family moved to a more capacious house in Haverstock Hill. The same year saw the founding of the International, work for which 'weighs upon me like an incubus' and which Marx considered to be of secondary importance to his economic studies.

By 1866 Marx decided at last to begin the final draft of Volume I of *Capital*. In spite of sleeplessness, illness and renewed debt, he managed to finish the manuscript by April 1867 and travelled to Hamburg in person to deliver the manuscript to the publisher. It was, wrote Marx, a work

to which I have sacrificed health, happiness and family ... I laugh at so-called 'practical' men and their wisdom. If one were willing to be an ox, one could naturally turn one's back on human suffering and look after one's own skin. But I would really have considered myself 'unpractical' if I caved in before making my book, or at least my manuscript, quite ready.

And when he had corrected the final proof in August he wrote to Engels:

It is you alone that I have to thank for making this possible! Without your sacrifice for me it would have been impossible to complete the enormous labour on the three volumes. I embrace you, full of thanks!

And in September Volume I of *Capital* appeared in Hamburg in an edition of 1,000 copies.

C. COMMENTARY

It is important to understand the place of *Capital* in the economic writings of Marx in the 1860s. Basically, at the time of writing the *Grundrisse*, Marx had thought of dividing his *Economics* into six volumes, the first of which was to be entitled *Capital*. The *Critique of Political Economy* published in 1859 was the first instalment of this volume and was to be completed by a section on 'Capital in General'. Marx's work on this section was interrupted in 1860 by his dispute with Karl Vogt, and when Marx started to work on it in 1861–3 he found – as usual – that he had produced an enormous manuscript (around 3,000 printed pages) that was quite unpublishable. Most of this manuscript was historical and dealt with past theories of value; it was eventually published by Kautsky in 1905 under the title *Theories of Surplus Value*, as the fourth volume of *Capital*. From 1863 onwards Marx was working directly on the three books of *Capital* eventually published.[1] Volume III was written mainly from 1863 to 1865, thus before the final drafting of Volume I. As for the manuscripts of Volume II, Marx worked on them both before and after the final drafting of Volume I. Thus although Volume I was completed, it was intended to be followed by Volumes II and III which remained incomplete both in content and in form; and the whole was to be followed by further volumes.

[1] These include an important fragment entitled 'Results of the Immediate Production Process' that was originally destined for vol I, but remained unpublished until the 1930s and is still untranslated in English. Two passages from this manuscript are quoted in Part II, Chapter 1, pp. 118 ff.

The only part of this immense task that Marx managed to complete in his lifetime – Volume I of *Capital* – consists of two very distinct parts. The first nine chapters are of an extremely abstract theoretical nature, whereas the rest of the book contains a description of the historical genesis of capitalism which is at times extremely vivid and readable.

The first nine chapters contain what Marx called in his 1857 *Introduction* 'the general abstract definitions which are more or less applicable to all forms of society'.[1] It is not only this abstract method that makes these chapters difficult; there is also the Hegelian cast of the book. In his *Afterword* to the second German edition of the book Marx explained that he was employing the Hegelian dialectic of which he had discovered the 'rational kernel' inside the 'mystical shell' by 'turning it right side up again'.[2] He even, he said in the same *Afterword*, went as far as 'coquetting with modes of expression peculiar to Hegel'. A third factor which makes the beginning of *Capital* difficult is the fact that the concepts used by Marx are ones quite familiar to economists in the mid-nineteenth century but thereafter abandoned by the orthodox schools of economics. Since the third quarter of the nineteenth century economists in Western Europe and America have tended to look at the capitalist system as given, construct models of it, assuming private property, profit and a more or less free market, and to discuss the functionings of this model, concentrating particularly on prices. This 'marginalist' school of economics has no concept of value apart from price. To Marx, this procedure seemed superficial for two reasons: firstly, he considered it superficial in a literal sense, in that it was only a description of phenomena lying on the surface of capitalist society without an analysis of the mode of production that gave rise to these phenomena. Secondly, this approach took the capitalist system for granted whereas Marx wished to analyse 'the birth, life and death of a given social organism and its replacement by another, superior order'.

In order to achieve these two aims, Marx took over the concepts of the 'classical' economists that were still the generally accepted tool of economic analysis, and used them to draw very different conclusions. Ricardo had made a distinction between

---

[1] *Marx's Grundrisse*, p. 42.
[2] K. Marx, *Capital* (Moscow, 1954) I 19 f.

use value and exchange value. The exchange value of an object was something separate from its price and consisted of the amount of labour embodied in the objects of production, though Ricardo thought that the price in fact tended to approximate to the exchange value. Thus – in contradistinction to later analyses – the value of an object was determined by the circumstances of production rather than those of demand. Marx took over these concepts, but, in his attempt to show that capitalism was not static but a historically relative system of class exploitation, supplemented Ricardo's views by introducing the idea of surplus value. Surplus value was defined as the difference between the value of the products of labour and the cost of producing that labour power, i.e. the labourer's subsistence; for the exchange value of labour power was equal to the amount of labour necessary to reproduce that labour power and this was normally much lower than the exchange value of the products of that labour power.

The theoretical part of Volume I divides very easily into three sections. The first section is a re-writing of the *Critique of Political Economy* of 1859 and analyses commodities, in the sense of external objects that satisfy human needs, and their value. Marx established two sorts of value – use value, or the utility of something, and exchange value which is determined by the amount of labour incorporated in the object. Labour is also of a twofold nature according to whether it creates use values or exchange values. There follows a difficult chapter on the form of value, and Marx concludes this section with an account of commodities as exchange values which he describes as the 'fetishism of commodities'.[1] The section ends with a chapter on exchange and an account of money as the means for the circulation of commodities, the material expression for their values and the universal measure of value.

The second section is a small one on the transformation of money into capital. Before the capitalist era people had sold commodities for money in order to buy more commodities. In the capitalist era, instead of selling to buy, people had bought to sell dearer: they had bought commodities with their money in order, by means of those commodities, to increase their money.

In the third section Marx introduces his key notion of surplus

[1] K. Marx, *Capital* (Moscow, 1954) I 91 ff.

value. He makes a distinction between *constant* capital which is 'that part of capital which is represented by the means of production, by the raw material, auxiliary material and instruments of labour, and does not, in the process of production, undergo any quantitative alteration of value' and *variable* capital. Of this Marx says: 'That part of capital, represented by labour power, does, in the process of production, undergo an alteration of value. It both reproduces the equivalent of its own value, and also produces an excess, a surplus value, which may itself vary, may be more or less according to the circumstances.'[1] A little further on Marx expanded on the nature of this surplus value:

> During the second period of the labour-process, that in which his labour is no longer necessary labour, the workman, it is true, labours, expends labour-power; but his labour being no longer necessary labour, he creates no value for himself. He creates surplus-value which, for the capitalist, has all the charms of a creation out of nothing. This portion of the working-day, I name surplus labour-time, and to the labour expended during that time, I give the name of surplus-labour. It is every bit as important, for a correct understanding of surplus-value, to conceive it as a mere congelation of surplus labour-time, as nothing but materialised surplus-labour, as it is, for a proper comprehension of value, to conceive it as a mere congelation of so many hours of labour, as nothing but materialised labour. The essential difference between the various economic forms of society, between, for instance, a society based on slave-labour, and one based on wage-labour, lies only in the mode in which this surplus-labour is in each case extracted from the actual producer, the labourer.[2]

Thus surplus value could only arise from variable capital, not from constant capital, as labour alone created value. Put very simply, Marx's reason for thinking that the rate of profit would decrease was that, with the introduction of machinery, labour time would become less and thus yield less surplus value. Of course, machinery would increase production and colonial markets would absorb some of the surplus, but these were only palliatives and an eventual crisis was inevitable.

[1] Ibid. 209.   [2] Ibid. 217.

These first nine chapters were complemented by a masterly historical account of the genesis of capitalism which illustrates better than any other writing Marx's approach and method. Marx particularly made pioneering use of official statistical information that came to be available from the middle of the nineteenth century onwards. Marx finished the book with a chapter on capitalist accumulation that reverts to the theme of the first part: the contradiction between the extraction of surplus value and the increasing tendency to accumulate capital in the form of machinery would lead to a cataclysm:

> Along with the constantly diminishing number of the magnates of capital, who usurp and monopolise all advantages of this process of transformation, grows the mass of misery, oppression, slavery, degradation, exploitation; but with this too grows the revolt of the working-class, a class always increasing in numbers, and disciplined, united, organised by the very mechanism of the process of capitalist production itself. The monopoly of capital becomes a fetter upon the mode of production, which has sprung up and flourished along with, and under it. Centralisation of the means of production and socialisation of labour at last reach a point where they become incompatible with their capitalist integument. This integument is burst asunder. The knell of capitalist private property sounds. The expropriators are expropriated.[1]

Volume II of *Capital* is a fairly finished piece of work but much less interesting than the other two volumes owing to its technical nature: it discusses the circulation of capital and its role in the genesis of economic crises. The first part of Volume III appears to be in a more or less final draft, but thereafter the book tails off without any final conclusion. It begins with a discussion of the conversion of surplus value into profit and thus the relationship between values and prices. Many people on reading Volume I had asked how it came about that, if values were measured by socially necessary labour, they should be so very different from market prices. The only answer that Marx provided to this problem was to assert that value was 'the centre of gravity around which prices fluctuate and around which their rise and fall tends to an equilibrium'.[2] He continued: 'No matter what may be the way in which

[1] K. Marx, *Capital*, I 763.   [2] *Capital*, vol. III (Chicago, 1909), p. 210.

prices are regulated, the result always is the following: the law of value dominates the movement of prices, since a reduction or increase of the labour-time required for production causes the prices of production to fall or to rise.'[1] Marx then enunciated in greater detail than in Volume I the falling tendency of the rate of profit. This law is expressed most succinctly by Marx as follows:

> . . . it is the nature of the capitalist mode of production, and a logical necessity of its development, to give expression to the average rate of surplus-value by a falling rate of average profit. Since the mass of the employed living labour is continually on the decline compared to the mass of materialised labour incorporated in productively consumed means of production, it follows that that portion of living labour, which is unpaid and represents surplus-value, must also be continually on the decrease compared to the volume and value of the invested total capital. Seeing that the proportion of the mass of surplus-value to the value of the invested total capital forms the rate of profit, this rate must fall continuously.[2]

Marx then deals with the factors that could slow down the fall in profits – principally increased production and foreign trade – and attempts to show that they can only be short-term palliatives. There follow two sections on interest-bearing capital and ground rent and the volume ends with the dramatically incomplete section on classes.[3]

The three volumes of the *Theories of Surplus Value* which Marx intended as a sort of Volume IV of *Capital* are less finished than any of the other three volumes. They consist mainly of excerpts from the classical economists and their disciples interspersed with commentary. In Part I Marx deals with the physiocrats and Adam Smith; in Part 2 he discusses Ricardo's work with a view to evaluating his theoretical merits; and in Part 3 he deals with the socialist followers of Ricardo, who had developed a concept of exploitation from his doctrines.

Thus Marx's economic writings of the 1860s are incomplete. Ill-health, the pressure of political activity and, perhaps, the sheer size of the task he had set himself, prevented him from completing anything but a fragment of his original project.

[1] Ibid. 211.   [2] Ibid. 249.   [3] See the extract on pp. 165f. below.

BIBLIOGRAPHY

TRANSLATIONS

Theories of Surplus Value
K. Marx, *Theories of Surplus Value*, 2 vols (Moscow, 1954–69).

Capital
K. Marx, *Capital*, 3 vols (Moscow, 1954).

Wages, Price and Profit
K. Marx, F. Engels, *Selected Works* (Moscow, 1962) vol. I.

COMMENTARIES

G. D. H. Cole, *A History of Socialist Thought*, vol. II (London, 1961) chap. 11.

M. Dobb, *Marx as an Economist* (London, 1943).

R. Garaudy, *Karl Marx: The Evolution of his Thought* (London, 1967) pt 3.

D. Horowitz (ed.), *Marx and Modern Economics* (London, 1968).

E. Mandel, *An Introduction to Marxist Economic Theory* (New York, 1969).

E. Roll, *A History of Economic Thought* (London, 1953), chap. 6.

J. Schumpeter, *Capitalism, Socialism and Democracy* (London, 1943) chap. 3.

Science and Society (1967): centenary number on *Capital*.

CHAPTER EIGHT

A. WRITINGS

Inaugural Address and Rules of the Working Men's International Association (1864)
Two Addresses on the Franco-Prussian War (1870)
Address on the Civil War in France (1871)
Comments on Bakunin's Statism and Anarchy (1875).
Critique of the Gotha Programme (1875)
Circular Letter to the Leaders of the German Social Democratic Party (1879)
Letter to Vera Sassoulitch (1881)
Preface to the Second Russian Edition of the 'Communist Manifesto' (1882)

B. BIOGRAPHY

MARX's writings during the last fifteen years of his life are mainly political owing to the involvement of Marx in the International and the growth of socialist parties. In 1864 Marx was invited to an international meeting in St Martin's Hall, London; here it was decided to found an International Working Men's Association whose statutes and *Inaugural Address* were composed by Marx. During the next few years Marx continued to be the leading figure in the International, drafting its various pronouncements on Continental movements (particularly in opposition to Lassalle's idea of workers' associations financed by the state), Polish independence as a bulwark against Russian barbarism, support for Irish Home Rule, the shortening of the working day, the transfer of land to common ownership, etc. This work took up the major part of Marx's time. In 1865 he wrote: 'Compared with my work on the book [i.e. *Capital*], the International Association takes up an enormous amount of time, because I am in fact in

charge of the whole business.'[1] However, as early as 1870 the split
in the International caused by the followers of the Russian anarchist Bakunin was already becoming apparent. In as far as they
held any coherent doctrine, Bakunin's followers opposed any
form of state, even a revolutionary workers' state, called for the
equalisation of classes, and proposed conspiratorial methods to
attain these ends.

The most important political event in the lifetime of the
International was the Franco-Prussian War and its aftermath.
The stability that Europe had enjoyed after the 1848 revolutions
was disturbed by the expansionist policy of Prussia under its
'Iron Chancellor', Bismarck. Prussia defeated Austria in a rapid
war in 1866, and proclaimed a united German Empire excluding
Austria. In 1870 Bismarck provoked a war with France in which
he very swiftly defeated and captured the Emperor Louis-
Napoleon. On behalf of the General Council of the International
Marx issued three addresses concerning the war: the first briefly
supported the view that the war was one of defence from Germany's
point of view and that a French defeat would bring about a
revolution in France; the second criticised Prussia for continuing
the war after the defeat of Napoleon, declared that the Prussian
annexation of Alsace and Lorraine only sowed the seeds of future
war and finally urged the Paris workers to support the provisional
government set up on the defeat of Napoleon. The third, and
much the longest address, entitled *On the Civil War in France*,
was written immediately following the bloody suppression of the
rising of the Paris workers against the provisional government,
known as the Paris Commune. Two earlier drafts of this address
survive.

By 1872 the quarrel inside the International with Bakunin
had become so serious that Marx was compelled to bring the
Association to an end by proposing the transfer of its seat to
New York.

During the last decade of his life, Marx was too ill to undertake
any protracted writing. He spent his time on taking notes from
his still enormous reading and on his wide correspondence. The
economic situation of the Marx family had greatly improved from
the mid-1860s onwards: Engels came to live in London and gave
Marx an annuity that enabled his family to move to a large house

[1] *MEW* xxxi 100.

on Haverstock Hill. During the 1870s, as well as working on the second edition of *Capital* and its French translation, Marx drew up a detailed criticism of the first common programme of the German socialists who met at Gotha in 1875 at a congress which united the Lassallean wing with the Eisenach party led by Liebknecht and Bebel. These criticisms were published by Engels in 1891 under the title *Critique of the Gotha Programme*. Particularly in his later years Marx began to be very interested in Russia, and among the correspondence of the last years of his life are letters containing a very balanced assessment of the possibilities of Russia's by-passing the capitalist stage of development and basing communism on existing peasant co-operatives.

In 1881 Marx's wife Jenny died. Marx never recovered from the blow and died two years later in March 1883.

C. Commentary

Marx began his *Inaugural Address* with the controversial statement that 'it is a great fact that the misery of the working masses has not diminished from 1848 to 1864' and attempted to prove it with material that he was later to use in *Capital*. This grim situation had been somewhat alleviated by the Ten Hours Bill and the co-operative movement. The International had been founded to carry this struggle further, both by encouraging working men of different countries to support each other's struggles, and by vindicating 'the simple laws of morals and justice' in foreign affairs. In the preamble to the General Rules, Marx declared that 'the emancipation of the working classes must be conquered by the working classes themselves' and that this 'involved the abolition of all class rule'. Further, the economic subjection of the worker was at the root of all other forms of servitude and therefore 'the economical emancipation of the working classes is the great end to which every political movement ought to be subordinate as a means'.[1] Marx also included some phrases about truth, justice, rights and duties to please members of the drafting committee, but informed Engels that they were 'so placed that they can't do any harm'.[2] The London Conference

[1] *MESW* i 386. [2] *MEW* xxxi 15.

of the International in 1871 strengthened the demand for independent action by workers by including in the Rules the statement that 'the proletariat can act as a class only by constituting itself a distinct political party, opposed to all the old parties formed by the possessing classes'.[1]

In the *First Address* prepared by Marx for the General Council of the International on the Franco-Prussian War, he claimed that the war was a defensive one on the German side but warned the German workers against allowing the war to lose its strictly defensive character. In the *Second Address*, written after the Prussian victory, Marx insisted that Prussian demands for the annexation of Alsace and Lorraine would 'contain within them the seed of fresh wars',[2] and doubted whether the republic recently proclaimed in France could be more than a stop-gap government. The third of the General Council's addresses was entitled *On the Civil War in France*. Marx began it with a long and mocking biography of Thiers, the head of the provisional government which had taken refuge at Versailles after the establishment of the Commune in Paris. Marx goes on to compare the orderliness and leniency of the Commune with the atrocities perpetrated by the Versailles Government, and asks the question: 'What is the Commune, that sphinx so tantalising to the bourgeois mind?'[3] He answers by quoting a statement of the Central Committee of the Commune that 'the proletarians of Paris have an absolute right to render themselves masters of their own destinies by seizing upon the governmental power'.[4] Marx continues: 'The working class cannot simply lay hold of the ready-made state machinery',[5] and analyses at length the historical development of centralised state power from the days of absolute monarchy until the end of the Second Empire. Marx's conclusion is that the Commune was the 'direct antithesis to the empire', in that it was the positive form of the republic aspired to by the revolution of February 1848. It proved its title to this claim by dealing resolutely with all the characteristics of the modern bourgeois state – army, police, bureaucracy, clergy and legislature: the standing army was replaced by the armed people; all churches were disestablished and disendowed; and free education was opened to all; like all other public servants, magistrates and

---

[1] *MESW* I 388.   [2] Ibid. 494.   [3] Ibid. 516.
[4] Ibid.   [5] Ibid.

judges were to be elective, responsible and revocable. The administration Marx summed up as follows:

> The Commune was formed of the municipal councillors, chosen by universal suffrage in the various wards of the town, responsible and revocable at short terms. The majority of its members were naturally working men, or acknowledged representatives of the working class. The Commune was to be a working, not a parliamentary, body, executive and legislative at the same time. Instead of continuing to be the agent of the Central Government, the police was at once stripped of its political attributes, and turned into the responsible and at all times revocable agent of the Commune. So were the officials of all other branches of the Administration. From the members of the Commune downwards, the public service had to be done at *workmen's wages*. The vested interests and the representation allowances of the high dignitaries of State disappeared along with the high dignitaries themselves. Public functions ceased to be the private property of the tools of the Central Government. Not only municipal administration, but the whole initiative hitherto exercised by the State was laid into the hands of the Commune.[1]

Marx then discussed the Commune as a model for the political organisation of France as a whole. He used the conditional tense here as these ideas were not able to be put into practice. The Commune was to be the form of local government from the great industrial centres down to the smallest village hamlet. The rural communes of each district would govern themselves by an assembly of delegates meeting in the central town; these district assemblies would send delegates to a national assembly in Paris; and each delegate, both at the local and at the national level, would be bound by the formal instructions of his constituents and revocable at any time by them. Marx continued: 'The few but important functions which still would remain for a central government were not to be suppressed . . . but were to be discharged by Communal, and therefore strictly responsible agents.'[2] The unity of the nation would not be broken, but the state would no longer be parasitic since its legitimate functions would be handed over to the responsible agents of society.

[1] Ibid. 519.   [2] Ibid. 520.

Instead of deciding once in three or six years which member of the ruling class was to misrepresent the people in Parliament, universal suffrage was to serve the people, constituted in Communes, as individual suffrage serves every other employer in the search for the workmen and managers in his business. And it is well known that companies, like individuals, in matters of real business, generally know how to put the right man in the right place, and, if they for once make a mistake, to redress it promptly. On the other hand, nothing could be more foreign to the spirit of the Commune than to supersede universal suffrage by hierarchic investiture.[1]

The Paris Commune was not to be confused with the communes of the Middle Ages, for it broke the state power whereas the communes of the Middle Ages supported it. Nor was the Commune to be associated with the age-old (and essentially reactionary) struggle against the centralisation of the state. The Commune was

. . . essentially a working-class government, the produce of the struggle of the producing against the appropriating class, the political form at last discovered under which to work out the economic emancipation of labour.[2]

On the other hand, the approach of the Commune was tentative and non-doctrinaire:

The working class did not expect miracles from the Commune. They have no ready-made utopias to introduce *par décret du peuple*. They know that in order to work out their own emancipation, and along with it that higher form to which present society is irresistibly tending by its own economical agencies, they will have to pass through long struggles, through a series of historic processes, transforming circumstances and men. They have no ideals to realise, but to set free the elements of the new society with which old collapsing bourgeois society itself is pregnant.[3]

Marx went on to describe the relationship of the Commune to other social groups. The lower middle classes were enthusiastic

[1] *MESW* i 520 ff.   [2] Ibid. 522.   [3] Ibid. 523.

supporters of the Commune, for the Empire had ruined them economically, excluded them politically and shocked them morally. For the peasants, the Commune would have lowered the burden of taxes and abolished the tyranny of local bureaucracies. As well as being the representative of all the 'healthy elements' of French society, the Commune was at the same time 'emphatically international', including Germans and Poles among its officers.

Turning to the actual measures taken by the Commune, Marx states that its greatest social measure was its own working existence; its particular measures – the abolition of night-work by journeyman bakers, the suppression of the habit of reducing wages by arbitrary fines, the surrender of closed factories to workers' associations, and various moderate inroads in excessive private property – were those of a government of the people by the people. Naturally certain undesirable elements did penetrate the Commune, but the general drop in the crime rate was striking.

The remainder of the *Address* recounted the hypocrisy of the Versailles Government and its barbarities on entering Paris.

Although the comments of Marx on the only working-class government of his day are of immense interest, it is still an open question as to how far Marx really approved of the Paris Commune. Certainly the atmosphere after the bloody defeat of the Commune was not such as to favour criticism. Previous drafts that Marx made of his *Address* were more reticent and Engels wrote later: 'That in *The Civil War* the *unconscious* tendencies of the Commune were put down to its credit as more or less conscious plans was justified and even necessary under the circumstances.' Indeed, Marx even went as far later as to say that the Commune 'was not socialist, nor could it be'.[1]

Marx's *Critique of the Gotha Programme* took the form of marginal notes, and contained two main points of which the one was criticism of the Programme's proposals for distributing the national product, the other, criticism of its views on the state. In the first, Marx objected to the attempt to reintroduce into the party 'dogmas, ideas which in a certain period had some meaning but which have now become obsolete verbal rubbish'.[2] Marx did

---

[1] K. Marx, F. Engels, *Selected Correspondence* (London, 1934) p. 338. (Hereafter referred to as *MESC*.)   [2] *MESW* ii 25.

not find very revolutionary the opening declaration that the proceeds of labour belonged to society as a whole since it was a proposition that had 'at all times been made use of by the champions of the state of society prevailing at any given time'.[1] Further, he criticised the Programme for not attacking land-owners together with capitalists. Talk about 'fair distribution' and 'equal rights' was vague; proposals that the workers should receive the 'undiminished proceeds of their labour' showed a complete disregard for necessary expenditure on capital replacement, administration of social services, poor relief, etc. In the future communist society the phrase 'proceeds of labour' would be meaningless, for

> Within the co-operative society based on common ownership of the means of production, the producers do not exchange their products; just as little does the labour employed on the products appear here as the value of these products, as a material quality possessed by them, since now, in contrast to capitalist society, individual labour no longer exists in an indirect fashion but directly as a component part of the total labour.[2]

Marx then offered a description of the distribution of the social product in the first stage of communist society 'as it emerges from capitalist society, which is thus in every respect, economically, morally and intellectually, still stamped with the birthmarks of the old society from whose womb it emerges'.[3] In this society the individual producer

> receives a certificate from society that he has furnished such and such an amount of labour (after deducting his labour for the common funds), and with this certificate he draws from the social stock of means of consumption as much as costs the same amount of labour. The same amount of labour which he has given to society in one form he receives back in another.[4]

Of course, Marx continued, this equality was, in effect, unequal. Measurement was made with an equal standard, that of labour,

[1] *MESW* II 19.   [2] Ibid. 22 f.   [3] Ibid. 23.
[4] Ibid.

whereas men's capacities, family situations, etc., were not the same and thus inequality would arise.

But [continued Marx in a famous passage] these defects are inevitable in the first phase of communist society as it is when it has just emerged after prolonged birth pangs from capitalist society. Right can never be higher than the economic structure of society and its cultural development conditioned thereby.

In a higher phase of communist society, after the enslaving subordination of the individual to the division of labour, and therewith also the antithesis between mental and physical labour, has vanished; after labour has become not only a means of life but life's prime want; after the productive forces have also increased with the all-round development of the individual, and all the springs of co-operative wealth flow more abundantly – only then can the narrow horizon of bourgeois right be crossed in its entirety and society inscribe on its banners: from each according to his ability, to each according to his needs![1]

Marx summed up his criticism of this section of the Programme by saying:

Vulgar socialism (and from it in turn a section of the democracy) has taken over from the bourgeois economists the consideration and treatment of distribution as independent of the mode of production and hence the presentation of socialism as turning principally on distribution. After the real relation has long been made clear, why retrogress again?[2]

Marx's second basic criticism was of the section where the Programme called for a 'free state' and 'the abolition of the wage system together with the iron law of wages'. Marx replied that wages were not the value of labour, but the value of labour power. This fact made it clear that

the whole capitalist system of production turns on the increase of this gratis labour by extending the working day or by developing the productivity, that is, increasing the intensity of labour power, etc.; that, consequently, the system of wage labour is a system of slavery, and indeed of a slavery which becomes more severe in proportion as the social productive

[1] Ibid. 24.   [2] Ibid. 25.

forces of labour develop, whether the worker receives better or worse payment.[1]

The Programme's solution to the problem was as misguided as its formulation: state-aided workers' co-operatives instead of the revolutionary transformation of society.

Turning to the proposal for a 'free state' Marx declared roundly that this could not be an aim of workers worthy of the name 'Socialist'. Marx put the question: 'What transformation will the state undergo in communist society? What social functions will remain in existence that are analogous to present functions of the state?' He did not answer this question specifically, but said:

> Between capitalist and communist society lies the period of the revolutionary transformation of the one into the other. There corresponds to this also a political transition period in which the state can be nothing but *the revolutionary dictatorship of the proletariat*.[2]

In fact the Programme contained, according to Marx, nothing but the 'old familiar democratic litany' – universal suffrage, direct legislation, popular rights, people's militia, etc., many of which had been realised in progressive bourgeois republics.

In the last years of his life Marx turned his attention particularly to the prospects of a social revolution in Russia. The emancipation of the serfs had occurred in 1861, and although the crushing of the Polish uprising in 1863 temporarily dampened his hopes, Marx's contacts with Russia grew and his optimism increased. Russian was the first language into which *Capital* was translated. Nevertheless his attitude to the possibilities of a Russian revolution was ambivalent. In his reply in 1877 to Mikhailovsky, a Russian populist who had reproached Marx with having a fatalist view of history, Marx wrote:

> What application to Russia could my critic make of this historical sketch? Only this: if Russia is tending to become a capitalist nation after the example of the West European countries – and during the last few years she has been taking a lot of trouble in this direction – she will not succeed without

[1] *MESW* ii 29.   [2] Ibid. 32 f.

having first transformed a good part of her peasants into proletarians; and after that, once taken to the bosom of the capitalist
regime, she will experience its pitiless laws like other profane
peoples.[1]

In his letter to Vera Sassoulitch four years later, Marx said:

The analysis given in *Capital* does not offer any reasons either
for or against the vitality of the rural commune, but the special
study that I have made of it, for which I have researched the
material in its original sources, has convinced me that this
commune is the starting point for the social regeneration of
Russia, but that, in order for it to function as such, it would be
necessary first of all to eliminate the deleterious influences that
assail it on all sides and then to assure it the normal conditions
for a spontaneous development.[2]

In one of the rough drafts for this letter, Marx went even
further:

To save the Russian commune, a Russian revolution is necessary.
Moreover, the Russian government and the 'new pillars of
society' are doing their best to prepare the masses for such a
catastrophe. If the revolution comes at an opportune moment,
if it concentrates all its forces to ensure the free development
of the rural commune, this commune will soon develop into
an element that regenerates Russian society and guarantees
superiority over countries enslaved by the capitalist regime.[3]

This point of view was reiterated in the last published writing
of Marx, the 1882 Preface to the second Russian edition of the
Communist Manifesto, where Marx declared that 'if the Russian
Revolution becomes the signal for a proletarian revolution in the
West, so that both complement each other, the present Russian
common ownership of land may serve as the starting point for a
communist development'.[4]

[1] K. Marx, F. Engels, *Basic Writings on Politics and Philosophy*, ed. L. Feuer
(New York, 1959) p. 440.
[2] K. Marx, *Œuvres*, ed. M. Rubel (Paris, 1968) ɪɪ 1558.
[3] Ibid. 1573.   [4] *MESW* ɪ 24.

BIBLIOGRAPHY

TRANSLATIONS

Inaugural Address
K. Marx, F. Engels, *Selected Works* (Moscow, 1962) vol. I.

The Civil War in France
K. Marx, F. Engels, *Selected Works* (Moscow, 1962) vol. I.
K. Marx, F. Engels, *Writings on the Paris Commune*, ed. H. Draper (New York, 1971).
K. Marx, F. Engels, *On the Paris Commune* (New York and London, 1971).

Critique of the Gotha Programme
K. Marx, F. Engels, *Selected Works* (Moscow, 1962) vol. II.

Preface to the Second Russian edition of the 'Communist Manifesto'
K. Marx, F. Engels, *Selected Works* (Moscow, 1962) vol. I.

COMMENTARIES

S. Avineri, *The Social and Political Thought of Karl Marx* (Cambridge, 1968).
H. Collins and C. Abramsky, *Karl Marx and the British Labour Movement* (London, 1965).
M. Johnstone, 'The Paris Commune and Marx's Concept of the Dictatorship of the Proletariat', *Massachusetts Review,* 1972.
J. Sanderson, *An Interpretation of the Political Ideas of Marx and Engels* (London, 1969).
B. Wolfe, *Marxism: 100 Years in the Life of a Doctrine* (London, 1967).

PART TWO

CHAPTER ONE

Alienation

MARX'S notion of alienation came most directly from Hegel, though its roots are much earlier. For Hegel, reality was Spirit realising itself. Later Spirit perceived this world to be its own creation. Spirit, which existed only in and through its productive activity, gradually became conscious that it was externalising or alienating itself. Alienation, for Hegel, consisted in this failure to realise that the world was not external to Spirit. Alienation would therefore cease when men saw that their environment and culture were creations of Spirit. When men saw this, they would be free, and this freedom was that aim of history. Marx summed up what he conceived to be Hegel's view as follows:

> For Hegel, the human essence, man, is the same as self-conscious-ness. All alienation of man's essence is therefore nothing but the alienation of self-consciousness. The alienation of self-consciousness is not regarded as the expression of the real alienation of man's essence reflected in knowledge and thought. The real alienation (or the one that appears to be real) in its inner concealed essence that has first been brought to the light by philosophy, is nothing but the appearance of the alienation of the real human essence, self-consciousness.[1]

Marx's central criticism of Hegel was that alienation would not cease with the supposed abolition of the external world. The external world, according to Marx, was part of man's nature and what was vital was to establish the right relationship between man and his environment.

> An objective being [Marx wrote] has an objective effect and it would not have an objective effect if its being did not include

[1] *Early Texts*, p. 165.

an objective element. It only creates and posits objects because
it is posited by objects, because it is by origin natural. Thus in
the act of positing it does not degenerate from its 'pure activity'
into creating an object; its objective product only confirms its
objective activity, its activity as an activity of an objective,
natural being.[1]

Marx thus rejected the notion of Spirit and replaced its supposed
antithesis to the external world by the antithesis between man
and his social being.

Particularly in his early writings Marx discusses several types
of alienation, moving, in the rapid process of secularisation
common to the thinking of all the Young Hegelians, from religious
alienation to philosophical, political and finally to economic
alienation. This last Marx considered to be fundamental in as
much as work was man's fundamental activity. In all fields the
common idea was that man had forfeited to someone or something
what was essential to his nature – principally to be in control of
his own activities, to be the initiator of the historical process.
In the different forms of alienation some other entity obtained
what was proper to man.

In religion, for example, it was God who had usurped man's own
position; religion served the double function of a compensation
for suffering and a projection of man's deepest desires. Religion
was 'the imaginary realisation of the human essence because the
human essence possesses no true reality'.[2] And Marx's conclusion
was: 'The abolition of religion as the illusory happiness of the
people is the demand for their real happiness. The demand to give
up the illusions about their condition is a demand to give up a
condition that requires illusion.'[3]

Philosophy, too (and here Marx had in mind particularly
Hegel's philosophy), could constitute an alienation. Speculative
philosophy reduced history and man to a mental process, and,
putting the Idea in the place of God, was no better than a secular-
ised theology. 'In Hegel', said Marx, 'the appropriation of man's
objectified and alienated faculties is thus firstly only an appropriation that occurs in the mind, in pure thought, i.e. in
abstraction.'[4]

Marx applied the same analysis to political alienation: the

---

[1] *Early Texts*, p. 167.   [2] Ibid. p. 116.   [3] Ibid.   [4] Ibid. p. 163.

state contained a description of human nature, but at the same time deprived man of the opportunity of attaining it:

> The political constitution was formerly the religious sphere, the religion of the people's life, the heaven of its universality over against the earthly and real existence. This political sphere was the only state sphere in the state, the only sphere in which the content as well as the form was a content of the species and the genuine universal; but at the same time this was in such a manner that, because this sphere stood over against the others, its content too became a formal and particular one. Political life in the modern state is the scholasticism of the people's life. Monarchy is the perfected expression of this alienation. Republicanism is its negative inside its own sphere.[1]

The passages where Marx talks most fully about alienation are contained in the *Paris Manuscripts*, where he first applied the notion to economics. Here, in the section on 'alienated labour', Marx divided the alienated situation of the worker under capitalism into four aspects.

> The worker [Marx wrote] is related to the product of his labour as to an alien object. The object he produces does not belong to him, dominates him, and only serves in the long run to increase his poverty. Alienation appears not only in the result, but also in the process of production and productive activity itself. The worker is not at home in his work which he views only as a means of satisfying other needs. It is an activity directed against himself, that is independent of him and does not belong to him. Thirdly, alienated labour succeeds in alienating man from his species. Species life, productive life, life creating life, turns into a mere means of sustaining the worker's individual existence, and man is alienated from his fellow men. Finally, nature itself is alienated from man, who thus loses his own inorganic body.[2]

Although the above passages refer to the workers, who were the most obviously alienated part of capitalist society, Marx conceived the state of alienation to be common to all members of that society. In the *Holy Family* he said: 'The propertied class and the class of the proletariat represent the same human self-alienation.

[1] Ibid. p. 67.   [2] Cf. ibid. pp. 137 ff.

But the former feels comfortable and confirmed in this self-alienation, knowing that this alienation is its own power and possessing in it the semblance of a human existence. The latter feels itself ruined in this alienation and sees in it its impotence and the actuality of an inhuman existence.'[1]

The concept of alienation is one that remains central to Marx's writings. He tended to use the actual word less, probably because of its exclusively philosophical connotation. Indeed, in the *Communist Manifesto* he poured scorn on the German *literati* who 'beneath the French criticism of the economic functions of money wrote *Alienation of Humanity*'.[2] However, the concept is obviously fundamental to the *Grundrisse* where Marx is concerned to underline 'not the state of objectification but the state of alienation, estrangement and abandonment, the fact that the enormous objectified power which social labour has opposed to itself as one of its elements belongs not to the worker but to the conditions of production that are objectified in capital'.[3]

The same notion reoccurs at the very beginning of *Capital* under the heading 'Fetishism of Commodities'. Marx says:

A commodity is therefore a mysterious thing, simply because in it the social character of men's labour appears to them as an objective character stamped upon the product of the labour; because the relation of the producers to the sum total of their own labour is presented to them as a social relation, existing not between them, but between the products of their labour. This is why the products of labour become commodities, social things whose qualities are at the same time perceptible and imperceptible by the senses. . . . There is a definite social relation between men that assumes, in their eyes, the fantastic form of a relation between things. . . . This I call the Fetishism which attaches itself to the products of labour, so soon as they are produced as commodities.[4]

Since several writers have stated that 'alienation' is a term only used by Marx in his philosophical youth, it is important to note that it occurs repeatedly in *Capital*.[5] Indeed, in so far as it

[1] *Writings of the Young Marx*, p. 367.   [2] *MESW* i 58.
[3] *Marx's Grundrisse*, p. 150.   [4] *Capital*, i 72.
[5] See, for example, the index to the London 1937 edition of *Capital*. The continuity of Marx's thought in terms of the concept of alienation has been

implies that relations between people have been replaced by relations between things, it may be said to be one of *Capital*'s basic themes. For example, Marx writes: 'The character of independence and estrangement which the capitalist modes of production as a whole give to the instruments of labour and the product, as against the workman, is developed by means of machinery into a thorough antagonism.'[1] Yet it is not only a question of terminology: the content, too, of *Capital* is a continuation of Marx's early thoughts. The main discussion of Volume I of *Capital* rests on the equation of work and value that goes back to the conception of man as a being who creates himself and the conditions of his life – a conception outlined in the *Paris Manuscripts*. It is man's nature, according to the Marx of the *Paris Manuscripts*, to be constantly developing, in co-operation with other men, himself and the world about him. What Marx in *Capital* is describing is how this fundamental role of man, to be the initiator and controller of the historical process, has been transferred, or alienated, and how it belongs to the inhuman power of capital. The counterpart of alienated man, the unalienated or 'total' man of the *Manuscripts*, also appears in *Capital*. In the chapter of Volume I on 'Machinery and Modern Industry' Marx makes the same contrast between the effects of alienated and unalienated modes of production on the development of human potentiality. He writes:

Modern industry, indeed, compels society, under penalty of death, to replace the detail-worker of today, crippled by the life-long repetition of one and the same trivial operation, and thus reduced to the mere fragment of a man, by the fully developed individual, fit for a variety of labours, ready to face any change of production, and to whom the different social functions he performs, are but so many modes of giving free scope to his own natural and acquired powers.[1]

The fact that, in *Capital*, the conclusion is supported by a detailed analysis of the effects of advanced technology should not obscure the continuity.

---

dealt with by R. Dunayevskaya, *Marxism and Freedom* (New York, 1958) pp. 103 ff., and E. Fromm, *Marx's Concept of Man* (New York, 1961) pp. 50 ff. and 69 ff.   [1] *Capital*, I 437.   [2] Ibid. 488.

However, the writing that best shows the centrality of the concept of alienation to Marx's thought is the *Grundrisse*, the thousand-page draft that served Marx as a basis for *Capital* but remained unpublished until 1941. The *Grundrisse*, of which the *Critique of Political Economy* and *Capital* are only partial elaborations, is the centrepiece of Marx's work. It is the basic work which permitted the generalisations in the famous *Preface* to the *Critique of Political Economy*. For *Capital* is only the first of the six volumes in which Marx wished to develop his *Economics*, the title by which he referred to his *magnum opus* on the alienation of man through capital and the state.

The scope of the *Grundrisse* being wider than that of *Capital*, Marx's thought is best viewed as a continuing meditation on themes begun in 1844, the high point in which meditation occurred in 1857–8. The continuity between the *Manuscripts* and the *Grundrisse* is evident. Marx himself talked of the *Grundrisse* as 'the result of fifteen years of research, thus the best period of my life'. This letter was written in November 1858, exactly fifteen years after Marx's arrival in Paris in November 1843. He also says, in the *Preface* of 1859: 'The total material lies before me in the form of monographs, which were written at widely separated periods, for self-clarification, not for publication, and whose coherent elaboration according to the plan indicated will depend on external circumstances.'[1] This can only refer to the *Paris Manuscripts* of 1844 and the London notebooks of 1850–2. Marx constantly used, and at the same time revised, material from an earlier date: for instance, he used his notebooks of 1843–5 while writing *Capital*.

The content of the *Grundrisse* only serves to confirm what is plain from the external evidence: the beginning of the chapter on Capital reproduces almost word for word the passages in the *Manuscripts* on human need, man as a species-being, the individual as a social being, the idea of nature as, in a sense, man's body, the parallels between religious and economic alienation, the utopian and almost millennial elements, etc. One point in particular emphasises this continuity: the *Grundrisse* is as Hegelian as the *Paris Manuscripts* and the central concept of both of them is alienation.[2]

---

[1] *MESW* I 361.
[2] See particularly *Marx's Grundrisse*, pp. 59 ff., 132 ff.

B. Texts

Selling is the practice of externalisation. As long as man is imprisoned within religion, he only knows how to objectify his essence by making it into an alien, imaginary being. Similarly, under the domination of egoistic need he can only become practical, only create practical objects by putting his products and his activity under the domination of an alien entity and lending them the significance of an alien entity – money.

On the Jewish Question (1843); *Early Texts*, p. 114.

What this fact expresses is merely this: the object that labour produces, its product, confronts it as an alien being, as a power independent of the producer. The product of labour is labour that has solidified itself into an object, made itself into a thing, the objectification of labour. The realisation of labour is its objectification. In political economy this realisation of labour appears as a loss of reality for the worker, objectification as a loss of the object or slavery to it, and appropriation as alienation, as externalisation. . . .

All these consequences follow from the fact that the worker relates to the product of his labour as to an alien object. For it is evident from this presupposition that the more the worker externalises himself in his work, the more powerful becomes the alien, objective world that he creates opposite himself, the poorer he becomes himself in his inner life and the less he can call his own. It is just the same in religion. The more man puts into God, the less he retains in himself. The worker puts his life into the object and this means that it no longer belongs to him but to the object. So the greater this activity, the more the worker is without an object. What the product of his labour is, that he is not. So the greater this product the less he is himself. The externalisation of the worker in his product implies not only that his labour becomes an object, an exterior existence but also that it exists outside him, independent and alien, and becomes a self-sufficient power opposite him, that the life that he has lent to the object affronts him, hostile and alien.

1844 Manuscripts; Early Texts, pp. 134f.

Religion, family, state, law, morality, science and art are only particular forms of production and fall under its general law. The positive abolition of private property and the appropriation of human life is therefore the positive abolition of all alienation, thus the return of man out of religion, family, state, etc., into his human, i.e. social being. Religious alienation as such occurs only in man's interior consciousness, but economic alienation is that of real life and its abolition therefore covers both aspects. It is obvious that the movement begins differently with different peoples according to whether the actual conscious life of the people is lived in their minds or in the outer world, is an ideal or a real life.

1844 Manuscripts; Early Texts, p. 149.

Supersession as an objective movement absorbing externalisation. This is the insight expressed within alienation of the reappropriation of objective being through the supersession of its alienation. It is the alienated insight into the real objectification of man, into the real appropriation of his objective essence through the destruction of the alienated character of the objective world, through its supersession in its alienated character of the objective world, through its supersession in its alienated existence. In the same way, atheism as the supersession of God is the emergence of theoretical humanism, and communism as the supersession of private property is the indication of real human life as man's property, which is also the emergence of practical humanism. In other words, atheism is humanism mediated with itself through the supersession of religion, and communism is humanism mediated with itself through the supersession of private property. Only through the supersession of this mediation, which is, however, a necessary precondition, does positive humanism that begins with itself come into being.

1844 Manuscripts; Early Texts, p. 173.

I have produced for myself and not for you, as you have produced for yourself and not for me. You are as little concerned by the result of my production in itself as I am directly concerned by the result of your production. That is, our production is not a production of men for men as such, that is, social production.

Thus, as a man none of us is in a position to be able to enjoy the product of another. We are not present to our mutual products as men. Thus, neither can our exchange be the mediating movement which confirms that my product is for you, because it is an objectification of your own essence, your need. For what links our production together is not the human essence. Exchange can only set in motion and activate the attitude that each of us has to his own product and thus to the product of another. Each of us sees in his own product only his own selfish needs objectified, and thus in the product of another he only sees the objectification of another selfish need independent and alien to him.

Of course as man you have a human relationship to my product; you have a need for my product. Therefore, it is present to you as an object of your desires and will. But your need, your desires, your will are powerless with regard to my product. This means, therefore, that your human essence, which as such necessarily has an intrinsic relationship to my production, does not acquire power and property over my production, for the peculiarity and power of the human essence is not recognised in my production. They are more a fetter that makes you depend on me because they manœuvre you into a position of dependence on my product. Far from being the means of affording you power over my production, they are rather the means of giving me power over you.

1844 Notebooks; Early Texts, pp. 199 f.

The propertied class and the class of the proletariat present the same human self-alienation. But the former class finds in this self-alienation its confirmation and its good, its own power: it has in it a semblance of human existence. The class of the proletariat feels annihilated in its self-alienation; it sees in it its own powerlessness and the reality of an inhuman existence. In the words of Hegel, the class of the proletariat is abased and indignant at that abasement, an indignation to which it is necessarily driven by the contradiction between its human nature and its condition of life, which is the outright, decisive and comprehensive negation of that nature.

Within this antithesis the private owner is therefore the conservative side, the proletarian, the destructive side. From the former arises the action of preserving the antithesis, from the latter, that of annihilating it.

The Holy Family (1845) p. 51.

The social character of activity, and the social form of the product, as well as the share of the individual in production, are here opposed to individuals as something alien and material; this does not consist in the behaviour of some to others, but in their subordination to relations that exist independently of them and arise from the collision of indifferent individuals with one another. The general exchange of activities and products, which has become a condition of living for each individual and the link between them, seems to them to be something alien and independent, like a thing.

In exchange value, the social relations of individuals have become transformed into the social connections of material things, personal power has changed into material power. The less social power the means of exchange possess and the closer they are still connected with the nature of the direct product of labour and the immediate needs of those exchanging, the greater must be the power of the community to bind the individuals together: the patriarchal relationship, the ancient communities, feudalism and the guild system. Each individual possesses social power in the form of a material object. If the object is deprived of its social power then this power must be exercised by people over people.

Relationships of personal dependence (which were at first quite spontaneous) are the first forms of society in which human productivity develops, though only to a slight extent and at isolated points. Personal independence founded on *material* dependence is the second great form: in it there developed for the first time a system of general social interchange, resulting in universal relations, varied requirements and universal capacities. Free individuality, which is founded on the universal development of individuals and the domination of their communal and social productivity, which has become their social power, is the third stage. The second stage creates the conditions for the third. Patriarchal and ancient societies (feudal also) decline as trade, luxury, money and exchange value develop, just as modern society has grown up simultaneously alongside these.

Grundrisse (1857–8) pp. 66 f.

The independent and autonomous existence of value as against living labour power –

hence its existence as capital –

the objective, self-centred indifference, the alien nature of objective conditions of labour as against living labour power, reaching the point that –

(1) these conditions face the worker, as a person, in the person of the capitalist (as personifications with their own will and interest), this absolute separation and divorce of owner-ship (i.e. of the material conditions of labour from living labour power); these conditions are opposed to the worker as alien property, as the reality of another legal person and the absolute domain of their will –

and that –

(2) labour hence appears as alien labour as opposed to the value personified in the capitalist or to the conditions of labour –

this absolute divorce between property and labour, between living labour power and the conditions of its realisation, between objectified and living labour, between the value and the activity that creates value –

hence also the alien nature of the content of the work vis-à-vis the worker himself –

this separation now also appears as the product of labour itself, as an objectification of its own elements.

For through the new act of production itself (which merely confirmed the exchange between capital and living labour that had preceded it), surplus labour and thus surplus value, surplus product, in brief, the total result of labour (that of surplus labour as well as of necessary labour) is established as capital, as exchange value which is independently and indifferently opposed both to living labour power and to its mere use value.

Labour power has only adopted the subjective conditions of necessary labour – subsistence indispensable for productive labour power, i.e. its reproduction merely as labour power divorced from the conditions of its realisation – and it has itself set up these conditions as objects and values, which stand opposed to it in an alien and authoritarian personification.

It comes out of this process not only no richer but actually poorer than when it entered it. For not only do the conditions of necessary labour that it has produced belong to capital; but also the possibility of creating values which is potentially present in labour power now likewise exists as surplus value, surplus product, in a word, as capital, as dominion over living labour power, as value endowed with its own strength and will as opposed to the abstract, purposeless, purely subjective poverty of labour power. Labour power has not only produced alien wealth and its own poverty, but also the relationship of this intrinsic wealth to itself as poverty, through the consumption of which wealth puts new life into itself and again makes itself fruitful. This all arose from the exchange in which labour power exchanged its living power for a quantity of objectified labour, except that this objectified labour – these conditions of its existence which exist outside it, and the independent external nature of these material conditions – appears as its own product. These conditions appear as though set up by labour power itself, both as its own objectification, and as the objectification of its own power which has an existence independent of it and, even more, rules over it, rules over it by its own doing.

Grundrisse (1857–8) pp. 98 ff.

Already in its simple form this relation is an inversion – personification of the thing and materialisation of the person; for what distinguishes this form from all previous forms is that the capitalist does not rule over the labourer through any personal qualities he may have, but only in so far as he is 'capital', his domination is only that of materialised labour over living labour, of the labourer's product over the labourer himself.

The relation grows still more complicated and apparently more mysterious because, with the development of the specifically capitalist mode of production, it is not only these directly material things (all products of labour; considered as use-values, they are both material conditions of labour and products of labour; considered as exchange-values, they are materialised general labour-time or money) that get up on their hind legs to the labourer and confront him as 'capital', but also the forms of socially developed labour – co-operation, manufacture (as a form of division of labour), the factory (as a form of social labour organised on machinery as its material basis) – all these appear as *forms of the development of capital*, and therefore the productive powers of labour built up on these forms of social labour – consequently also science and the forces of nature – appear as *productive powers of capital*. In fact, the unity [of labour] in co-operation, the combination of labour through the division of labour, the use for productive purposes in machine industry of the forces of nature and science alongside the products of labour – all this confronts the individual labourers themselves as something *extraneous* and *objective*, as a mere form of existence of the means of labour that are independent of them and control them, just as the means of labour themselves confront them, in their simple visible form as materials, instruments, etc., as functions of *capital* and consequently of the *capitalist*.

In this process, in which the *social* character of their labour confronts them to a certain degree as *capitalised* (as for example in machinery the visible products of labour appear as dominating labour), the same naturally takes place with the forces of nature and science, the product of general historical development in its abstract quintessence – they confront the labourers as *powers* of capital. They are separate in fact from the skill and knowledge of the individual labourer – and although, in their origin, they too are the product of labour – wherever they enter into the labour-process they appear as *embodied in capital*. The capitalist who makes use of a machine need not understand it. But science realised *in the machine* appears as *capital* in relation to the labourers. And in fact all these applications of science, natural forces and products of labour on a large scale, these applications founded on *social labour*, themselves appear only as *means for the exploitation* of labour, as means of appropriating surplus-labour, and hence confront labour as *powers* belonging to capital. Capital naturally uses all these means only to exploit labour; but in order to exploit it, it must apply them in production. And so the development of the *social* productive powers of labour and the conditions for this development appear as *acts of capital*, towards which the individual labourer not only maintains a passive attitude, but which take place in opposition to him.

Theories of Surplus Value (1862) i 390 ff.

Capital shows itself more and more as a social power, whose agent the capitalist is, and which stands no longer in any possible

relation to the things which the labour of any single individual
can create. Capital becomes a strange, independent, social power,
which stands opposed to society as a thing, and as the power of
capitalists by means of this thing. The contradiction between
capital as a general social power and as a power of private capitalists over the social conditions of production develops into an ever
more irreconcilable clash, which implies dissolution of these
relations and the elaboration of the conditions of production into
universal, common, social conditions. This elaboration is performed by the development of the productive powers under
capitalist production, and by the course which this development
pursues.

Capital, vol. III (1864–5) p. 310.

Capital is not a thing. It is a definite interrelation belonging to a
definite historical formation of society. . . . Capital signifies the
means of production monopolised by a certain part of society,
the products and material requirements of labour made independent of labour-power in living human beings and antagonistic to
them, and personified in capital by this antagonism. Capital
means not merely the products of the labourers made independent
of them and turned into social powers, the products turned into
rulers and buyers of their own producers, but also the forces and
social relations – forms of this labour – which antagonise the
producers in the shape of qualities of their products. Here, then,
we have a definite and, at first sight, very mystical, social form
of one of the factors in a historically produced process of social
production.

Capital, vol. III (1864–5) pp. 947 f.

The capitalist fulfils his function only as personified capital;
he is capital turned into a person. Similarly, the worker is only the
personification of labour. . . . In material production, therefore,
we have exactly the same relationship that obtains, in the domain
of ideology, with religion: the subject transformed into object and
vice versa.

From the historical point of view, this inversion appears as
a transitional stage that is necessary in order to obtain, by
force and at the expense of the majority, the creation of wealth
as such, i.e. the unlimited productivity of social labour which

alone is able to constitute the material basis of a free human society. It is necessary to traverse this antagonistic form just as it is inevitable that man begin by giving his spiritual forces a religious form by erecting them opposite himself as autonomous powers.

This is the *process of alienation* of man's own labour. From the start, the worker is superior to the capitalist in that the capitalist is rooted in his *process of alienation* and is completely content therein, whereas the worker who is its victim finds himself from the beginning in a state of rebellion against it and experiences the process as one of enslavement. . . . The self-valorisation of capital – the creation of surplus value – is the determining, supreme and dominant aim of the capitalist, the complete motive and content of his actions, the rationalised instinct and aim of the miser – a poor content which demonstrates that the capitalist is in the same slavish relation to capital as the worker, although at the opposite pole.

> *Results of the Immediate Process of Production* (1865); *Arkhiv Marksa i Engelsa,* vol. ii (7) (Moscow, 1933) pp. 197 f.

On examination, we notice that capital regulates, according to its need to exploit, this production of the labour force itself, the production of human masses to be exploited. Thus capital does not only produce capital, it also produces a growing mass of workers, the substance thanks to which it can function alone as additional capital. Consequently, not only does labour produce, on an ever widening scale and in opposition to itself, the conditions of labour in the form of capital, but also capital produces, on an ever growing scale, the productive wage labourers that it needs. Labour produces its conditions of production as capital, and capital produces labour as a means of realising capital, as wage labour. Capitalist production is not simply a reproduction of this relationship, it is its reproduction on an ever increasing scale; and precisely to the extent that, with the capitalist mode of production, the social productivity of labour increases, the wealth over against the worker grows and dominates him as capital. Opposite him is deployed the world of wealth, this world which is alien to him and oppresses him, and his poverty, shame and personal subjection increase in the same proportion. His nakedness is the correlative of this plenitude. At the same time there increases the mass of capital's living means of production: the labouring proletariat.

> *Results of the Immediate Process of Production* (1865); *Arkhiv Marksa i Engelsa*, vol. ii (7) (Moscow, 1933) pp. 213 ff.

A commodity is therefore a mysterious thing, simply because in it the social character of men's labour appears to them as an objective character stamped upon the product of that labour; because the relation of the producers to the sum total of their own labour is presented to them as a social relation, existing not between themselves, but between the products of their labour. This is the reason why the products of labour become commodities, social things whose qualities are at the same time perceptible and imperceptible by the senses. . . . To find an analogy, we must have recourse to the mist-enveloped regions of the religious world. In that world the productions of the human brain appear as independent beings endowed with life, and entering into relation both with one another and the human race. So it is in the world of commodities with the products of men's hands. This I call the Fetishism which attaches itself to the products of labour, so soon as they are produced as commodities, and which is therefore inseparable from the production of commodities.

This Fetishism of commodities has its origin, as the foregoing analysis has already shown, in the peculiar social character of the labour that produces them.

> *Capital*, vol. i (1867) p. 72.

Further Reading

D. Bell, 'The Debate on Alienation', in *Revisionism*, ed. L. Labedz (London, 1962).

D. Braybrooke, 'Diagnosis and Remedy in Marx's Doctrine of Alienation', *Social Research* (autumn 1958).

L. Easton, 'Alienation and History in the Early Marx', *Philosophy and Phenomenological Research* (Dec 1961).

L. Easton, 'Alienation and Empiricism in Marx's Thought', *Social Research* (autumn 1970).

K. Löwith, 'Self-alienation in the Early Writings of Marx', *Social Research* (1954).

S. Lukes, 'Alienation and Anomie', in *Philosophy, Politics, and Society*, 3rd series, ed. P. Laslett and W. G. Runciman (Oxford, 1967).

D. McLellan, 'Marx's View of the Unalienated Society', *Review of Politics* (Oct 1969).

B. Ollman, *Alienation: Marx's Critique of Man in Capitalist Society* (Cambridge, 1971).

J. O'Neill, 'Alienation, Class Struggle and Marxian Anti-politics', *Review of Metaphysics* (1964).

J. O'Neill, 'The Concept of Estrangement in the Early and Later Writings of Karl Marx', *Philosophy and Phenomenological Research* (Sep 1964).

R. Schacht, *Alienation*, London, 1971.

Also the books by Avineri, Fromm, McLellan and Tucker cited in the General Bibliography.

CHAPTER TWO

Historical Materialism

A. Commentary

ENGELS said that his and Marx's materialist conception of history was composed of three elements: German idealist philosophy, French socialism and English classical economics. In German philosophy Kant had talked of progress to a free and peaceful society and Fichte had considered human history as a rational development. But it was Hegel who presented German idealism at its most systematic and complete. For Hegel, history was the development and conflict of abstract 'principles' – cultures, religions and philosophies. In this development he spoke of 'the power of the negative', thinking that there was always a tension between any present state of affairs and what it was becoming: every state of affairs contained within itself the seeds of its own destruction and transformation to a higher stage. Each stage was a progress beyond those that had preceded, and contained elements from them. This process Hegel called the dialectic, a concept that Marx took over but stood on its head, considering that, instead of abstract principles, the changing economic basis of society – and the social classes to which it gave rise – was the key to grasping the unfolding of human history.

In France, Gracchus Babeuf had in 1796 attempted to establish communism by means of a revolutionary *coup*; and socialist ideas had been elaborated in some detail by two other thinkers. Charles Fourier had preached the essential goodness of man, the free expression of whose passions was currently frustrated by industry which dehumanised man's labour, and by marriage which limited sexual drives and kept women in a subordinate state. Fourier's solution was the establishment of small-scale communities called *phalanges* where men would be able to develop all their capacities harmoniously. The eccentric nobleman Saint-Simon, on the other hand, welcomed the advent of industry but wanted the means of production to be held in a 'social fund' for the benefit of the deprived mass of the population and administered by a government of bankers and technicians appointed by the state.

In England Marx made full use of the materials there present for the study of capitalism. Adam Smith had explained the functioning of *laissez-faire* capitalism and Ricardo had worked out a labour theory of value which enabled Marx to demonstrate the exploitation of one class in society by another.

'Historical materialism' was a term never used by Marx, who would have felt even less happy with the later expression 'dialectic materialism'. He preferred to talk of 'the materialist conception of history' or 'the materialist conditions of production', i.e. it was viewed more as a method or approach than as a fully developed system of ideas. The tentative nature of Marx's thought is shown by an interesting passage at the end of the *Introduction* of 1857 where Marx asks why classical art, whose economic base was a slave society, should 'still constitute for us a source of aesthetic enjoyment and in certain respects prevail as the standard and model beyond attainment'.[1] The manuscript breaks off before Marx can answer the question beyond remarking that the Greeks were the childhood of humanity and everyone loves a child. The central idea of this materialist conception was that the key to change in society was to be found in the way men produce their life in common. This productive activity was fundamental, and the ideas and concepts – political, philosophical, religious – with which men interpreted and organised this activity were secondary. To take a particular example, the rights of man as proclaimed in the French Revolution and the first constitution of the United States were not eternal truths about the nature of man that happened to be discovered at that particular time; they could only be fully understood if viewed in the context of demands by new commercial groups for the end of the feudal restrictions and for free competition in economic affairs. It is in this sense of ideas propagated to serve a particular class interest that Marx usually uses the term 'ideology'. In the *Communist Manifesto* these ideas are put in a simplified form:

Does it require deep intuition to comprehend that man's ideas, views and conceptions, in one word, man's consciousness,

[1] *Marx's Grundrisse*, p. 45.

changes with every change in the conditions of his material existence, in his social relations and in his social life?

What else does the history of ideas prove, than that intellectual production changes its character in proportion as material production is changed? The ruling ideas of each age have ever been the ideas of its ruling class.[1]

The theory is worked out at greatest length in the first part of the *German Ideology*, and the best summary of it is in the *Preface* to the *Critique of Political Economy*. Thus historical materialism is sharply distinguished from the mechanistic materialism which claims that only matter exists. Marx strongly criticised the eighteenth-century French materialists for leaving the human element out of account in their doctrines of the influence of material conditions. In the third *Thesis on Feuerbach* he wrote: 'The materialist doctrine concerning the changing of circumstances and upbringing forgets that circumstances are changed by man and the educator must himself be educated.'[2]

Thus history was viewed not as the result of accident, nor as shaped by the acts of great men, and still less by supernatural powers, but as the – mostly unconscious – creation of men subject to observable laws. There were, of course, elements in Marx's thought that tended to overemphasise the necessity and predetermination of these laws, and Engels wrote later that 'Marx and I are ourselves partly to blame for the fact that the younger people sometimes lay more stress on the economic side than is due to it. We had to emphasise the main principle vis-à-vis our adversaries, who denied it, and we had not always the time, the place, or the opportunity to give their due to the other elements involved in the interaction. But when it came to presenting a section of history, that is, to making a practical application, it was a different matter and there no error was permissible.'[3] The bourgeoisie were sometimes described as the involuntary agents of their own destruction, and Marx and Engels often compared the necessity of their theses with that of laws obtaining in natural science. They also talked, in their letters, of the similarity of their ideas on society and those of Darwin on natural evolution.

The ultimately determining element in history was most often

<hr>

[1] *MESW* I 52.   [2] *The German Ideology*, p. 660.
[3] *Basic Writings on Politics and Philosophy*, pp. 399 f.

stated by Marx to be the sum total of the relations of production which 'constitutes the economic structure of society, the real foundation, on which rises a legal and political superstructure and to which correspond definite forms of social consciousness'.[1] Occasionally the determining factor was narrowed down to the actual instruments of production as in the statement that 'the hand mill will give you a society with the feudal lord, the steam mill a society with the industrial capitalist'.[2] It is obviously illicit to generalise such phrases and credit Marx with a theory of 'technological determinism'. Some of the most trenchant criticisms of Marx's ideas have concentrated on pointing out that any theory of historical materialism which separates the base from the superstructure was invalid since any description of the base involved elements of the superstructure – for example, it is impossible to conceive of an economic organisation of society without some concept of rules and obligations.[3] This is, of course, an extremely powerful objection, but it is doubtful whether Marx ever formulated his theory as a strictly causal one in the sense attributed to him by his critics. Marx sometimes included the workers themselves among the instruments of production and even calls the revolutionary class 'the greatest productive power of all the instruments of production'.[4]

He also makes it clear that the instruments of production can never be isolated from their social context. The core of the Marxian dialectic is the unity of subjective and objective factors that is present, to some extent, throughout history and increasingly so as the revolution approaches. 'History does nothing; it does not possess immense riches, it does not fight battles. It is men, real, living men, who do all this, who possess things and fight battles. It is not 'history' which uses men as a means of achieving – as if it were an individual person – its own ends. History is nothing but the activity of men in pursuit of their ends.'[5] Or again: 'Men make their own history, but they do not make it just as they please; they do not make it under circumstances chosen by themselves, but under circumstances directly encountered, given and transmitted from the past.'[6]

[1] *MESW* I 363.   [2] *The Poverty of Philosophy*, p. 196.
[3] See particularly J. Plamenatz, *Man and Society* (London, 1963) II 274 ff.
[4] *The Poverty of Philosophy*, p. 167.
[5] *The Holy Family*, p. 125.   [6] *MESW* I 247.

Marx also took pains to emphasise that his ideas had their origin in his study of the development of Western Europe and should not be extrapolated beyond without further thought. His remark about not being a Marxist is particularly in point here. When his followers wished to apply his theory enthusiastically to Russia he objected to the metamorphosis of his 'historical sketch of the genesis of capitalism in Western Europe into a historico-philosophical theory of the general path every people is fated to tread, whatever the historical circumstances in which it finds itself', and goes on to declare that one will never understand history 'by using as one's master key a general historico-philosophical theory, the supreme virtue of which consists in being supra-historical'.[1]

Engels advised a correspondent who asked about historical materialism to read the *Eighteenth Brumaire.* The best understanding of Marx's ideas is to be gained by looking at his own application of this method in historical analysis, as, for example, in *The Class Struggles in France* or the second half of the first volume of *Capital.*

B. Texts

It is above all necessary to avoid restoring society as a fixed abstraction opposed to the individual. The individual is the social being. Therefore, even when the manifestation of his life does not take the form of a communal manifestation performed in the company of other men, it is still a manifestation and confirmation of social life. The individual and the species-life of man are not different, although, necessarily, the mode of existence of individual life is a more particular or a more general mode of species-life or the species-life is a more particular or more general individual life.

1844 Manuscripts; Early Texts, pp. 150 f.

Industry is the real historical relationship of nature, and therefore of natural science, to man. If then it is conceived of as the open revelation of human faculties, then the human essence of

[1] *Basic Writings on Politics and Philosophy*, pp. 440 f.

nature or the natural essence of man will also be understood. Natural science will then lose its one-sidedly materialist, or rather idealistic, orientation and become the basis of human science as it has already, though in an alienated form, become the basis of actual human life. And to have one basis for life and another for science would be in itself a falsehood.

1844 Manuscripts; Early Texts, p. 154.

There is no need of any great penetration to see from the teaching of materialism on the original goodness and equal intellectual endowment of men, the omnipotence of experience, habit and education, and the influence of environment on man, the great significance of industry, the justification of enjoyment, etc., how necessarily materialism is connected with communism and socialism. If man draws all his knowledge, sensation, etc., from the world of the senses and the experience gained in it, the empirical world must be arranged so that in it man experiences and gets used to what is really human and that he becomes aware of himself as man. If correctly understood interest is the principle of all morals, man's private interest must be made to coincide with the interest of humanity. If man is unfree in the materialist sense, i.e. is free not through the negative power to avoid this or that, but through the positive power to assert his true individuality, crime must not be punished in the individual, but the anti-social source of crime must be destroyed, and each man must be given social scope for the vital manifestation of his being. If man is shaped by his surroundings, his surroundings must be made human. If man is social by nature, he will develop his true nature only in society, and the power of his nature must be measured not by the power of separate individuals but by the power of society.

The Holy Family (1845) pp. 175 f.

The premises from which we begin are not arbitrary ones, not dogmas, but real premises from which abstraction can only be made in the imagination. They are the real individuals, their activity and the material conditions under which they live, both those which they find already existing and those produced by their activity. These premises can thus be verified in a purely empirical way.

The first premise of all human history is, of course, the existence of living human individuals. Thus the first fact to be established is the physical organisation of these individuals and their consequent relation to the rest of nature. Of course, we cannot here go either into the actual physical nature of man, or into the natural conditions in which man finds himself – geological, oro-hydrographical, climatic and so on. The writing of history must always set out from these natural bases and their modification in the course of history through the action of men.

Men can be distinguished from animals by consciousness, by religion or anything else you like. They themselves begin to distinguish themselves from animals as soon as they begin to *produce* their means of subsistence, a step which is conditioned by their physical organisation. By producing their means of subsistence men are indirectly producing their actual material life.

The way in which men produce their means of subsistence depends first of all on the nature of the actual means of subsistence they find in existence and have to reproduce. This mode of production must not be considered simply as being the reproduction of the physical existence of the individuals. Rather it is a definite form of activity of these individuals, a definite form of expressing their life, a definite *mode of life* on their part. As individuals express their life, so they are. What they are, therefore, coincides with their production, both with *what* they produce and with *how* they produce. The nature of individuals thus depends on the material conditions determining their production.

The German Ideology (1845–6) pp. 31 f.

This conception of history depends on our ability to expound the real process of production, starting out from the material production of life itself, and to comprehend the form of intercourse connected with this and created by this mode of production (i.e. civil society in its various stages), as the basis of all history; and to show it in its action as State, to explain all the different theoretical products and forms of consciousness, religion, philosophy, ethics, etc., etc., and trace their origins and growth from that basis; by which means, of course, the whole thing can be depicted in its totality (and therefore, too, the reciprocal action of these various sides on one another). It has not, like the idealistic view of history, in every period to look for a category, but remains constantly on the real *ground* of history; it does not explain practice from the idea but explains the formation of ideas from material practice; and accordingly it comes to the conclusion that all forms and products of consciousness cannot be dissolved by mental criticism, by resolution into 'self-consciousness' or transformation into 'apparitions', 'spectres'. 'fancies', etc., but only by the practical overthrow of the actual social relations which gave rise to this idealistic humbug; that not criticism but revolution is the driving force of history, also of religion, of philosophy and all other types of theory. It shows that history does not end by being resolved into 'self-consciousness' as 'spirit of the spirit', but that in it at each stage there is found a material result: a sum of productive forces, a historically created relation of individuals to nature and to one another, which is handed down to each generation from its predecessor; a mass of productive forces, capital funds and conditions, which, on the one hand, is indeed modified by the new generation, but also on the other prescribes for it its conditions of life and gives it a definite development, a special character. It shows that circumstances make men just as much as men make circumstances.

The German Ideology (1845–6) pp. 50 f.

The materialist doctrine concerning the changing of circumstances and upbringing forgets that circumstances are changed by men and that it is essential to educate the educator himself. This doctrine must, therefore, divide society into two parts, one of which is superior to society.

The coincidence of the changing of circumstances and of human activity or self-changing can be conceived and rationally understood only as *revolutionary practice*.

The German Ideology (1845–6) p. 660.

What is society, whatever its form may be? The product of men's reciprocal action. Are men free to choose this or that form of society for themselves? By no means. Assume a particular state of development in the productive forces of man and you will get a particular form of commerce and consumption. Assume particular stages of development in production, commerce and consumption and you will have a corresponding social constitution, a corresponding organisation of the family, of orders or of classes, in a word, a corresponding civil society. Assume a particular civil society and you will get particular political conditions which are only the official expression of civil society. M. Proudhon will never understand this because he thinks he is doing something great by appealing from the state to society – that is to say, from the official résumé of society to official society.

It is superfluous to add that men are not free to choose their *productive forces* – which are the basis of all their history – for every productive force is an acquired force, the product of former activity. The productive forces are therefore the result of practical human energy; but this energy is itself conditioned by the circumstances in which men find themselves, by the productive forces already acquired, by the social form which exists before they do, which they do not create, which is the product of the preceding generation. Because of this simple fact that every succeeding generation finds itself in possession of the productive forces acquired by the previous generation, which serve it as the raw material for new production, a coherence arises in human history, a history of humanity which takes shape is all the more a history of humanity as the productive forces of man and therefore his social relations have been more developed. Hence it necessarily follows that the social history of men is never anything but the history of their individual development, whether they are conscious of it or not. Their material relations are the basis of all their relations. These material relations are only the necessary forms in which their material and individual activity is realised.

The Poverty of Philosophy (1847) pp. 202 f.

In production, men not only act on nature but also on one another. They produce only by co-operating in a certain way and mutually exchanging their activities. In order to produce, they enter into definite connections and relations with one another and only within these social connections and relations does their action on nature, does production, take place.

These social relations into which the producers enter with one another, the conditions under which they exchange their activities and participate in the whole act of production, will naturally vary according to the character of the means of production. With the invention of a new instrument of warfare, firearms, the whole internal organisation of the army necessarily changed: the relationships within which individuals can constitute an army and act as an army were transformed and the relations of different armies to one another also changed.

Thus the social relations within which individuals produce, the social relations of production, change, are transformed, with the change and development of the material means of production, the productive forces. The relations of production in their totality constitute what are called the social relations, society, and, specifically, a society at a definite stage of historical development, a society with a peculiar, distinctive character. Ancient society, feudal society, bourgeois society are such totalities of production relations, each of which at the same time denotes a special stage of development in the history of mankind.

Wage Labour and Capital (1849); *MESW* I 89 f.

Notes on the points to be mentioned here and not to be omitted:

1. *War* attains complete development before peace; how certain economic phenomena, such as wage-labour, machinery, etc., are developed at an earlier date through war and in armies than within bourgeois society. The connection between productive force and commercial relationships is made especially plain in the case of the army.

2. The relation between the previous idealistic methods of writing history and the realistic method; namely, the so-called history of civilisation, which is all a history of religion and states. In this connection something may be said of the different methods hitherto employed in writing history. The so-called objective method. The subjective (the moral and others). The philosophical.

3. *Secondary and tertiary.* Conditions of production which have been taken over or transplanted; in general, those that are not original. Here the effect of international relations must be introduced.

4. Objections to the materialistic character of this view. Its relation to naturalistic materialism.

5. The dialectic of the conceptions of productive force (means of production) and relation of production, a dialectic whose limits are to be determined and which does not do away with the concrete difference.

6. The unequal relation between the development of material production and art, for instance. In general, the conception of progress is not to be taken in the sense of the usual abstraction.

In the case of art, etc., it is not so important and difficult to understand this disproportion as in that of practical social relations, e.g. the relation between education in the United States and Europe. The really difficult point, however, that is to be discussed here is that of the unequal development of relations of production as legal relations. As, for example, the connection between Roman civil law (this is less true of criminal and public law) and modern production.

7. This conception of development appears to imply necessity. On the other hand, justification of accident. How. (Freedom and other points.) (The effect of means of communication.) World history has not always existed; history as world history is a result.

8. The starting point is to be found in certain facts of nature embodied subjectively and objectively in clans, races, etc.

It is well known that certain periods of the highest development of art stand in no direct connection to the general development of society, or to the material basis and skeleton structure of its organisation. Witness the example of the Greeks as compared with the modern nations, or even Shakespeare. As regards certain forms of art, e.g. the epos, it is admitted that they can never be produced in the universal epoch-making form as soon as art as such has come into existence; in other words, that in the domain of art certain important forms of it are possible only at a low stage of its development. If that be true of the mutual relations of different forms of art within the domain of art itself, it is far less surprising that the same is true of the relation of art as a whole to the general development of society. The difficulty lies only in the general formulation of these contradictions. No sooner are they specified than they are explained.

Let us take for instance the relation of Greek art, and that of Shakespeare's time, to our own. It is a well-known fact that Greek mythology was not only the arsenal of Greek art, but also the very ground from which it had sprung. Is the view of nature and of social relations which shaped Greek imagination and Greek art possible in the age of automatic machinery and railways and locomotives and electric telegraphs? Where does Vulcan come in as against Roberts & Co.? Jupiter, as against the lightning conductor? and Hermes, as against the *Crédit Mobilier*? All mythology masters and dominates and shapes the forces of nature in and through the imagination; hence it disappears as soon as man gains mastery over the forces of nature. What becomes of the Goddess Fama side by side with Printing House Square? Greek art presupposes the existence of Greek mythology, i.e. that nature and even the form of society are wrought up in popular fancy in an unconsciously artistic fashion. That is its material. Not, however, any mythology taken at random, nor any accidental unconsciously artistic elaboration of nature (including under the latter all objects, hence also society). Egyptian mythology could never be the soil or womb which would give birth to Greek art. But in any event there had to be a mythology. In no event could Greek art originate in a society which excludes any mythological explanation of nature, any mythological attitude towards it, or which requires of the artist an imagination free from mythology.

Looking at it from another side: is Achilles possible side by side with powder and lead? Or is the *Iliad* at all compatible with the printing press and even printing machines? Do not singing and reciting and the muses necessarily go out of existence with the appearance of the printer's bar, and do not, therefore, the prerequisites of epic poetry disappear?

But the difficulty is not in grasping the idea that Greek art and epos are bound up with certain forms of social development. It lies rather in understanding why they still constitute for us a source of aesthetic enjoyment and in certain respects prevail as the standard and model beyond attainment.

A man cannot become a child again unless he becomes childish. But does he not enjoy the artless ways of the child, and must he not strive to reproduce its truth on a higher plane? Is not the character of every epoch revived, perfectly true to nature, in the child's nature? Why should the childhood of human society, where it had obtained its most beautiful development, not exert an eternal charm as an age that will never return? There are ill-bred children and precocious children. Many of the ancient nations belong to the latter class. The Greeks were normal children. The charm their art has for us does not conflict with the primitive character of the social order from which it had sprung. It is rather the product of the latter, and is due rather to the fact that the immature social conditions under which the art arose and under which it alone could appear can never return.

Grundrisse (1857–8) pp. 43 ff.

It is just as certain that individuals cannot dominate their own social relationships until they have created them. But it is absurd to interpret these *purely material* relationships as natural relationships, inseparable from the nature of individuality (in contrast to reflected knowledge and desire) and inherent in it. These relationships are produced by individuals, produced historically. They belong to a definite phase of the development of the individual. The heterogeneity and independence in which these relationships still stand opposed to individuals, prove only that these individuals are still engaged in the production of the conditions of their social life, rather than that they began that life starting from those conditions. This is the natural and spontaneous interrelationship of individuals inside production relations that are determined and narrowly limited. Universally developed individuals, whose social relationships are subject, as their own communal relationships, to their own collective control, are the product not of nature but of history. The extent and universality of the development of capacities which make possible this sort of individuality, presupposes precisely production on the basis of exchange values. The universal nature of this production creates an alienation of the individual from himself and others, but also for the first time the general and universal nature of his relationships and capacities. At early stages of development the single individual appears to be more complete, since he has not yet elaborated the abundance of his relationships, and has not established them as powers and autonomous social relationships that are opposed to himself. It is as ridiculous to wish to return to that primitive abundance as it is to believe in the continuing necessity of its complete depletion. The bourgeois view has never got beyond opposition to this romantic outlook and thus will be accompanied by it, as a legitimate antithesis, right up to its blessed end.

Grundrisse (1857–8) pp. 70f.

The development of science, of this ideal and at the same time practical wealth, is however only one aspect, one form, of the *development of human productive forces* (i.e. wealth). *Ideally* considered, the disintegration of a particular form of consciousness was enough to kill an entire epoch. In reality, this limitation of consciousness corresponds to a *definite stage of development of material productive forces*, and thus of wealth. Of course, development occurred not only on the old basis; there was development of the basis itself. The highest development of this basis, the point of flowering at which it changes (it is nevertheless still *this* basis, this plant in flower, and therefore it fades after flowering and as a consequence of flowering), is the point at which it has been elaborated to a form in which it can be united with the *highest development of productive* forces, and thus also with the richest development of the individual. As soon as this point has been reached, any further development takes place from a new basis. We saw earlier that ownership of the means of production was identified with a limited, determined form of community and thus also of individuals possessing qualities and a development as limited as those of the community that they form.

Grundrisse (1857–8) pp. 120 f.

In the *method* of treatment the fact that by mere accident I again glanced through Hegel's *Logic* has been of great service to me – Freiligrath found some volumes of Hegel which originally belonged to Bakunin and sent them to me as a present. If there should ever be time for such work again, I would greatly like to make accessible to the ordinary human intelligence, in two or three printer's sheets, what is *rational* in the method which Hegel discovered but at the same time enveloped in mysticism. . . .

Marx to Engels (1858); *MESC* p. 100.

He knows very well that my method of development is *not* Hegelian, since I am a materialist and Hegel is an idealist. Hegel's dialectics is the basic form of all dialectics, but only *after* it has been stripped of its mystical form, and it is precisely this which distinguishes my method.

Marx to Kugelmann (1868); *MESC* p. 199.

Now what application to Russia could my critic make of this historical sketch? Only this: If Russia is tending to become a capitalist nation after the example of the West European countries – and during the last few years she has been taking a lot of trouble in this direction – she will not succeed without having first transformed a good part of her peasants into proletarians; and after that, once taken to the bosom of the capitalist regime, she will experience its pitiless laws like other profane peoples. That is all. But that is too little for my critic. He feels

he absolutely must metamorphose my historical sketch of the
genesis of capitalism in Western Europe into a historico-
philosophic theory of the general path every people is fated to
tread, whatever the historical circumstances in which it finds itself,
in order that it may ultimately arrive at the form of economy
which ensures, together with the greatest expansion of the
productive powers of social labor, the most complete development
of man. But I beg his pardon. (He is both honouring and shaming
me too much.) Let us take an example.

In several parts of *Capital* I allude to the fate which overtook
the plebeians of ancient Rome. They were originally free peasants,
each cultivating his own piece of land on his own account. In the
course of Roman history they were expropriated. The same
movement which divorced them from their means of production
and subsistence involved the formation not only of big landed
property but also of big money capital. And so one fine morning
there were to be found on the one hand free men, stripped of
everything except their labour power, and on the other, in order
to exploit this labour, those who held all the acquired wealth in
their possession. What happened? The Roman proletarians
became not wage laborers but a *mob* of do-nothings more abject
than the former 'poor whites' in the South of the United States,
and alongside of them there developed a mode of production
which was not capitalist but based on slavery. Thus events
strikingly analogous but taking place in different historical
surroundings led to totally different results. By studying each of
these forms of evolution separately and then comparing them one
can easily find the clue to this phenomenon, but one will never
arrive there by using as one's master key a general historico-
philosophical theory, the supreme virtue of which consists in being
supra-historical.

Reply to Mikhailovsky (1877);
Basic Writings on Politics and Philosophy, pp. 440 ff.

If capitalist production must establish its reign in Russia, the
great majority of Russian people, that is, of the Russian peasants,
must be converted into wage earners, and consequently expropriated by the preliminary abolition of its communist property.
But in any case the western precedent would not prove anything
at all concerning the 'historical fatality' of this process.

In this western movement, we are concerned with the transformation of one form of private property into another form of private property. Whether one affirms or denies the fatality of this transformation the reasons for or against have nothing to do with my analysis of the genesis of the capitalist regime. At most one could infer that, considering the present state of the great majority of Russian peasants, their conversion into small-scale proprietors would merely be the prologue to their rapid expropriation. . . .

At the same time as the commune is being bled and tortured, its land sterilised and pauperised, the literary lacqueys of the 'new columns of society' ironically characterise the wounds inflicted on the commune as so many symptoms of its spontaneous and incontestable decrepitude, and argue that it is dying a natural death and that a good turn will be served by shortening its agony. Here there is no longer a problem to be solved; it is a question very simply of fighting an enemy. Thus it is no longer a theoretical problem. To save the Russian commune, there must be a Russian revolution. Moreover, the Russian government and the 'new columns of society' are doing their best to prepare the masses for just such a catastrophe. If the revolution occurs at an opportune moment, if it concentrates all its forces to ensure the free development of the rival commune, this commune will soon become an element that regenerates Russian society and renders it superior to the countries enslaved by the capitalist regime.

Drafts of letter to Vera Zassoulitch (1881);
Œuvres, ed. Rubel, II 1560, 1573.

Further Reading

H. Acton, *The Illusion of the Epoch* (London, 1955).

H. Acton and G. Cohen, 'Some Criticisms of Historical Materialism', *Proceedings of the Aristotelian Society* (1970).

M. Bober, *Karl Marx's Interpretation of History*, 2nd ed. (New York, 1965).

Z. Jordan, *The Evolution of Dialectical Materialism* (London, 1967).

J. Plamenatz, *Man and Society*, vol. II (London, 1963).

J. Sanderson, *An Interpretation of the Political Ideas of Marx and Engels* (London, 1969).

I. Zeitlin, *Marxism: A Re-examination* (New York, 1967).

See also the reading list attached to Part I, Chapter 6.

CHAPTER THREE

Labour

A. COMMENTARY

LABOUR was, for Marx, the instrument of man's self-creation. Quoting Vico, he said that 'human history differs from natural history in this, that we have made the former but not the latter'.[1] Marx summed up this process very well in *Capital*: 'Labour is, in the first place, a process in which both man and nature participate, and in which man of his own accord starts, regulates and controls the material reactions between himself and Nature . . . by thus acting on the external world and changing it, he at the same time changes his own nature. He develops his slumbering powers and compels them to act in obedience to his sway.'[2]

This conception was present in Marx from his early writings onwards: in fact, he took it over, at least in part, from Hegel and it was the key point on which he came to terms with Hegel in the *Paris Manuscripts*. Marx praised Hegel in that 'he grasps the nature of labour and understands objective man, true, because real, man as the result of his own labour'.[3] On the other hand, however, Hegel 'sees only the positive side of labour, not its negative side. Labour is the means by which man becomes himself inside externalisation or as externalised man. The only labour that Hegel knows and recognises is abstract, mental labour.'[4]

Previously Marx had seen the most important sphere of alienation as being religion or politics and it was only in 1844 that he came to the conclusion that the labour process constituted the area of man's fundamental alienation, a view that he never abandoned. In the *Paris Manuscripts* Marx offered a description of the condition of alienated labour in capitalist society where the worker felt that not only did the product of his labour not belong to him but actually came to possess a power hostile to his interests.

[1] *Capital*, I 372.   [2] Ibid. 177.   [3] *Early Texts*, p. 164.   [4] Ibid.

From this it followed that the worker could not feel at ease in the act of producing; that the natural world and the faculties that he shared with other men became alien to him; and lastly that men became alienated from, and hostile to, their fellow men.[1] Marx also outlined again, in four points, his picture of unalienated labour in his *Notes on James Mill* which describe – albeit in an almost poetical manner – how labour could become the central activity creating and enriching the human essence.[2]

Marx's most explicit statements about the nature of labour in the future communist society occur in the *Grundrisse*. Here Marx presented his position as a middle way between the extreme views of Adam Smith and Fourier. According to Adam Smith labour was necessarily a burden and a sacrifice, and rest was the fitting state of man; whereas Fourier in his ideal picture of the future had equated work with amusement and play. As against Adam Smith, Marx pointed out that a normal quantity of work is essential for any human being and that the result of labour in its proper context was 'the self-realisation and objectification of the subject, therefore real freedom, whose activity is precisely labour'. Yet, as against Fourier, Marx insisted that 'really free labour, the composing of music for example, is at the same time damned serious and demands the greatest effort. The labour concerned with material production can only have this character if (1) it is of a social nature and (2) it has a scientific character.'[3]

The precise function allotted to labour is not always clear: in the *Paris Manuscripts* labour seems to be – at least ideally – co-extensive with all man's activities. However, one of the main themes of the *Grundrisse* in this connection is that the development of machinery and automation would give men so much free time that they would be able to develop, in a communist society, many of the capacities hitherto stunted by the necessity of working long hours in an alienating situation. This point is further emphasised in *Capital* where Marx contrasts the realm of freedom with the realm of necessity. The realm of freedom, he says, 'only begins, in fact, where that labour which is determined by need and external purposes, ceases; it is therefore, by its very nature, outside the sphere of material production proper'. Even under a communist organisation of production, Marx continues,

[1] Cf. ibid. pp. 133 ff.   [2] Cf. ibid. pp. 202 f.
[3] *Marx's Grundrisse*, p. 124.

man's struggle with nature 'always remains a realm of necessity. Beyond it begins that development of human potentiality for its own sake, the true realm of freedom, which however can only flourish upon that realm of necessity as its basis. The shortening of the working day is its fundamental prerequisite.'[1]

Nevertheless it is clear that Marx considered that the nature of labour would change fundamentally in a future communist society. He even talked about the eventual 'abolition of labour'. In the *Grundrisse* he mentioned the capacity of capital 'with its restless striving after the general form of wealth' to 'drive labour out beyond the limit of its natural needs and thus produce the material elements needed for the development of the rich individuality, which is just as universal in its production as consumption, and whose labour thus itself appears not to be labour any more but a full development of activity, in which the natural necessity has disappeared in its direct form.'[2] And in the *German Ideology* Marx declared succinctly: 'Labour is free in all civilised countries; it is not a matter of freeing labour but of abolishing it.'[3]

One fundamental factor in Marx's concept of labour was his view of the nefarious influence of the division of labour. This notion was basic to Marx's philosophy of history. The whole state apparatus was the result of the appearance of the division of labour and would be dissolved with its disappearance. And the disappearance of the division of labour would also dissolve the distinction between physical and mental labour. Thus would arise a society in which one would 'hunt in the morning, fish in the afternoon, rear cattle in the evening, and criticise after dinner'. This remark (which obviously only fits a very rural society) should perhaps not be taken too seriously, though Marx did think that the progress of technology and automation would simplify the tasks to be performed and permit rapid transfer from job to job. 'In a communist society,' said Marx, 'there are no painters but at most people who engage in painting among other activities.'[4] And, whatever the practical difficulties posed by advanced technological society, Marx's model for the labourer remained the 'all-round man' of the *Paris Manuscripts* and the 'social individual' of the *Grundrisse*.

[1] *Capital* (Moscow, 1954) III 934.   [2] *Marx's Grundrisse*, pp. 85 f.
[3] *The German Ideology*, p. 224.   [4] Ibid. p. 443.

B. TEXTS

So when we ask the question: what relationship is essential to labour, we are asking about the relationship of the worker to production.

Up till now we have only considered one aspect of the alienation, or externalisation, of the worker, his relationship to the products of his labour. But alienation shows itself not only in the result, but also in the act of production, inside productive activity itself. How would the worker be able to affront the product of his work as an alien being if he did not alienate himself in the act of production itself? For the product is merely the summary of the activity of production. So if the product of labour is externalisation, production itself must be active externalisation, the externalisation of activity, the activity of externalisation. The alienation of the object of labour is only the resumé of the alienation, the externalisation in the activity of labour itself.

What does the externalisation of labour consist of then?

Firstly, that labour is exterior to the worker, that is, it does not belong to his essence. Therefore he does not confirm himself in his work, he denies himself, feels miserable instead of happy, deploys no free physical and intellectual energy, but mortifies his body and ruins his mind. Thus the worker only feels at home outside his work and in his work he feels a stranger. He is at home when he is not working and when he works he is not at home. His labour is therefore not voluntary but compulsory, forced labour. It is therefore not the satisfaction of a need but only a means to satisfy needs outside itself. How alien it really is is very evident from the fact that when there is no physical or other compulsion, labour is avoided like the plague. External labour, labour in which man externalises himself, is a labour of self-sacrifice and mortification. Finally, the external character of labour for the worker shows itself in the fact that it is not his own but someone else's, that it does not belong to him, that he does not belong to himself in his labour but to someone else. As in religion the human imagination's own activity, the activity of man's head and his heart, reacts independently on the individual as an alien activity of gods or devils, so the activity of the worker

is not his own spontaneous activity. It belongs to another and is
the loss of himself.

1844 Manuscripts; Early Writings, p. 137.

It is true that the animal, too, produces. It builds itself a nest,
a dwelling, like the bee, the beaver, the ant, etc. But it only
produces what it needs immediately for itself or its offspring;
it produces one-sidedly whereas man produces universally; it
produces only under the pressure of immediate physical need,
whereas man produces free from physical need and only truly
produces when he is thus free; it produces only itself whereas
man reproduces the whole of nature. Its product belongs immediately to its physical body whereas man can freely separate
himself from his product. The animal only fashions things according to the standards and needs of the species it belongs to,
whereas man knows how to produce according to the measure of
every species and knows everywhere how to apply its inherent
standard to the object; thus man also fashions things according
to the laws of beauty.

Thus it is in the working over of the objective world that man
first really affirms himself as species-being. This production is his
active species-life. Through it nature appears as his work and his
reality. The object of work is therefore the objectification of the
species-life of man; for he duplicates himself not only intellectually, in his mind, but also actively in reality and thus can look
at his image in a world he has created.

1844 Manuscripts; Early Texts, pp. 139 f.

But the exercise of labour power, labour, is the worker's own life-
activity, the manifestation of his own life. And this *life-activity*
he sells to another person in order to secure the necessary *means
of subsistence*. Thus his life-activity is for him only a means to
enable him to exist. He works in order to live. He does not even
reckon labour as part of his life, it is rather a sacrifice of his life.
It is a commodity which he has made over to another. Hence, also,
the product of his activity is not the object of his activity. What
he produces for himself is not the silk that he weaves, not the gold
that he draws from the mine, not the palace that he builds. What
he produces for himself is *wages*, and silk, gold, palace resolve
themselves for him into a definite quantity of the means of

subsistence, perhaps into a cotton jacket, some copper coins and a lodging in a cellar. And the worker, who for twelve hours weaves, spins, drills, turns, builds, shovels, breaks stones, carries loads, etc. – does he consider this twelve hours' weaving, spinning, drilling, turning, building, shovelling, stone-breaking as a manifestation of his life, as life? On the contrary, life begins for him where this activity ceases, at table, in the public house, in bed. The twelve hours' labour, on the other hand, has no meaning for him as weaving, spinning, drilling, etc., but as earnings, which bring him to the table, to the public house, into bed.

Wage Labour and Capital (1849); *MESW* I 82f.

The greater division of labour enables one worker to do the work of five, ten, or twenty; it therefore multiplies competition among the workers fivefold, tenfold and twentyfold. The workers do not only compete by one selling himself cheaper than another; they compete by one doing the work of five, ten, twenty; and the division of labour, introduced by capital and continually increased, compels the workers to compete among themselves in this way.

Further, as the division of labour increases, labour is simplified. The special skill of the worker becomes worthless. He becomes transformed into a simple, monotonous productive force that does not have to use intense bodily or intellectual faculties. His labour becomes a labour that anyone can perform. . . .

Therefore, as labour becomes more unsatisfying, more repulsive, competition increases and wages decrease. The worker tries to keep up the amount of his wages by working more, whether by working longer hours or by producing more in one hour. Driven by want, therefore, he still further increases the evil effects of the division of labour. The result is that the more he works the less wages he receives, and for the simple reason that he competes to that extent with his fellow workers, hence makes them into so many competitors who offer themselves on just the same bad terms as he does himself, and that, therefore, in the last resort he competes with himself, with himself as a member of the working class.

Machinery brings about the same results on a much greater scale by replacing skilled workers by unskilled, men by women, adults by children. It brings about the same results, where it is newly introduced, by throwing the hand workers on to the streets in masses, and, where it is developed, improved and replaced by more productive machinery, by discharging workers in smaller batches.

Wage Labour and Capital (1849); *MESW* i 102 f.

The indifference as to the particular kind of labour implies the existence of a highly developed aggregate of different species of concrete labour, none of which is any longer the predominant one. So the most general abstractions commonly arise only where there is the highest concrete development, where one feature appears to be jointly possessed by many and to be common to all. Then it cannot be thought of any longer in one particular form. On the other hand, this abstraction of labour is only the result of a concrete aggregate of different kinds of labour. The indifference to the particular kind of labour corresponds to a form of society in which individuals pass with ease from one kind of work to another, which makes it immaterial to them what particular kind of work may fall to their share. Labour has become here, not only categorially but really, a means of creating wealth in general and has no longer coalesced with the individual in one particular manner. This state of affairs has found its highest development in the most modern of bourgeois societies, the United States. It is only here that the abstraction of the category 'labour', 'labour in general', labour *sans phrase*, the starting point of modern political economy, becomes realised in practice. Thus the simplest abstraction which modern political economy sets up as its starting point, and which expresses a relation dating back to antiquity and prevalent under all forms of society, appears truly realised in this abstraction only as a category of the most modern society. It might be said that what appears in the United States as a historical product – viz. the indifference as to the particular kind of labour – appears among the Russians, for example, as a spontaneously natural disposition. But it makes all the difference in the world whether barbarians have a natural predisposition which makes them applicable alike to everything, or whether civilised people apply themselves to everything. And, besides, this indifference of the Russians as to the kind of work they do corresponds to their traditional practice of remaining in the rut of a quite definite occupation until they are thrown out of it by external influences.

Grundrisse (1857–8) pp. 38 f.

The development of heavy industry means that the basis upon which it rests – the appropriation of the labour time of others – ceases to constitute or to create wealth; and at the same time direct labour as such ceases to be the basis of production, since it is transformed more and more into a supervisory and regulating activity; and also because the product ceases to be made by individual direct labour, and results more from the combination of social activity. 'As the division of labour develops, almost all the work of any individual is a part of the whole, having no value or utility of itself. There is nothing on which the labourer can seize: this is my produce, this I will keep to myself.' In direct exchange between producers, direct individual labour is found to be realised in a particular product, or part of a product, and its common social character – as the objectification of general labour and the satisfaction of general need – is only established through exchange. The opposite takes place in the production process of heavy industry: on the one hand, once the productive forces of the means of labour have reached the level of an automatic process, the prerequisite is the subordination of the natural forces to the intelligence of society, while on the other hand individual labour in its direct form is transformed into social labour. In this way the other basis of this mode of production vanishes.

Grundrisse (1857–8) pp. 145 f.

Real economy – savings – consists in the saving of working time (the minimum, and reduction to the minimum, of production costs); but this saving is identical with the development of productivity. Economising, therefore, does not mean the giving up of pleasure, but the development of power and productive capacity, and thus both the capacity for and the means of enjoyment. The capacity for enjoyment is a condition of enjoyment and therefore its primary means; and this capacity is the development of an individual's talents, and thus of the productive force. To economise on labour time means to increase the amount of free time, i.e. time for the complete development of the individual, which again reacts as the greatest productive force on the productive force of labour. From the standpoint of the immediate production process it may be considered as production of fixed capital; this fixed capital being man himself. It is also self-evident that immediate labour time cannot remain in its abstract contradiction to free time – as in the bourgeois economy. Work cannot become a game, as Fourier would like it to be; his great merit was that he declared that the ultimate object must be to raise to a higher level not distribution but the mode of production. Free time – which includes leisure time as well as time for higher activities – naturally transforms anyone who enjoys it into a different person, and it is this different person who then enters the direct process of production. The man who is being formed finds discipline in this process, while for the man who is already formed it is practice, experimental science, materially creative and self-objectifying knowledge, and he contains within his own head the accumulated wisdom of society. Both of them find exercise in it, to the extent that labour requires practical manipulation and free movement, as in agriculture.

Grundrisse (1857–8) pp. 148 f.

No special sagacity is required in order to understand that, beginning with free labour or wage-labour for example, which arose after the abolition of slavery, machines can only develop in opposition to living labour, as a hostile power and alien property, i.e. they must, as capital, oppose the worker. But it is equally easy to see that machines do not cease to be agents of social production, once they become, for example, the property of associated workers. But in the first case, their means of distribution (the fact that they do not belong to the workers) is itself a condition of the means of production that is founded on wage-labour. In the second case, an altered means of distribution will derive from a new, altered basis of production emerging from the historical process.

Grundrisse (1857–8) p. 152.

The social forms of their own labour or the forms of their own social labour are relations that have been formed quite independently of the individual labourers; the labourers, as subsumed under capital, become elements of these social formations – but these social formations do not belong to them. They therefore confront them as *forms* of capital itself, as combinations belonging to capital, as distinct from their individual labour-power, arising from capital and incorporated in it. And this takes on a form that is all the more real the more on the one hand their labour-power itself becomes so modified by these forms that it is powerless as an independent force, that is to say, *outside* this capitalist relationship, and that its independent capacity to produce is destroyed. And on the other hand, with the development of machinery the conditions of labour seem to dominate labour also technologically while at the same time they replace labour, oppress it, and make it superfluous in its independent forms.

Theories of Surplus Value (1862) I 391.

But there was in store a still greater victory of the political economy of labour over the political economy of property. We speak of the co-operative movement, especially the co-operative factories raised by the unassisted efforts of a few bold 'hands'. The value of these great social experiments cannot be over-rated. By deed, instead of by argument, they have shown that production on a large scale, and in accord with the behests of modern science, may be carried on without the existence of a class of masters employing a class of hands; that to bear fruit, the means of labour need not be monopolised as a means of dominion over, and of extortion against, the labouring man himself; and that, like slave labour, like serf labour, hired labour is but a transitory and inferior form, destined to disappear before associated labour plying its toil with a willing hand, a ready mind, and a joyous heart. In England, the seeds of the co-operative system were sown by Robert Owen; the working men's experiments, tried on the Continent, were, in fact, the practical upshot of the theories, not invented, but loudly proclaimed, in 1848.

Inaugural Address (1864); *MESW* I 383.

Let us now picture to ourselves, by way of change, a community of free individuals, carrying on their work with the means of production in common, in which the labour-power of all the different individuals is consciously applied as the combined labour-power of the community. All the characteristics of Robinson's labour are here repeated, but with this difference, that they are social, instead of individual. Everything produced by him was exclusively the result of his own personal labour, and therefore simply an object of use for himself. The total product of our community is a social product. One portion serves as fresh means of production and remains social. But another portion is consumed by the members as means of subsistence. A distribution of this portion amongst them is consequently necessary. The mode of this distribution will vary with the productive organisation of the community, and the degree of historical development attained by the producers. We will assume, but merely for the sake of a parallel with the production of commodities that the share of each individual producer in the means of subsistence is determined by his labour time. Labour-time would, in that case, play a double part. Its apportionment in accordance with a definite social plan maintains the proper proportion between the different kinds of work to be done and the various wants of the community. On the other hand, it also serves as a measure of the portion of the common labour borne by each individual, and of his share in the part of the total product destined for individual consumption. The social relations of the individual producers, with regard both to their labour and to its products are in this case perfectly simple and intelligible, and that with regard not only to production but also to distribution.

Capital, vol. i (1867) pp. 78 f.

Labour is, in the first place, a process in which both man and Nature participate, and in which man of his own accord starts, regulates, and controls the material reactions between himself and Nature. He opposes himself to Nature as one of her own forces, setting in motion arms and legs, head and hands, the natural forces of his body, in order to appropriate Nature's productions in a form adapted to his own wants. By thus acting on the external world and changing it, he at the same time changes his own nature. He develops his slumbering powers and compels them to act in obedience to his sway. We are not now dealing with those primitive instinctive forms of labour that remind us of the mere animal. An immeasurable interval of time separates the state of things in which a man brings his labour-power to market for sale as a commodity, from that state in which human labour was still in its first instinctive stage. We presuppose labour in a form that stamps it as exclusively human. A spider conducts operations that resemble those of a weaver, and a bee puts to shame an architect in the construction of her cells. But what distinguishes the worst architect from the best of bees is this, that the architect raises his structure in imagination before he erects it in reality. At the end of every labour-process, we get a result that already existed in the imagination of the labourer at its commencement. He not only effects a change of form in the material on which he works, but he also realises a purpose of his own that gives the law to his *modus operandi*, and to which he must subordinate his will. And this subordination is no mere momentary act. Besides the exertion of the bodily organs, the process demands that, during the whole operation, the workman's will be steadily in consonance with his purpose. This means close attention. The less he is attracted by the nature of the work, and the mode in which it is carried on, and the less, therefore, he enjoys it as something which gives play to his bodily and mental powers, the more close his attention is forced to be.

The elementary factors of the labour-process are (1) the personal activity of man, i.e., work itself, (2) the subject of that work, and (3) its instruments.

The soil (and this, economically speaking, includes water) in the virgin state in which it supplies man with necessaries or the means of subsistence ready to hand, exists independently of him, and is the universal subject of human labour. All these things which labour merely separates from immediate connection with their environment, are subjects of labour spontaneously provided by Nature. Such are fish which we catch and take from their element, water, timber which we fell in the virgin forest, and ores which we extract from their veins. If, on the other hand, the subject of labour has, so to say, been filtered through previous labour, we call it raw material; such is ore already extracted and ready for washing. All raw material is the subject of labour but not every subject of labour is raw material; it can only become so, after it has undergone some alteration by means of labour.

An instrument of labour is a thing, or a complex of things, which the labourer interposes between himself and the subject of his labour, and which serves as the conductor of his activity. He makes use of the mechanical, physical, and chemical properties of some substances in order to make other substances subservient to his aims. Leaving out of consideration such ready-made means of subsistence as fruits, in gathering which a man's own limbs serve as the instruments of his labour, the first thing of which the labourer possesses himself is not the subject of labour but its instrument. Thus Nature becomes one of the organs of his activity, one that he annexes to his own bodily organs, adding stature to himself in spite of the Bible. As the earth is his original larder, so too it is his original tool house. It supplies him, for instance, with stones for throwing, grinding, pressing, cutting, etc. The earth itself is an instrument of labour, but when used as such in agriculture implies a whole series of other instruments and a comparatively high development of labour. No sooner does labour undergo the least development, than it requires specially prepared instruments. Thus in the oldest caves we find stone implements and weapons. In the earliest period of human history domesticated animals, i.e. animals which have been bred for the purpose, and have undergone modifications by means of labour, play the chief part as instruments of labour along with specially prepared stones, wood, bones, and shells. The use and fabrication of instruments of labour, although existing in the germ among certain species of animals, is specifically characteristic of the human labour-process, and Franklin therefore defines man as a tool-making animal. Relics of bygone instruments of labour possess the same importance for the investigation of extinct economical forms of society, as do fossil bones for the determination of extinct species of animals. It is not the articles made, but how they are made, and by what instruments, that enables us to distinguish different economical epochs.

Capital, vol. i (1867) pp. 177 ff.

FURTHER READING

S. Avineri, *The Social and Political Thought of Karl Marx* (Cambridge, 1968).

D. Braybrooke, 'Diagnosis and Remedy in Marx's Doctrine of Alienation', *Social Research* (autumn 1958).

B. Ollman, *Alienation: Marx's Critique of Man in Capitalist Society* (Cambridge, 1971).

CHAPTER FOUR

Class

A. COMMENTARY

CLASSES are obviously of immense importance in Marx's view of history. The opening words of the *Communist Manifesto* are: 'The history of all hitherto existing societies is the history of class struggles'. For Marx, classes were the basic social groups by means of whose conflict society developed in accordance with changes in its economic substructure. In the past Marx thought that revolutions had occurred when one class had been able to identify its own interests with those of society as a whole. In the *German Ideology* he wrote: 'Each new class which puts itself in place of the one ruling before it, is compelled, merely in order to carry through its aims, to represent its interest as the common interest of all the members of society. . . . The class making a revolution appears from the very start . . . not as a class but as the representative of the whole of society.'[1] These 'identifications' had in the past proved to be of very short duration; but in the coming revolution the proletarian class really was in a position, both because of the simplification of the class system and because of its sheer numbers, to represent the interests of society as a whole. Thus the next revolution would, in time, inaugurate a classless society. Class, like the state or alienation, was a transitory phenomenon portrayed to its fullest extent in capitalist society.

Considering the importance of the idea of class for Marx, it is surprising that he offers no systematic analysis of the concept. The only place where he attempts this is at the end of Volume III of *Capital*; it is, however, incomplete, interrupted by his death.[2] Marx begins this passage by asking: how many classes are there? He answers that there are three large classes in capitalist society – wage labourers, capitalists and landowners. Yet he immediately

[1] *The German Ideology*, p. 62.   [2] *Capital* (Moscow, 1962) III 832 f.

qualifies this by saying that in England, where capitalist society is at its most developed, 'the stratification of classes does not appear in its pure form. Middle and intermediate strata even here obliterate lines of demarcation everywhere (although incomparably less in rural districts than in the cities).' However, the development of capitalist society was rapidly simplifying the situation by producing two and only two classes: bourgeoisie and proletariat. Not only were the 'middle and intermediate' strata being squeezed out: the landowners, too, would undergo the same process. All the workers would eventually become wage-labourers, and competition among capitalists would increase the wealth of some and force the rest down into the proletariat.

Marx then asks a second question: what makes the three groups referred to above into the three great social classes? His answer is: 'At first glance – the identity of revenues and sources of revenues. There are three great social groups whose numbers, the individuals forming them, live on wages, profit and ground rent, respectively, on the realisation of their labour-power, their capital, and their landed property.' He then puts the objection that this criterion would make, for example, doctors and civil servants into separate classes; and the same would be true of other groups inside the three classes mentioned above. The objection is unanswered, however, as the manuscript breaks off here.

The less systematic statements on class in the rest of Marx's writings help to answer the questions raised in *Capital*. In the *Communist Manifesto* Marx uses the model of two classes: 'society as a whole is more and more splitting up into two great hostile camps, into two great classes directly facing each other: bourgeoisie and proletariat'.[1] The bourgeoisie are defined as the owners of the means of production and the employers of wage-labour, the proletariat as those who own no means of production and live by selling their wage-labour. Thus the criterion for belonging to a class is one's position in the prevailing mode of production.

It is also this two-class model that lies behind Marx's idea on the immiserisation of the proletariat. Marx never claimed that the proletariat would become immiserised in any absolute sense.[2]

[1] K. Marx, F. Engels, *The Communist Manifesto*, *MESW* i 35.
[2] The passage from *Capital* usually quoted in this respect refers, as is obvious from the wider context, only to an increasing mass of unemployed.

Such an idea would not have harmonised well with his view of all human needs as mediated through society. What he did claim was that the gap in resources between those who owned the means of production and those who did not would widen. He makes this clear in his parable of the house and the place in *Wage Labour and Capital*:

> A house may be large or small; as long as the surrounding houses are equally small it satisfies all social demands for a dwelling. But let a palace arise beside the little house, and it shrinks from a little house to a hut. The little house shows now that its owner has only very slight or no demands to make; and however high it may shoot up in the course of civilization, if the neighbouring palace grows to an equal or even greater extent, the occupant of the relatively small house will feel more and more uncomfortable, dissatisfied and cramped within its four walls.[1]

But this two-class model is not Marx's only use of the word 'class'. He uses the term of other economic groups, and particularly of the petty-bourgeoisie and the peasants. These groups seem to render the neat division of the *Communist Manifesto* inapplicable, for these two groups obviously merge into bourgeoisie and the proletariat according to how many workers they employ or how much land they own. Marx even foresaw, with the increased use of machinery and the multiplication of service industries, the advent of a new middle class, and criticised Ricardo for forgetting 'the constantly growing number of the middle classes, those who stand between the workman on the one hand and the capitalist and landlord on the other.'[2]

There are other groups that are still more intermediate: farm-labourers, for example, seem to be half-way between peasants and proletariat. Although Marx's normal characterisation of the proletariat only applies to industrial workers, yet sometimes he says that the proletariat comprises the vast majority of people in capitalist society and so must include farm-labourers; and in a comment on Bakunin in 1875 he spoke of the possibility of a situation in which 'the capitalist tenant has ousted the peasants, and the real tiller of the soil is just as much a proletarian, a wage worker, as is the urban worker and thus shares with him interests

[1] K. Marx, *Wage Labour and Capital*, *MESW* I 93 f.
[2] K. Marx, *Theories of Surplus Value*, vol. II (Moscow, 1969) p. 573.

that are directly the same'.[1] He also, in the same comment, says that sometimes even the landowning peasant belongs to the proletariat, though he is not conscious of it. The burden of mortgage on his land means that he does not really own it and is, in effect, working for someone else. If then the peasants are held to be proletarians and landowners to be capitalists, then we have the two-class model again. Nevertheless, Marx thought that politically the peasants were a reactionary group and was unwilling to group them with the urban proletariat: the most recent peasant movements in Western Europe had had feudal or monarchist inclinations.

A second intermediate group that Marx found difficult to classify was the one he himself belonged to – the intelligentsia. He often referred to them as the 'ideological representatives and spokesmen' of the bourgeoisie. They were those 'who make the perfecting of the illusion of the class about itself their chief source of livelihood'.[2] And in the *Communist Manifesto* he called the intellectuals the 'paid wage-labourers' of the bourgeoisie, though obviously in a sense different from that in which the proletarians were. Marx also considered that certain intellectuals could achieve an objective assessment of at least certain aspects of society in spite of their class backgrounds – in particular he credited the classical economists, such as Ricardo, or the British factory inspectors, with such an objective view.

The fact that Marx quite often referred to intellectuals as the 'ideological classes' shows that he sometimes used the expression without particular reference to the position of a group in the mode of production. Marx spoke, for example, of a 'lower middle class' as consisting of 'the small tradespeople, shopkeepers, the handicraftsmen and peasants'.[3] In Britain Marx talked of the 'ruling classes', and he even went so far as to say that finance capitalists and industrial capitalists 'form two distinct classes'. At the other end of the social scale there is what Marx called the *Lumpenproletariat*. In the *Class Struggles in France* Marx described them as 'a recruiting ground for thieves and criminals of all kinds, living on the crumbs of society, people without a definite trade, vagabonds, people without a hearth or a home'.[4] In other

---

[1] *MEW* xviii 633.   [2] *The German Ideology*, p. 61.
[3] *The Communist Manifesto, MESW* i 41.
[4] K. Marx, *The Class Struggles in France, MESW* i 155.

words, the *Lumpenproletariat* were the drop-outs of society who
had no stake in the development of society and so no historical
role to play. They were at times reactionary since they were
willing to sell their services to the bourgeoisie.

Thus Marx's definition of class seems to vary greatly, not only
with the development of his thought but even within the same
period. Marx often uses the term, in common with the usage of
his time, as a synonym for faction or group.

Nevertheless two general points can be made: firstly, the tri-
partite division of society into capitalists, proletariat and landowners is the most usual one in Marx. He did not consider himself
to be analysing a static society and many of the groups he sometimes referred to as 'classes' were in fact rapidly disappearing.
The petty-bourgeoisie and the peasants were in this position.
Even the landowning class will finally, according to Marx, dissolve
into either the capitalist or the proletarian class, the only two
classes in developed capitalist society.

Secondly, Marx also had a dynamic or subjective element in
his definition of class: a class only existed when it was conscious
of itself as such, and this always implied common hostility to
another social group. A class always viewed its own interests as
opposed to those of other groups and had to be organised
politically to fight for them. Thus, Marx was sometimes hesitant
as to whether even the capitalists formed a class. In the *German
Ideology* he said of them that 'the separate individuals form a
class in so far as they have to carry on a common battle against
another class; otherwise they are on hostile terms with each other
as competitors'.[1] The same applied to the proletariat: in the
Poverty of Philosophy Marx speaks of utopian socialism as typical
of the time when 'the proletariat is not yet sufficiently developed
to constitute itself into a class' and 'consequently . . . the struggle
itself between proletariat and bourgeoisie does not yet have a
political character'. And in the same work he says of the proletariat
that 'this mass is already a class in opposition to capital, but not
yet a class for itself'.[2] In the *Communist Manifesto* he said that
'this organisation of the proletarians into a class, and consequently
into a political party, is continually being upset again by the
competition between the workers themselves':[3] and as late as 1866

[1] *The German Ideology*, pp. 48 f.
[2] *The Poverty of Philosophy*, pp. 140, 195.   [3] *MESW*, i 43.

Marx talked of the International as an instrument for 'the organisation of the workers into a class'.[1] Marx puts this most clearly in his description of the French peasantry in *The Eighteenth Brumaire of Louis Bonaparte*:

> In so far as millions of families live under economic conditions of existence that separate their mode of life, their interests and their culture from those of the other classes and put them in hostile opposition to the latter, they form a class. In so far as there is merely a local interconnection among those smallholding peasants and the identity of their interests begets no community, no national bond, and no political organisation among them, they do not form a class. They are consequently incapable of enforcing their class interest in their own name . . . .[2]

It should be noted in this connection that although Marx talks in the *Communist Manifesto* of the workers' having no fatherland, he also uses the concept of a 'national class'. He says, also in the *Communist Manifesto*, that 'since the proletariat must first of all acquire political supremacy, must rise to be the leading class of the nation, must constitute itself the nation, it is, so far, itself national.[3]

Thus Marx has many criteria for the application of the term 'class' and not all of them apply all the time. The two chief criteria are relationship to the prevailing mode of production and a group's consciousness of itself as a class with its attendant political organisation.

Marx categorically disclaimed any credit for having discovered either the existence of classes in modern society or their struggle: bourgeois historians and economists had already done that. What Marx saw as novel in his ideas was that he thought he had shown the existence of classes to be linked to particular historical periods in the development of production, and that the class struggle would lead to the dictatorship of the proletariat and a classless society.[4]

[1] Marx to Kugelmann, *MEW* xxxi 529.
[2] K. Marx, *The Eighteenth Brumaire of Louis Bonaparte*, *MESW* i 334.
[3] *The Communist Manifesto*, *MESW* i 51.
[4] Cf. Marx to Weydemeyer, 5 Mar. 1852, *MESC* p. 86.

B. TEXTS

It is not the radical revolution that is a Utopian dream for Germany, not universal human emancipation; it is the partial, purely political revolution, the revolution which leaves the pillars of the house still standing. What is the basis of a partial, purely political revolution? It is that a part of civil society emancipates itself and attains to universal domination, that a particular class undertakes the general emancipation of society from its particular situation. This class frees the whole of society, but only under the presupposition that the whole of society is in the same situation as this class, that it possesses, or can easily acquire, for example, money and education.

No class in civil society can play this role without arousing a moment of enthusiasm in itself and among the masses. It is a moment when the class fraternises with society in general and dissolves itself into society; it is identified with society and is felt and recognised as society's general representative. Its claims and rights are truly the claims and rights of society itself of which it is the real social head and heart. A particular class can only vindicate for itself general supremacy in the name of the general rights of society. Revolutionary energy and intellectual self-confidence alone are not enough to gain this position of emancipator and thus to exploit politically all spheres of society in the interest of one's own sphere. So that the revolution of a people and the emancipation of a particular class of civil society may coincide, so that one class can stand for the whole of society, the deficiency of all society must inversely be concentrated in another class, a particular class must be a class that rouses universal scandal and incorporates all limitations: a particular social sphere must be regarded as the notorious crime of the whole society, so that the liberation of this sphere appears as universal self-liberation. So that one class *par excellence* may appear as the class of liberation, another class must inversely be the manifest class of oppression. The universally negative significance of the French nobility and clergy determined the universally positive significance of the class nearest to them and opposed to them: the bourgeoisie.

Introduction to a Critique of Hegel's Philosophy of Right (1844);
Early Texts, pp. 125 f.

So where is the real possibility of a German emancipation?

We answer: in the formation of a class with radical chains, a class in civil society that is not a class of civil society, of a social group that is the dissolution of all social groups, of a sphere that has a universal character because of its universal sufferings and lays claim to no particular right, because it is the object of no particular injustice but of injustice in general. This class can no longer lay claim to a historical status, but only to a human one. It is not in a one-sided opposition to the consequences of the German political regime, it is in total opposition to its presuppositions. It is, finally, a sphere that cannot emancipate itself without emancipating itself from all other spheres of society and thereby emancipating these other spheres themselves. In a word, it is the complete redemption of humanity. This dissolution of society, as a particular class, is the proletariat.

Introduction to a Critique of Hegel's Philosophy of Right (1844); *Early Texts*, pp. 127 f.

The ideas of the ruling class are in every epoch the ruling ideas: i.e. the class which is the ruling *material* force of society, is at the same time its ruling *intellectual* force. The class which has the means of material production at its disposal, has control at the same time over the means of mental production, so that thereby, generally speaking, the ideas of those who lack the means of mental production are subject to it. The ruling ideas are nothing more than the ideal expression of the dominant material relationships, the dominant material relationships grasped as ideas; hence of the relationships which make the one class the ruling one, therefore, the ideas of its dominance. The individuals composing the ruling class possess among other things consciousness and therefore think. Insofar, therefore, as they rule as a class and determine the extent and compass of an epoch, it is self-evident that they do this in its whole range, hence among other things rule also as thinkers, as producers of ideas, and regulate the production and distribution of the ideas of their age: thus their ideas are the ruling ideas of the epoch.

The German Ideology (1845–6) p. 61.

In the Middle Ages the citizens in each town were compelled to unite against the landed nobility to save their skins. The extension of trade, the establishment of communications, led the separate towns to get to know other towns, which had asserted the same interests in the struggle with the same antagonist. Out of the many local corporations of burghers there arose only gradually the burgher *class*. The conditions of life of the individual burghers became, on account of their contradiction to the existing relationships and of the mode of labour determined by these, conditions which were common to them all and independent of each individual. The burghers had created the conditions insofar as they had torn themselves free from feudal ties, and were created by them insofar as they were determined by their antagonism to the feudal system which they found in existence. When the individual towns began to enter into associations, these common conditions developed into class conditions. The same conditions, the same contradiction, the same interests necessarily called forth on the whole similar customs everywhere. The bourgeoisie itself, with its conditions, develops only gradually, splits according to the division of labour into various fractions and finally absorbs all propertied classes it finds in existence (while it develops the majority of the earlier propertyless and a part of the hitherto propertied classes into a new class, the proletariat) in the measure to which all property found in existence is transformed into industrial or commercial capital. The separate individuals form a class only insofar as they have to carry on a common battle against another class; otherwise they are on hostile terms with each other as competitors. On the other hand, the class in its turn achieves an independent existence over against the individuals, so that the latter find their conditions of existence predestined, and hence have their position in life and their personal development assigned to them by their class, become subsumed under it. This is the same phenomenon as the subjection of the separate individuals to the division of labour and can only be removed by the abolition of private property and of labour itself. We have already indicated several times how this subsuming of individuals under the class brings with it their subjection to all kinds of ideas, etc.

The German Ideology (1845–6) pp. 69 f.

In the development of productive forces there comes a stage when productive forces and means of intercourse are brought into being, which, under the existing relationships, only cause mischief, and are no longer productive but destructive forces (machinery and money); and connected with this a class is called forth, which has to bear all the burdens of society without enjoying its advantages, which, ousted from society, is forced into the most decided antagonism to all other classes; a class which forms the majority of all members of society, and from which emanates the consciousness of the necessity of a fundamental revolution, the communist consciousness, which may, of course, arise among the other classes too through the contemplation of the situation of this class.

The German Ideology (1845–6) p. 86.

An oppressed class is the vital condition for every society founded on the antagonism of classes. The emancipation of the oppressed class thus implies necessarily the creation of a new society. For the oppressed class to be able to emancipate itself it is necessary that the productive powers already acquired and the existing social relations should no longer be capable of existing side by side. Of all the instruments of production, the greatest productive power is the revolutionary class itself. The organisation of revolutionary elements as a class supposes the existence of all the productive forces which could be engendered in the bosom of the old society.

Does this mean that after the fall of the old society there will be a new class domination culminating in a new political power? No.

The condition for the emancipation of the working class is the abolition of every class, just as the condition for the liberation of the third estate of the bourgeois order, was the abolition of all estates and all orders.

The working class, in the course of its development, will substitute for the old civil society an association which will exclude classes and their antagonism, and there will be no more political power properly so-called, since political power is precisely the official expression of antagonism in civil society.

Meanwhile the antagonism between the proletariat and the bourgeoisie is a struggle of class against class, a struggle which carried to its highest expression is a total revolution. Indeed, is it at all surprising that a society founded on the opposition of classes should culminate in brutal *contradiction*, the shock of body against body, as its final *dénouement*?

Do not say that social movement excludes political movement. There is never a political movement which is not at the same time social.

It is only in an order of things in which there are no more classes and class antagonisms that *social evolutions* will cease to be *political revolutions*. Till then, on the eve of every general reshuffling of society, the last word of social science will always be:

> *Le combat ou la mort; la lutte sanguinaire ou le néant.*
> *C'est ainsi que la question est invinciblement posée.*

> *The Poverty of Philosophy* (1847) pp. 196 ff.

After vouchsafing such profound explanations about the 'connection of politics with social conditions' and the 'class relations' with the State power, Mr Heinzen exclaims triumphantly: 'The "communistic narrow-mindedness" which divides men into classes, or antagonises them according to their handicraft, has been avoided by me. I have left open the "possibility" that "humanity" is not always determined by "class" or the "length of one's purse".' Bluff common sense transforms the class distinction into the 'length of the purse' and the class antagonism into trade quarrels. The length of the purse is a purely quantitative distinction, which may perchance antagonise any two individuals of the same class. That the medieval guilds confronted each other on the basis of handicraft is well known. But it is likewise well known that the modern class distinction is by no means based on handicraft; rather the division of labour within the same class produces very different methods of work.

It is very 'possible' that particular individuals are not always influenced in their attitude by the class to which they belong, but this has as little effect upon the class struggle as the secession of a few nobles to the *tiers état* had on the French Revolution. And then these nobles at least joined a class, the revolutionary class, the bourgeoisie. But Mr Heinzen sees all classes melt away before the solemn idea of 'humanity'.

If he believes that entire classes, which are based upon economic conditions independent of their will, and are set by these conditions in a relation of mutual antagonism, can break away from their real relations, by virtue of the quality of 'humanity' which is inherent in all men, how easy it should be for a prince to raise

himself above his 'princedom', above his 'princely handicraft' by
virtue of 'humanity'?

Moralising Criticism and Critical Morality (1847);
Selected Essays, pp. 155 ff.

The history of all hitherto existing society is the history of class
struggles.

Freeman and slave, patrician and plebeian, lord and serf,
guild-master and journeyman, in a word, oppressor and oppressed,
stood in constant opposition to one another, carried on an uninter-
rupted, now hidden, now open fight, a fight that each time ended,
either in a revolutionary re-constitution of society at large, or in
the common ruin of the contending classes.

In the earlier epochs of history, we find almost everywhere a
complicated arrangement of society into various orders, a manifold
gradation of social rank. In ancient Rome we have patricians,
knights, plebeians, slaves; in the Middle Ages, feudal lords,
vassals, guild-masters, journeymen, apprentices, serfs; in almost
all of these classes, again, subordinate gradations.

The modern bourgeois society that has sprouted from the ruins
of feudal society has not done away with class antagonisms. It has
but established new classes, new conditions of oppression, new
forms of struggle in place of the old ones.

Our epoch, the epoch of the bourgeoisie, possesses, however,
this distinctive feature: it has simplified the class antagonisms.
Society as a whole is more and more splitting up into two great
hostile camps, into two great classes directly facing each other:
Bourgeoisie and Proletariat.

The Communist Manifesto (1848); *MESW* I 34 f.

This organisation of the proletarians into a class, and consequently into a political party is continually being upset again
by the competition between the workers themselves. But it ever
rises up again, stronger, firmer, mightier. It compels legislative
recognition of particular interests of the workers, by taking
advantage of the divisions among the bourgeoisie itself. Thus the
ten-hours' bill in England was carried.

Altogether collisions between the classes of the old society
further, in many ways, the course of development of the proletariat.
The bourgeoisie finds itself involved in a constant battle. At first
with the aristocracy; later on, with those portions of the

bourgeoisie itself, whose interests have become antagonistic to the progress of industry; at all times, with the bourgeoisie of foreign countries. In all these battles it sees itself compelled to appeal to the proletariat, to ask for its help, and thus to drag it into the political arena. The bourgeoisie itself, therefore, supplies the proletariat with its own elements of political and general education, in other words, it furnishes the proletariat with weapons for fighting the bourgeoisie.

Further, as we have already seen, entire sections of the ruling classes are, by the advance of industry, precipitated into the proletariat, or are at least threatened in their conditions of existence. These also supply the proletariat with fresh elements of enlightenment and progress.

Finally, in times when the class struggle nears the decisive hour, the process of dissolution going on within the ruling class, in fact within the whole range of old society, assumes such a violent, glaring character, that a small section of the ruling class cuts itself adrift, and joins the revolutionary class, the class that holds the future in its hands. Just as, therefore, at an earlier period, a section of the nobility went over to the bourgeoisie, so now a portion of the bourgeoisie goes over to the proletariat, and in particular, a portion of the bourgeois ideologists, who have raised themselves to the level of comprehending theoretically the historical movement as a whole.

The Communist Manifesto (1848); *MESW* i 43.

The small-holding peasants form a vast mass, the members of which live in similar conditions but without entering into manifold relations with one another. Their mode of production isolates them from one another instead of bringing them into mutual intercourse. In so far as millions of families live under economic conditions of existence that separate their mode of life, their interests and their culture from those of the other classes, and put them in hostile opposition to the latter, they form a class. In so far as there is merely a local interconnection among these small-holding peasants, and the identity of their interests begets no community, no national bond and no political organisation among them, they do not form a class.

The Eighteenth Brumaire of Louis Bonaparte (1852)
MESW i 334.

No credit is due to me for discovering the existence of classes in modern society or the struggle between them. Long before me bourgeois historians had described the historical development of this class struggle and bourgeois economists the economic anatomy of the classes. What I did that was new was to prove: (1) that the *existence of classes* is only bound up with *particular historical phases in the development of production*, (2) that the class struggle necessarily leads to the *dictatorship of the proletariat*, (3) that this dictatorship itself only constitutes the transition to the *abolition of all classes* and to a *classless society*.

Marx to Weydemeyer (1852); *MESC* p. 69.

The owners of mere labour-power, the owners of capital, and the landlords, whose respective sources of income are wages, profit and ground-rent, in other words, wage-labourers, capitalists and landlords, form the three great classes of modern society resting upon the capitalist mode of production.

In England, modern society is indisputably developed most highly and classically in its economic structure. Nevertheless the stratification of classes does not appear in its pure form even there. Middle and transition stages obliterate even here all definite boundaries, although much less in the rural districts than in the cities. However, this is immaterial for our analysis. We have seen that the continual tendency and law of development of capitalist production is to separate the means of production more and more from labour, and to concentrate the scattered means of production more and more in large groups, thereby transforming labour into wage-labour and the means of production into capital. In keeping with this tendency we have, on the one hand, the independent separation of private land from capital and labour, or the transformation of all property in land into a form of landed property corresponding to the capitalist mode of production.

The first question to be answered is this: What constitutes a class? And this follows naturally from another question, namely: What constitutes wage-labourers, capitalists and landlords into three great social classes?

At first glance it might seem that the identity of their revenues and their sources of revenue does that. They are three great social groups, whose component elements, the individuals forming them, live on wages, profit and ground-rent, or by the utilisation of their labour-power, their capital and their private land.

However, from this point of view, physicians and officials would also form two classes, for they belong to the two distinct social groups, and the revenue of their members flow from the same common source. The same would also be true of the infinite dissipation of interests and positions created by the social division of labour among labourers, capitalists and landlords. For instance, the landlords are divided into owners of vineyards, farms, forests, mines and fisheries.

[Here the manuscript breaks off.]

Capital, vol. III (1864–5) pp. 1031 ff.

The Commune does not do away with the class struggles, through which the working classes strive to the abolition of all classes and, therefore, of all class rule (because it does not represent a peculiar interest. It represents the liberation of 'labour', that is the fundamental and natural condition of individual and social life which only by usurpation, fraud and artificial contrivances can be shifted from the few upon the many), but it affords the rational medium in which that class struggle can run through its different phases in the most rational and human way. It could start violent reactions and as violent revolutions. It begins the *emancipation of labour* – its great work of the state parasites, by cutting away the springs which sacrifice an immense portion of the national produce to the feeding of the statemonster on the one side, by doing, on the other, the real work of administration, local and national, for workingmen's wages. It begins therefore with an immense saving, with economical reform as well as political transformation.

Drafts for the Civil War in France (1871).[1]

FURTHER READING

S. Bloom, *The World of Nations*, 2nd ed. (New York, 1967) pp. 57 ff.
R. Dahrendorf, *Class and Class Conflict in Industrial Society.* (London, 1959) chap. 1.

[1] This – and subsequent passages from the *Drafts* – are based on a fresh collation of the original manuscript made by my colleague Joseph O'Malley.

G. Cohen, 'Bourgeois and Proletarians', *Journal of the History of Ideas* (Jan 1968).

D. Hodges, 'The Intermediate Classes in Marxian Theory', *Social Research* (1961).

S. Lipset and R. Bendix, 'Karl Marx's Theory of Social Classes', in *Class, Status and Power*, ed. Lipset and Bendix (Glencoe, Ill., 1953).

H. Mayer, 'Marx, Engels and the Politics of the Peasantry', *Études de Marxologie* (1960).

M. Nicolaus, 'Proletariat and Middle Class in Marx', *Studies in the Left* (1967).

B. Ollman, 'Marx's Use of "Class"', *American Journal of Sociology* (1968).

H. Rosenberg, 'The Pathos of the Proletariat', *Kenyon Review* (1949).

W. Wesolowski, 'Marx's Theory of Class Domination', in *Marx and the Western World*, ed. N. Lobkowicz (Notre Dame, Ind., 1967).

CHAPTER FIVE

The Party

A. COMMENTARY

M ARX offered no more systematic an account of the political party that he conceived to be necessary for working-class action, than he did of his views on classes or on the state. Marx never founded a party and was only a member of any party organisation for a few years. Although from very early on he saw the proletariat as the agent of social change, he always based his political activity on existing organisations, and particularly in his later years offered much advice to the growing workers' parties. Two difficulties inherent in giving an account of Marx's views are, firstly, that it was only during Marx's lifetime that the idea of the political party in the modern sense developed; secondly, that Marx himself used the term in widely differing senses. The two periods in which he was most active were those of the Communist League (1847–52) and the First International (1864–73).

The communist correspondence committees that Marx and Engels initiated in 1846 were not political parties, but only means of exchanging ideas among revolutionary groups in the European cities. Describing the organisation in a letter to Proudhon, Marx said that the aim was 'to link German socialists with French and English socialists, to keep foreigners informed of the socialist movements that will develop in Germany, and Germans informed of the progress of socialism in France and England'.[1] In 1847, however, on the invitation of its leaders, Marx became a member of the League of the Just, though he insisted that it abandon its character as a small international conspiratorial organisation. He wrote much later: 'When for the first time Engels and I joined the secret society of Communists, we did so on the condition *sine qua non* that everything that could favour a cult

[1] Marx to Proudhon, 5 May 1846, *MEW* XXVII 442.

of authority be banished from the statutes.'[1] In 1847 it was
renamed the Communist League and given a new and thoroughly
democratic constitution stipulating that all officers were elected
by, and continually responsible to, the members, the sovereign
body being the annual congress.

It was the League that commissioned the *Communist Manifesto*
in which Marx and Engels outlined their conception of the
Communist Party. The communists' claim to be the vanguard of
the working class was not based, according to Marx, on any
interests separate from those of the proletariat as a whole or on
any sectarian principles of their own. 'The Communists are
distinguished from other working-class parties by this only:
1. In the national struggles of the proletarians of the different
countries they point out and bring to the front the common
interests of the entire proletariat, independent of all nationality.
2. In the various stages of development which the struggle of the
working class against the bourgeoisie has to pass through, they
always and everywhere represent the interests of the movement
as a whole.'[2] Thus they were both 'the most advanced and resolute
section' of the working class and also 'theoretically, they have
over the great mass of the proletariat the advantage of clearly
understanding the line of march, the conditions and the ultimate
general results of the proletarian movement'.[3] With regard to
other opposition parties, the communists, while instilling into
their members the exclusiveness of their class interests, 'support
every revolutionary movement against the existing social and
political order of things'. In France they supported the social
democrats, in Switzerland the radicals, in Germany the liberal
bourgeoisie, etc. In spite of its programme being called the
Manifesto of the Communist Party, the League in 1848–9 never
functioned as a real political party, even in the sense in which
Marx and Engels used the term in the *Communist Manifesto*, nor
could it have done so in the circumstances: it had only 300
members at most, and was always forced to operate in a semi-
clandestine manner. The League appears to have been dissolved
by Marx in June 1848 since he preferred to work through the
Press; and when, in April 1849, Marx for the first time saw the
need and potential for a separate organised workers' party, it was

[1] Marx to Blos, 10 Nov 1877, *MESC* p. 310.
[2] *The Communist Manifesto*, *MESW* i 46.   [3] Ibid.

already too late, for the defeat of the insurrection in south-west Germany meant the end of the revolution.

In 1850 the League was reorganised with London as its centre. During the two years of its existence, Marx was responsible for several directives from the Central Committee to the groups. The most important of these, the *Address* written in March 1850, called for the establishment of an 'independent, secret and public organisation of the workers' party'. This party would be separate from other opposition parties and formed from the nucleus of already existing workers' associations which were normally of a social or educational nature. Marx did conclude an abortive alliance with Blanqui at about this time, but his conception of the communist party was very different from Blanqui's: in Marx's view the party should aim at being a party of the masses and should not try to gain power by a revolutionary *putsch*, nor be highly centralised; he also warned the workers of a lengthy revolutionary struggle to achieve class consciousness. 'They themselves', he wrote, 'must do the utmost for their final victory by clarifying their minds as to what their class interests are, by taking up their position as an independent party as soon as possible and by not allowing themselves to be seduced for a single moment by the hypocritical phrases of the democratic petty bourgeoisie . . . .'[1] By the summer of 1850, Marx had become convinced that an immediate revolution was not possible. The League split into two factions on this issue: a minority of the Central Committee wished to continue activities aimed at promoting an immediate revolution, whereas Marx told the workers that they might have as much as fifty years of civil war to go through before they were ready for revolution. Marx subsequently referred to the League as only an 'episode in the history of the Party which grows naturally from the soil of modern society'[2].

From the early 1850s until the mid-1860s, Marx was not a member of any party. He wrote to Engels in February 1851: 'I am very happy with the public and authentic isolation in which we two, you and I, now find ourselves. It entirely corresponds to our position and our principles. The system of mutual concessions, of inadequacies endured for the sake of appearances, and the obligation of appearing ridiculous before the public in the party with

[1] K. Marx, *Address of the Central Committee to the Communist League*, *MESW* i 117.   [2] Marx to Freiligrath, 29 Feb 1860, *MEW* xxx 490.

all these asses, has now ceased.'¹ Marx did, however, continue to
refer to his 'party', and that in two senses. Firstly, when he talked
about 'recruiting our party afresh' or 'insisting on party discipline',
he was referring to his small group of intimate followers often
called by their acquaintances the 'Marx party'. Secondly, Marx
used the term in a wider sense, as when, in the letter to Freiligrath
quoted above, he talks of 'the party in the great historical sense'
or later talks of the Paris Commune as 'the most glorious deed of
our Party since the June insurrection in Paris'.²

The second period of Marx's activity as a member of a political
party was occasioned by the First International. Marx's policies
here give a fair indication of his ideas on the organisation of
working-class parties. The International Association of Working
Men was not founded by Marx; it sprang up spontaneously, and
its chief purpose originally was to protect English trade unions
against the importations of foreign labour. It was in no way a
communist party, nor did Marx's followers form a separate group
inside it. Marx opposed secret groupings inside the International
even in countries where no right of association existed. 'This type
of organisation', he declared, 'is opposed to the proletarian
movement because these associations, instead of educating the
workers, subject them to authoritarian and mystical laws that
impede their independence and misguide their minds.'³ The rules
of the Association were intended by Marx to have as wide a scope
as possible, including, for example, the followers of Proudhon and
Lassalle. Marx wished the International only to deal with those
matters, as he wrote to Kugelmann, 'which allow of immediate
agreement and concerted action by the workers and give direct
nourishment and impetus to the requirements of the class struggle
and the organisation of the workers into a class'.⁴ Even after the
defeat of the Paris Commune in 1871 had convinced Marx of the
need for more discipline and independence in proletarian parties,
he still did not press for further centralisation of the International:
the demand of the London Conference of 1871 for the 'constitution
of the working class into a political party' only referred to
independent national parties. The quarrel with Bakunin and his

---

¹ Marx to Engels, 11 Feb 1851, *MEW* xxvii 184 f.
² Marx to Kugelmann, 12 Apr 1871, *MEW* xxxiii 206.
³ Speech to the London Conference of 1871, *MEW* xvii 655.
⁴ Marx to Kugelmann, 9 Oct 1866, *MEW* xxxi 529.

followers which brought about the end of the International was a quarrel about organisation, not about ideology: Marx was for a democratic, open organisation guided by decisions taken by majority vote at annual congresses, whereas Bakunin was in favour of a secret society with a hierarchical organisation. In its later years, owing to the growth of reaction outside the International and of disruptive elements inside it, Marx was forced to fight for a more effective central control.

Marx's comments on the German Social Democratic Party and its forerunners show the same concerns. He strongly criticised the followers of Lassalle for creating too disciplined and dogmatic a party. But for all his misgivings about the Gotha Programme of 1875 (which united the two hitherto opposed wings of the German workers), Marx recognised the German Social Democratic Party as a genuinely socialist party and even referred to it as 'our party'. In one of his last pronouncements on this theme, Marx sent a circular to the party leaders in 1879 urging them to preserve the party from all contamination with foreign values.[1]

To sum up, Marx's concept of the party was never some ideal institution, but always based on what political organisation was already in existence. However, he did insist that this party should have a completely democratic internal organisation; that it should be the independent creation of the workers themselves; that it was distinguished by a theoretical understanding of working-class goals; and that (usually) its organisation was not to be a part of, or dependent on, any other political party.

B. TEXTS

Now and then the workers are victorious, but only for a time. The real fruit of their battles lies, not in the immediate result, but in the ever-expanding union of the workers. This union is helped on by the improved means of communication that are created by modern industry and that place the workers of different localities in contact with one another. It was just this contact that was needed to centralise the numerous local struggles, all of the same character, into one national struggle between classes. But

[1] Cf. *MESC*, Circular Letter of 1879, pp. 375 f.

every class struggle is a political struggle. And that union, to attain which the burghers of the Middle Ages, with their miserable highways, required centuries, the modern proletarians, thanks to railways, achieve in a few years.

This organisation of the proletarians into a class, and consequently into a political party, is continually being upset again by the competition between the workers themselves. But it ever rises up again, stronger, firmer, mightier. It compels legislative recognition of particular interests of the workers, by taking advantage of the divisions among the bourgeoisie itself. Thus the ten-hours' bill in England was carried.

The Communist Manifesto (1848); *MESW* I 42f.

The Communists do not form a separate party opposed to other working-class parties.

They have no interests separate and apart from those of the proletariat as a whole.

They do not set up any sectarian principles of their own, by which to shape and mould the proletarian movement.

The Communists are distinguished from the other working-class parties by this only: 1. In the national struggles of the proletarians of the different countries, they point out and bring to the front the common interests of the entire proletariat, independently of all nationality. 2. In the various stages of development which the struggle of the working class against the bourgeoisie has to pass through, they always and everywhere represent the interests of the movement as a whole.

The Communists, therefore, are on the one hand, practically, the most advanced and resolute section of the working-class parties of every country, that section which pushed forward all others; on the other hand, theoretically, they have over the great mass of the proletariat the advantage of clearly understanding the line of march, the conditions, and the ultimate general results of the proletarian movement.

The immediate aim of the Communists is the same as that of all the other proletarian parties: formation of the proletariat into a class, overthrow of the bourgeois supremacy, conquest of political power by the proletariat.

The Communist Manifesto (1848); *MESW* I 46.

The relation of the revolutionary workers' party to the petty-bourgeois democrats is this: it marches together with them against the faction which it aims at overthrowing, it opposes them in everything whereby they seek to consolidate their position in their own interests.

Address of the Central Committee to the Communist League (1850);
MESW I 109.

After the failure of the 1848–49 revolution, the proletarian party on the continent lost all the rights that it had – exceptionally – possessed during this short period, rights such as the press, free speech, right of association, i.e. the legal means for the organisation of a party. The liberal bourgeois party and the petty-bourgeois democratic party found, in the social situation of the classes that they represented and in spite of the reaction, the possibility of a *rapprochement* under one form or another and of more or less advancing the interests that they held in common. But the proletarian party, after 1849 as before 1848, had only one means at its disposition: secret association. This is why, since 1849, there have arisen on the continent a whole series of secret proletarian societies which, discovered by the police, condemned by the tribunals, and disorganised by prison sentences, are ceaselessly reborn by the circumstances . . . .

The *Communist League* was therefore not a society of conspirators, but a society which prepared in secret the organisation of the proletarian party since the German proletariat was openly and forcibly deprived of the right to publish, speak and associate. If such a society conspires, it is only in the sense in which steam and electricity conspire against the status quo.

It is self-evident that such a secret society, whose aim is not to constitute the party of government but the opposition party of the future, could scarcely seduce individuals who wish to display the nullity of their personalities under the theatrical cloak of conspiracy . . . .

The Cologne Communist Trial (1853); *MEW* VIII 458 ff.

After the League was dissolved, at my request, in November 1852, I did not belong any more, nor do I, to any organisation whether secret or public; thus the party, in this quite ephemeral sense, ceased to exist for me eight years ago . . . .

The League, like the Society of Seasons in Paris and a hundred other associations, was only an episode in the history of the party which grows everywhere spontaneously from the soil of modern society . . . .

Under the term 'party', I understand party in the great historical sense of the word.

Marx to Freiligrath (1860); *MEW* xxx 489 ff.

During my first stay in Paris I entered into personal contact with the Paris leaders of the League [i.e. of the Just] and also with the leaders of most of the French secret societies without ever actually joining any of them. When I settled in Brussels, whither I was exiled by Guizot, I founded, with Engels, W. Wolff and some others, the German Workers' Educational Society which still exists today. At the same time we published a series of pamphlets, printed or cyclostyled, in which we submitted to implacable criticism the mixture of Anglo-French socialism and communism and German philosophy which then constituted the esoteric doctrine of the League. Instead, the scientific understanding of the economic structure of bourgeois society was established as the only acceptable theoretical basis; finally, in our public lectures we stressed that the point was not to realise any particular utopian system but to intervene with full knowledge in the historical process of social upheaval that was taking place before our eyes.

Herr Vogt (1860); *MEW* xiv 439.

Coalitions which give birth to trade unions are not only of the utmost importance as a means of organising the working class in its struggle against the bourgeoisie, an importance underlined by the example, among others, of the workers of the United States who cannot do without unions, in spite of universal suffrage and the republic; further, in Prussia and in Germany in general, the right of coalition breaks the rule of the police and the bureaucracy and shatters the feudal laws and rule by the nobles in the countryside; in short, it is a measure for the emancipation of 'subjects', a measure that the progressive party, that is, any bourgeois opposition party in Prussia, could, unless it were mad, accord a hundred times more easily than the Prussian government, above all the government of a Bismarck! On the other hand, any help given to co-operative societies by the Prussian government . . . is ineffective from an economic point of view, extends at the same time the tutelary system, corrupts a part of the working class and emasculates the movement. Just as the Prussian bourgeois party has made a blunder and has provoked its present appalling situation by imagining that, with the 'new era', the government had, by the grace of the Prince Regent, fallen into its lap; so the workers' party will make a still bigger blunder in imagining that, thanks to the Bismarck era or any other Prussian era, golden apples will fall into its mouth by the King's grace. It is beyond all doubt that Lassalle's unhappy illusion concerning socialist measures undertaken by a Prussian government will be disappointed. The logic of things will pronounce. But the honour of the workers' party demands that it reject these hallucinations before experience demonstrates their inanity. The working class is revolutionary or it is nothing.

Letter to Schweitzer (1865); *MEW* xxxi 445 f.

The starting points for the programme of a serious working-class movement should be as follows: agitation for complete political liberty, regulation of the working day, and international and systematic co-operation of the working class in the great historical task that it must accomplish for the benefit of society as a whole.

Article in the *Social Democrat* (1868); *MEW* xvi 316.

If they wish to accomplish their task, trade unions ought never to be attached to a political association or place themselves under its tutelage; to do so, would be to deal themselves a mortal blow. Trade unions are the schools of socialism. It is in trade unions that workers educate themselves and become socialists because under their very eyes and every day the struggle with capital is taking place. Any political party, whatever its nature and without exception, can only hold the enthusiasm of the masses for a short time, momentarily; unions, on the other hand, lay hold on the masses in a more enduring way; they alone are capable of representing a true working-class party and opposing a bulwark to the power of capital. The great mass of workers, whatever party they belong to, have at last understood that their material situation must become better. But once the worker's material situation has become better, he can consecrate himself to the education of his children; his wife and children do not need to go to the factory, he himself can cultivate his mind more, look after his body better, and he becomes socialist without noticing it.

Speech to a delegation of German trade unionists (1869)

Do not let him [i.e. Verlet] give any sectarian name – whether communist or anything else – to the new section that he wants to form. We must avoid sectarian 'labels' in the International Association. The general aims and tendencies of the working class spring from the real conditions in which it finds itself. Therefore these aims and tendencies are present in the whole class although the movement is reflected in their heads in widely different forms, more or less imaginary, and more or less in accordance with the conditions. Those who best understand the hidden meaning of the class struggle unfolding before our eyes – the Communists – are the last to commit the error of agreeing to or furthering sectarianism.

Marx to Paul and Laura Lafargue (1870); *MEW* xxxii 671.

Every movement in which the working class comes out as a *class* against the ruling classes and tries to coerce them by pressure from without is a political movement. For instance, the attempt in a particular factory or even in a particular trade to force a shorter working day out of individual capitalists by strikes, etc., is a purely economic movement. On the other hand the movement to force through an eight-hour, etc., *law*, is a *political* movement. And in this way, out of the separate economic movements of the workers there grows up everywhere a *political* movement, that is to say, a movement of the *class*, with the object of enforcing its interests in a general form, in a form possessing general, socially coercive force. While these movements presuppose a certain degree of previous organisation, they are in turn equally a means of developing this organisation.

Marx to Bolte (1871); *MESC* pp. 270 f.

In its struggle against the collective power of the possessing classes the proletariat can act as a class only by constituting itself a distinct political party, opposed to all the old parties formed by the possessing classes.

This constitution of the proletariat into a political party is indispensable to ensure the triumph of the social revolution and of its ultimate goal: the abolition of classes.

The coalition of the forces of the working class, already achieved by the economic struggle, must also serve, in the hands of this class, as a lever in its struggle against the political power of its exploiters.

As the lords of the land and of capital always make use of their political privileges to defend and perpetuate their economic monopolies and to enslave labour, the conquest of political power becomes the great duty of the proletariat.

Decision of London Conference (1871); *MESW* I 388 f.

The first phase in the struggle of the proletariat against the bourgeoisie is marked by sectarian movements. These are justified in an age when the proletariat is not yet developed enough to act as a class. Individual thinkers give a critique of social antagonisms and provide imaginary solutions that the mass of workers has only to accept, propagate and put into action. By their very nature, the sects formed by these initiators are abstentionist, hostile to any real action, to politics, to strikes, to coalitions, in short to any collective movement . . . . This is the infancy of the proletarian movement, as astrology and alchemy are the infancy of science. In order for the foundation of the International to be possible, it was necessary that the proletariat should have progressed beyond this phase.

In face of the fantastical and mutually antagonistic organisation of the sects, the International is the real and militant organisation of the proletarian class in all countries linked together in their common struggle against the capitalists, the landed proprietors and their class power organised in the state.

Also the statutes of the International only recognise simple 'workers' societies, all pursuing the same aim and all accepting the same programme which is restricted to outlining the main characteristics of the proletarian movement and leaves the theoretical elaboration to the impulse afforded by the necessities of practical struggle and to the exchange of ideas that takes place in the sections, allowing without distinction all socialist convictions in their organs and their congresses.

The Alleged Splits in the International (1872);
La Première Internationale, ed. J. Freymond (Geneva, 1962)
II 284.

The international activity of the working classes does not in any way depend on the existence of the *International Working Men's Association*. This was only the first attempt to create a central organ for that activity; an attempt which was a lasting success on account of the impulse which it gave but which was no longer realisable in its *first historical form* after the fall of the Paris Commune.

Critique of the Gotha Programme (1875); *MESW* ii 28.

As for ourselves, in view of our whole past there is only one road open to us. For almost forty years we have stressed the class struggle as the immediate driving power of history, and in particular the class struggle between bourgeoisie and proletariat as the great lever of the modern social revolution; it is, therefore, impossible for us to co-operate with people who wish to expunge this class struggle from the movement. When the International was formed we expressly formulated the battle-cry: The emancipation of the working classes must be conquered by the working classes themselves. We cannot therefore co-operate with people who openly state that the workers are too uneducated to emancipate themselves and must be freed from above by philanthropic big bourgeois and petty bourgeois.

Circular Letter (1879); *MESC* p. 327.

FURTHER READING

J. Braunthal, *History of the International* (London, 1967) pp. 44 ff., 85 ff.

H. Collins and C. Abramsky, *Karl Marx and the British Labour Movement* (London, 1965).

R. Garaudy, *Karl Marx: The Evolution of his Thought* (London, 1967) pp. 190 ff.

M. Johnstone, 'Marx and Engels and the Concept of the Party', *Socialist Register* (1967).

B. Nicolaevsky, 'Towards a History of the Communist League', *International Review of Social History* (1956).

B. Wolfe, *Marxism: 100 Years in the Life of a Doctrine* (London, 1967) esp. chap. 11.

CHAPTER SIX

The State

A. COMMENTARY

MARX was first led to formulate his views on the state, which was in many ways for him the most characteristic institution of man's alienated condition, by his early journalistic experiences. Marx experienced the impact of the state chiefly as censor of his articles for the *Rheinische Zeitung*. In opposition to the contemporary Prussian state, Marx conceived of the possibility of forming a truly free association of men in an idealised state conceived, on the Hegelian model, as the incarnation of reason.

By the summer of 1843, two factors led Marx to modify this view: one was his reading of Feuerbach's critique of Hegel's philosophy, the second his practical experience as editor of the *Rheinische Zeitung* which showed him the importance of socio-economic factors in the framing of legislation. With this in mind, Marx elaborated his ideas on the state in a long manuscript which was a critique of Hegel's political philosophy. According to Hegel, the state was logically prior to, and ethically superior to its two constituent elements, the family and civil society. Marx set out to show that it was an illusion to suppose that the state had a universal character capable of harmonising the discordant elements of civil society and uniting them on a higher level. By describing the state prior to any analysis of civil society, Hegel presupposed a gap between them and so had to work out institutions to bridge the gap. All these institutions, however – monarchy, representative assemblies, bureaucracy – were in fact cloaks for particular interests in civil society: the state was no more than an empty ideal sphere which created the illusion of belonging to a community. This opposition between civil society and the state was characteristic of the bourgeois epoch but not of the Middle Ages. The form of government that Marx recommended, in contrast to Hegel, was one where there was no separation between civil society and the state and which directly corresponded to 'the essence of socialised man'. He called this 'true democracy' and characterised it as follows:

> In all states that are not democracies, the state, the law, the constitution is the dominant factor without really dominating, i.e. materially penetrating all the other spheres that are not political. In a democracy the constitution, the law and the state itself are only a self-determination of the people and a particular content of them in so far as it is a political constitution.[1]

With his conversion to communism in 1844, Marx came to the conclusion that the state was essentially the negation of man. In the *Paris Manuscripts* he declared the state to be an expression of human alienation similar to religion, law and morality, and equally based on a particular mode of production. But at the same time the state did contain positive elements. Marx's analysis here is similar to his analysis of religion which in many respects acted as a paradigm for his political views. Marx considered America as 'the most perfect example of a modern state' and went as far as to say:

> . . . as regards actual life, the political state, even where it is not yet consciously impregnated with socialist principles, contains in all its modern forms the demands of reason. . . . Inside its republican form the political state expresses all social struggles, needs and truths.[2]

Thus Marx viewed the state, like religion, as a statement of man's ideal aims and also a compensation for their lack of realisation. The state was limited just because its aims remained ideal. Marx found confirmation of his view in the documents of the French and American revolutions which claimed to emancipate man as a *political citizen*, but left him in bondage as a *man*, or member of civil society, i.e. economic society. It was this paradox that Marx analysed in his 1843 essay *On the Jewish Question* in which he gave his most accessible critique of liberalism. In his article against Ruge in 1844 Marx went as far as to say that the more political

---

[1] *The Early Texts*, p. 66.   [2] Ibid. p. 81.

a state was, and the more it constituted a separate sphere, the more incapable it was of solving society's problems:

> The state cannot abolish the contradiction which exists between the role and good intentions of the administration on the one hand and the means at its disposal on the other, without abolishing itself, for it rests on this contradiction. It rests on the contrast between public and private life, on the contrast between general and particular interests. The administration must therefore limit itself to a formal and negative activity, for its power ceases just where civil life and work begin.

Thus:

> If the modern state wished to do away with the impotence of its administration, it would have to do away with the contemporary private sphere for it only exists in contrast to the private sphere.[1]

Marx actually signed a contract in 1844 for a book on politics which would have incorporated his *Critique of Hegel's Philosophy of the State* and readings on the French Revolution; but he seems to have got no further than the table of contents.

Although Marx in his later writings did not abandon the idea of the state as compensation, as alienated social power, he concentrated more and more on an analysis of the function of the state in society. Whereas in his earlier writings he had tended to emphasise the gap between the state and society, he later considered the state as part of society. His fullest formulation of this idea was in the *German Ideology*. Marx's programme of analysis, stated at the beginning of the work, was:

> Definite individuals who are productively active in a specific way enter into these definite social and political relations. In each particular instance, empirical observation must show empirically, without any mystification or speculation, the connection of the social and political structure with production. The social structure and the state continually evolve out of the life-process of definite individuals, individuals . . . as they work,

[1] *Ibid.* pp. 213 f.

produce materially, and act under definite material limitations, presuppositions, and conditions independent of their work.[1]

In the *German Ideology* Marx traced the origin of the state, together with other social institutions, to the division of labour: the state was in contradiction to the real interests of all members of society, constituting as it did an illusory community serving as a screen for the real struggles waged by classes against each other. In the course of history each method of production gave rise to a typical political organisation furthering the interests of the dominant class. The large-scale industry and universal competition of modern capitalism had created their own political organisation – the modern state which was dependent on the bourgeoisie for taxes and public credit. The state in turn moulded other social institutions:

> Since the state is the form in which the individuals of a ruling class assert their common interests and the entire civil society of an epoch is epitomised, the state acts as an intermediary in the formation of all communal institutions and gives them a political form. Hence, there is the illusion that law is based on will, that is, on will divorced from its real basis, on free will. In similar fashion, right in turn is reduced to statute law.[2]

This is the view that Marx summed up in the *Communist Manifesto*: 'The executive of the modern state is but a committee for managing the common affairs of the whole bourgeoisie.'[3] It should be noted, however, that Marx himself considered this correlation between economic substructure and political formations to be a very loose one: for example, though he thought England the most advanced country economically, France was for him politically more advanced in many respects.

Marx does admit exceptions to his general description of the state as an instrument of class domination, and especially in two of his most striking analyses of contemporary events – *The Class Struggles in France* and *The Eighteenth Brumaire of Louis Bonaparte*. Sometimes Marx says that the state need not be representative of the whole of a class but only of a section of that class (for example, the financiers under Louis-Philippe); or that

---

[1] *Writings of the Young Marx*, pp. 413 f.   [2] Ibid. p. 470.
[3] *The Communist Manifesto*, MESW I 36.

one class can control the state for the benefit of another class (for example, the Whigs on behalf of the middle class in England). In relatively backward countries, where classes were not fully developed, Marx thought that the state could play an independent role; also in the European absolute monarchies in the transition between feudal and bourgeois classes. He says of France under Louis Bonaparte, in contrast to his predecessors: 'only under the second Bonaparte does the state seem to have made itself completely independent'. He goes on: 'And yet the state power is not suspended in mid-air. Bonaparte represents a class, and the most numerous class of French society at that, the small-holding peasants.'[1]

Yet Bonaparte was not controlled by the peasants and governed by no means exclusively in their interests. Indeed, Marx said that the state simply as an instrument of class domination was to be found only in North America, 'where the state, unlike all other national structures, was from the start subordinated to bourgeois society and bourgeois production'.[2]

The second broad exception in Marx to the idea of the state as an instrument of class domination occurs in Asian societies – India, China, and to some extent Russia. Owing to the lack of private property in land, 'the despot here appears as the father of all the numerous lesser communities, thus revealing the common unity of all'.[3]

Marx considered bureaucracy to be the most essential part of this modern state apparatus. His views on bureaucracy are contained chiefly in his *Critique of Hegel's Philosophy of the State* written in 1843 and in *The Eighteenth Brumaire of Louis Bonaparte* written in 1851. In the latter Marx writes of bureaucracy as originating with the rise of absolute monarchy and thus originally as a progressive force which destroyed the corporations of medieval society and made for centralisation and equality of treatment for all citizens. In the 1843 manuscript, with his eye principally on Prussia, Marx described how the bureaucracy had eventually become a caste which claimed to possess, through higher education, the monopoly of the interpretation of the state's interests. The bureaucracy, finding itself challenged by the

---

[1] *The Eighteenth Brumaire, MESW* I 333.
[2] *Marx's Grundrisse*, p. 48.
[3] K. Marx, *Pre-Capitalist Economic Formations* (London, 1964) p. 69.

very spirit of equality that originally it had fostered, had turned itself into a medieval corporation, taking refuge in the trinity of mystery, hierarchy and authority. In France, Marx considered that the bureaucracy, which had prepared the way for the rule of the bourgeoisie, had largely become an instrument in their hands, though they conserved a tendency to independence, unlike the bureaucracies of Britain and the United States where parliaments were stronger and bureaucracy had not played such an important role in the transition from feudalism. Under Louis Napoleon, owing to the weakness of the bourgeoisie, the bureaucracy was able to control the state, being more than a match for the isolated peasantry that formed the basis of Bonaparte's power. This point is expanded in Marx's draft versions of *The Civil War in France*.[1]

Any successful revolution was bound to involve the breaking of the power of the state and its bureaucracy. In 1871 Marx reminded Kugelmann of the passage in *The Eighteenth Brumaire* where he talked of the destruction of the bureaucratic-military machinery and described it as 'the precondition of any real popular revolution on the continent'.[2] In 1872 he wrote:

> What all socialists understand by anarchism is this: as soon as the goal of the proletarian movement, the abolition of classes, shall have been reached, the power of the state, whose function it is to keep the great majority of producers beneath the yoke of a small minority of exploiters, will disappear and governmental functions will be transformed into simple administrative functions.[3]

The distinction made here between 'government' and 'administration' is never completely spelled out by Marx but he seems to have thought that the abolition of the state would at least involve the disappearance of its most typical manifestations – the bureaucracy, the army and the judicature. The phrase that most often comes to mind in this connection is that 'the state is not abolished, it withers away', although the words are not actually by Marx but by Engels. Nevertheless, the variety of terms that Marx uses to refer to the disappearance of the state is too great

---

[1] See the quotation on pp. 192 f. below.
[2] Marx to Kugelmann, 12 Apr 1871, *MEW* xxxiii 205.
[3] K. Marx, *The Alleged Splits in the International*, in *La Première Internationale*, ed. J. Freymond (Geneva, 1962) ii 295.

to yield any precise meaning and the term most often employed is, in fact, 'abolition'.[1]

Marx's conception of the future role of the state has to be pieced together from remarks made solely *en passant*. Some statements of Marx seem to reveal an 'authoritarian' attitude, but these are usually devoted to what aspects of the bourgeois revolution the proletariat should support. When, for example, in the *Address* of March 1850 he says 'the workers . . . must not only strive for a single and indivisible German republic, but also within this republic for the most determined centralisation of power in the hands of the state authority',[2] this is a recommendation of policy in a country on the eve of a bourgeois revolution.

For Marx's view of the state after a successful proletarian revolution, there are two main sources. The first is Marx's comments on the Paris Commune, contained in his *Civil War in France*. This essay cannot be taken as entirely representative of Marx's thought as it was written immediately after the bloody failure of the Commune and could not but have been an attempt at justification. Moreover, the rising had taken place against Marx's advice, he knew that the majority of its leaders were not communist and he went so far later as to say that its policies 'were not socialist, nor in the circumstances could they have been'.[3] Nevertheless, some of the policies of the Commune seem to have met with Marx's approval and he also considered it to have important potentialities. Marx welcomed the Commune's proposals to have all officials, including judges, elected by universal suffrage and revocable at any time; to pay officials the same wages as workmen; to replace the standing army by the armed people; and to divest the police and clergy of their political influence. Marx also considered that the initiative of the Commune could have yielded a decentralised, federal political structure and an economy based on co-operatives united by a common plan. Naturally during the arguments inside the International Marx rejected the anarchist views of Bakunin and his followers, but this does not support the view that he was an authoritarian.

The second main source for Marx's view of government after a

---

[1] Cf. M. Evans, 'Marx Studies', *Political Studies* (Dec 1970). Also see further Chapter 8 below.

[2] *Address to the Communist League*, *MESW* i 115.

[3] Marx to Domela-Nieuwenhuis, 22 Feb 1881, *MESC* p. 410.

proletarian revolution is in the *Critique of the Gotha Programme.*
Here Marx asserts that 'freedom consists in converting the state
from an organ superior to society into one completely subordinate
to it'.[1] Commenting on the role of the state in communist society,
Marx merely says that the question as to what social functions
analogous to those of the contemporary state will still subsist in
communist society can only be answered scientifically. Marx's
only further statement is that there will exist 'a period of revolutionary transformation' between capitalist and communist society
and that in this period 'the state can be nothing but the revolutionary dictatorship of the proletariat'.[2] As has been previously
pointed out, it is difficult to read any particular political
implications into the term 'dictatorship'.[3]

In the six-volume treatise entitled *Economics* that Marx
intended to write, but never even half completed, the fourth
volume was to have been devoted to the state; and it is the lack of
this volume that constitutes the major gap in Marx's later writings.
The general outline of its contents has to be reconstructed from
the tangential remarks in writings devoted to other subjects.

B. Texts

Since it is of the essence of bureaucracy to be the 'state as for-
malism', so its aim implies this also. The real aim of the state thus
appears to bureaucracy as an aim against the state. The spirit of
bureaucracy is therefore the 'formal spirit of the state'. Thus it
makes the 'formal spirit of the state' or the real lack of spirit by
the state into a categorical imperative. Bureaucracy counts in its
own eyes as the final aim of the state. Because it makes its 'formal'
ends into its content, it enters into conflict everywhere with 'real'
ends. It is therefore compelled to claim the formal for its content
and its content as the formal. The aims of the state are transformed into the aims of the bureaux and the aims of the bureaux
into the aims of the state. Bureaucracy is a circle from which no
one can escape. Its hierarchy is a hierarchy of knowledge. The
apex entrusts the lower circles with insight into the individual

---

[1] K. Marx, *Critique of the Gotha Programme, MESW* II 32.
[2] Ibid. 33.   [3] See also p. 202 below.

while the lower circles leave insight into the universal to the apex, so they deceive each other reciprocally.

Bureaucracy constitutes an imaginary state beside the real state and is the spiritualism of the state. Thus every object has a dual meaning, a real one and a bureaucratic one, just as knowledge is dual, a real and a bureaucratic (it is the same with the will). But the real thing is treated according to its bureaucratic essence, its otherworldly spiritual essence. Bureaucracy holds in its possession the essence of the state, the spiritual essence of society, it is its private property. The general spirit of bureaucracy is secret, mystery, safeguarded inside itself by hierarchy and outside by its nature as a closed corporation. Thus public political spirit and also political mentality appear to bureaucracy as a betrayal of its secret. The principle of its knowledge is therefore authority, and its mentality is the idolatry of authority. But within bureaucracy the spiritualism turns into a crass materialism, the materialism of passive obedience, faith in authority, the mechanism of fixed and formal behaviour, fixed principles, attitudes, traditions. As far as the individual bureaucrat is concerned, the aim of the state becomes his private aim, in the form of a race for higher posts, of careerism.

Critique of Hegel's Philosophy of Right (1843); *Early Texts*, p. 69.

Democracy is the solution to the riddle of all constitutions. Here the constitution is constantly, not only in itself and essentially but also in its existence and reality, brought back to its real basis, the real man, the real people, and set up as its own work. The constitution appears as what it is, the free product of man; one could say that this is valid in certain respects for constitutional monarchy also, but the specific difference of democracy is that in it the constitution is nothing more than one element in the being of the people, that the political constitution does not explicitly form the state.

Hegel starts from the state and makes man into the subjective aspect of the state; democracy starts from man and makes the state into objectified man. Just as religion does not make man, but man makes religion, so the constitution does not make the people, but the people makes the constitution. In a certain respect democracy has the same relation to all the other forms of state as

Christianity has to all other forms of religion. Christianity is the religion *par excellence*, the essence of religion, deified man as a particular religion. Similarly democracy is the essence of all constitutions of the state, socialised man as a particular constitution of the state; it has the same relationship to other constitutions as the species has to its types, only that in this case, the species itself appears as a particular existence and thus over against existences that do not correspond to the essence, it appears as a particular type. Democracy is the Old Testament in relation to other political forms. Man is not there for the benefit of the law, but the law for the benefit of man, it is a human existence, whereas in other political forms man has only a legal existence. That is the fundamental character of democracy.

> *Critique of Hegel's Philosophy of Right* (1843);
> *Early Texts*, p. 65.

The perfected political state is by its nature the species-life of man in opposition to his material life. All the presuppositions of this egoistic life continue to exist in civil society outside the sphere of the state, but as proper to civil society. When the political state has achieved its true completion, man leads a double life, a heavenly one and an earthly one, not only in thought and consciousness but in reality, in life. He has a life both in the political community, where he is valued as a communal being, and in civil society where he is active as a private individual, treats other men as means, degrades himself to a means and becomes the plaything of alien powers. Political emancipation is of course a great progress. Although it is not the final form of human emancipation in general, it is nevertheless the final form of human emancipation inside the present world order. It is to be understood that I am speaking here of real, practical emancipation. . . .

But we should not be deceived about the limitations of political emancipation. The separation of man into a public and a private man, the displacement of religion from the state to civil society is not a stage but the completion of political emancipation, which thus does not abolish or even try to abolish the actual religiosity of man.

> *On the Jewish Question* (1843); *Early Texts*, pp. 93 ff.

All emancipation is bringing back man's world and his relationships to man himself.

Political emancipation is the reduction of man, on the one hand to a member of civil society, an egoistic and independent individual, on the other hand to a citizen, a moral person.

The actual individual man must take the abstract citizen back into himself and, as an individual man in his empirical life, in his individual work and individual relationships become a species-being; man must recognise his own forces as social forces, organise them and thus no longer separate social forces from himself in the form of political forces. Only when this has been achieved will human emancipation be completed.

On the Jewish Question (1843); *Early Texts*, p. 108.

From the political point of view the state and any organisation of society are not two distinct things. The state is the organisation of society. In so far as the state admits the existence of social abuses, it seeks their origin either in natural laws that no human power can control or in the private sector which is independent of it or in the inadequacy of the administration that depends on the state. . . .

The state cannot abolish the contradiction which exists between the role and good intentions of the administration on the one hand and the means at its disposal on the other, without abolishing itself, for it rests on this contradiction. It rests on the contrast between public and private life, on the contrast between general and particular interests. The administration must therefore limit itself to a formal and negative activity, for its power ceases just where civil life and work begin. Indeed, in the face of the consequences that spring from the unsocial nature of this civil life, this private property, this commerce, this industry, this reciprocal plundering of different civil groups, in face of these consequences, impotence is the natural law of the administration. For this tearing apart, this baseness, this slavery of civil society is the natural basis on which the modern state rests, as the civil society of slavery was the natural basis on which the classical state rested. The existence of the state and the existence of slavery are inseparable. The classical state and classical slavery – frank and open class oppositions – were not more closely forged together than the modern state and modern world of haggling, hypocritical, Christian oppositions. If the modern state wished to do away with the impotence of its administration, it would have to do away with

the contemporary private sphere for it only exists in contrast to
the private sphere.

Critical Notes on 'The King of Prussia and Social Reform' (1844);
Early Texts, pp. 213f.

The more powerful the state, and thus the more political a country
is, the less is it inclined to look in the state itself, that is in the
present organisation of society whose active, self-conscious and
official expression is the state, for the cause of social evils, and
thus understand their general nature. Political intelligence is
political just because it thinks inside the limits of politics. The
sharper and livelier it is the less capable it is of comprehending
social evils. The classical period of political intelligence is the
French Revolution. Far from seeing the source of social defects
in the state, the heroes of the French Revolution see in social
defects the source of political misfortunes. Thus Robespierre sees
in extremes of poverty and riches only an impediment to pure
democracy. So he wishes to establish a general Spartan frugality.
The principle of politics is the will. The more one-sided, and thus
the more perfect political intelligence is, the more it believes in the
omnipotence of the will, the blinder it is to the natural and
intellectual limits of the will, and thus the more incapable it is of
discovering the sources of social evils.

Critical Notes on 'The King of Prussia and Social Reform' (1844);
Early Texts, p. 214.

The recognition of the Rights of Man by the modern state means
nothing more than did the recognition of slavery by the state of
old. In the same way, in other words, as the state of old had slavery
as its natural basis, the modern state has civil society and the
man of civil society, i.e. the independent man depending on other
men only by private interest and unconscious natural necessity,
the slave of earning his living and of his own as well as other men's
selfish need. The modern state has recognised this as its natural
basis in the universal rights of man. It did not create it. As it was
the product of civil society driven beyond its bounds by its own
development, it now recognises the womb it was born of and its
basis by the declaration of the rights of man.

The Holy Family (1845) pp. 152f.

The fact is, therefore, that definite individuals who are productively active in a definite way enter into these definite social and political relations. Empirical observation must in each separate instance bring out empirically, and without any mystification and speculation, the connection of the social and political structure with production. The social structure and the State are continually evolving out of the life process of definite individuals, but of individuals, not as they may appear in their own or other people's imagination, but as they really are; i.e. as they operate, produce materially, and hence as they work under definite material limits, presuppositions and conditions independent of their will.

The German Ideology (1845–6) pp. 36 f.

Out of this very contradiction between the interest of the individual and that of the community the latter takes an independent form as the *State*, divorced from the real interests of individual and community, and at the same time as an illusory communal life, always based, however, on the real ties existing in every family and tribal conglomeration – such as flesh and blood, language, division of labour on a larger scale, and other interests – and especially, as we shall enlarge upon later, on the classes, already determined by the division of labour, which in every such mass of men separate out, and of which one dominates all the others. It follows from this that all struggles within the State, the struggle between democracy, aristocracy, and monarchy, the struggle for the franchise, etc., etc., are merely the illusory forms in which the real struggles of the different classes are fought out among one another.

The German Ideology (1845–6) p. 45.

If power is taken as the basis of right, as Hobbes, etc., do, then right, law, etc., are merely the symptom, the expression of *other* relations upon which State power rests. The material life of individuals, which by no means depend merely on their 'will', their mode of production and form of intercourse, which mutually determine each other – this is the real basis of the State and remains so at all the stages at which division of labour and private property are still necessary, quite independently of the *will* of individuals. These actual relations are in no way created by the State power; on the contrary they are the power creating it. The individuals who rule in these conditions, besides having to constitute their power in the form of the State, have to give their will, which is determined by these definite conditions, a universal expression as the will of the State, as law – an expression whose content is always determined by the relations of this class, as the civil and criminal law demonstrates in the clearest possible way.

The German Ideology (1845–6) p. 366.

Each step in the development of the bourgeoisie was accompanied by a corresponding political advance of that class. An oppressed class under the sway of the feudal nobility, an armed and self-governing association in the medieval commune; here independent urban republic (as in Italy and Germany), there taxable 'third estate' of the monarchy (as in France), afterwards, in the period of manufacture proper, serving either the semi-feudal or the absolute monarchy as a counterpoise against the nobility, and, in fact, corner-stone of the great monarchies in general, the bourgeoisie has at last, since the establishment of Modern Industry and of the world-market, conquered for itself, in the modern representative State, exclusive political sway. The executive of the modern State is but a committee for managing the common affairs of the whole bourgeoisie.

The Communist Manifesto (1848); *MESW* i 35 f.

The bourgeois state is nothing but a mutual insurance pact of the bourgeois class both against its members taken individually and against the exploited class; this insurance becomes inevitably more and more costly and, in appearance, more and more independent vis-à-vis bourgeois society, for it is more and more difficult to bridle the exploited class. . . .

The abolition of the state only has a meaning for communists as a necessary result of the suppression of classes whose disappearance automatically entails the disappearance of the need for an organised power of one class for the suppression of another.

Review of E. Girardin, *Socialism and Taxes* (Paris, 1850);
MEW vii 288.

The middling bourgeoisie and the petty middle class were by their economical conditions of life excluded from initiating a new revolution and induced to follow in the track of the ruling classes or to become the followers of the working class. The peasants were the passive economical basis of the Second Empire, of that last triumph of a *state* separate of and independent from society. Only the proletarians, fired by a new social task to be accomplished by them for all society, to do away with all classes and class rule, were the men to break the instrument of that class rule – the state, the centralised and organised governmental power usurping to be the master instead of the servant of society.

Drafts for *The Civil War in France* (1871).

The *Commune* – the reabsorption of the state power by society as its own living forces instead of as forces controlling and subduing it, by the popular masses themselves, forming their own force instead of the organised force of their suppression, the political form of their social emancipation instead of the artificial force – appropriated by their oppressors (their own force opposed to an organised force against them) – of society wielded for their oppression by their enemies. The form was simple like all great things. . . . The general suffrage, till now abused either for the parliamentary sanction of the Holy State Power, or a play in the hands of the ruling classes, only employed by the people to choose the instruments of parliamentary class rule once in so many years, now adapted to its real purposes: to choose by the communes their own functionaries of administration and initiation. The delusion as if administration and political governing were mysteries, transcendent functions only to be trusted to the hands of a trained caste – state parasites, richly paid sycophants and sinecurists, in the higher posts, absorbing the intelligence of the masses and turning them against themselves in the lower places of the hierarchy. Doing away with the state hierarchy altogether and replacing the haughty masters of the people with always removable servants, a mock responsibility by a real responsibility, as they act continuously under public supervision.

Drafts for *The Civil War in France* (1871).

The Paris Commune was, of course, to serve as a model to all the great industrial centres of France. The communal *régime* once established in Paris and the secondary centres, the old centralised Government would in the provinces, too, have to give way to the self-government of the producers. In a rough sketch of national organisation which the Commune had no time to develop, it states clearly that the Commune was to be the political form of even the smallest country hamlet, and that in the rural districts the stand- ing army was to be replaced by a national militia, with an extremely short term of service. The rural communes of every district were to administer their common affairs by an assembly of delegates in the central town, and these district assemblies were again to send deputies to the National Delegation in Paris, each delegate to be at any time revocable and bound by the *mandat impératif* (formal instructions) of his constituents. The few but important functions which still would remain for a central government were not to be suppressed, as has been intentionally mis-stated, but were to be discharged by Communal, and therefore strictly responsible agents. The unity of the nation was not to be broken, but, on the contrary, to be organised by the Communal Constitution and to become a reality by the destruction of the State power which claimed to be the embodiment of that unity independent of, and superior to, the nation itself, from which it was but a parasitic excrescence. While the merely repressive organs of the old governmental power were to be amputated, its legitimate functions were to be wrested from an authority usurping pre-eminence over society itself, and restored to the responsible agents of society. Instead of deciding once in three or six years which member of the ruling class was to misrepresent the people in Parliament, universal suffrage was to serve the people, constituted in Communes, as individual suffrages serves every other employer in the search for the workmen and managers in his business. And it is well known that companies, like individ- uals, in matters of real business generally know how to put the right man in the right place, and, if they for once make a mistake, to redress it promptly. On the other hand, nothing could be more foreign to the spirit of the Commune than to super- sede universal suffrage by hierarchic investiture.

> *The Civil War in France* (1871); *MESW* i 520f.

By *anarchy* all socialists understand this: once the aim of the proletarian movement, the abolition of classes, is attained, . . . the state power disappears and governmental functions are trans- formed into simple administrative functions.

> *The Alleged Splits in the International* (1872);
> *La Première Internationale*, ii 295.

Bakunin: There are about 40 million Germans. Will, for example, all the forty million be members of the government?

Marx: Certainly! For the thing begins with the self-government of the Commune.

Bakunin: The whole people will govern and there will be no one to be governed.

Marx: According to this principle, when a man rules himself, he does not rule himself; since he is only himself and no one else.

Bakunin: Then there will be no government, no State, but if there is a State in existence there will also be governors and slaves.

Marx: This merely means: when class rule has disappeared, there will no longer be any state in the present political sense of the word.

Marx on Bakunin (1875); *MEW* xviii 634.

Further Reading

R. Adamiak, 'The "Withering Away" of the State: A Reconsideration', *Journal of Politics* (Feb, 1970).

S. Avineri, 'The Hegelian Origins of Marx's Political Thought', *Review of Metaphysics* (1967).

S. Bloom, 'The Withering Away of the State', *Journal of the History of Ideas* (1946).

J. Hyppolite, *Studies on Marx and Hegel* (London, 1969) chap. 5.

R. Miliband, 'Marx and the State', *Socialist Register* (1965).

M. Rubel, 'Marx's Concept of Democracy', *New Politics* (1962).

J. Sanderson, 'Marx and Engels on the State', *Western Political Quarterly* (Dec 1963).

J. Sanderson, *An Interpretation of the Political Ideas of Marx and Engels* (London, 1969).

R. Tucker, *The Marxian Revolutionary Idea* (London, 1970) chap. 3.

CHAPTER SEVEN

Revolution

A. COMMENTARY

MARX's ideas on revolution are a direct consequence of his general materialist views on historical development, that is, that the development of society was determined by changes in its economic basis, in its forces of production and its corresponding relations of production. He wrote:

> At a certain stage of their development the material forces of production in society come into conflict with the existing relations of production, or – what is but a legal expression for the same thing – with the property relations within which they had been at work before. From forms of development of the forces of production these relations turn into their fetters. Then comes the period of social revolution.[1]

Thus Marx could call the revolution 'the driving force of history',[2] and all his studies in other fields were devoted to uncovering the springs of that 'driving force'.

When in past history the fetters of the relations of production had been broken by the developing forces of production, the resulting revolutions had only been partial ones. In one of his early writings Marx said:

> What is the basis of a partial, purely political revolution? It is that a part of civil society emancipates itself and attains to universal domination, that a particular class undertakes the general emancipation of society from its particular situation. This class frees the whole of society, but only under the presupposition that the whole of society is in the same situation

[1] *MESW* I 363.   [2] *The German Ideology*, p. 50.

as this class, that it possesses, or can easily acquire for example, money and education.[1]

What Marx had in mind particularly here was the French Revolution, which exercised over him the fascination that it did over most of his contemporaries. Indeed, during his formative years he spent more time studying the French Revolution than anything else and the whole of his thought could be seen as an attempted answer to the question: why had the French Revolution, that seemed so progressive, entirely failed to cure social evils and in particular to achieve a redistribution of the wealth of society? Marx saw much that was positive in the French Revolution: it had destroyed feudalism and abolished the formal importance of social position in politics; men were proclaimed equal in their common citizenship. But – and this was Marx's central criticism – this social aspect, men's common membership of the state, had no influence on their real life which was anti-social in the extreme. Here, 'liberty' was 'not based on the association of man with man but rather on the separation of man from man'. It was 'the right to this separation, the rights of the limited individual who is limited to himself'.[2] And 'equality' was merely the equal right to this sort of liberty.

This contradiction between the principles of the state and the real life of the citizens was what, for Marx, characterised a 'merely political' revolution. In his attack on Ruge in 1844 he wrote:

> Political intelligence is political just because it thinks inside the limits of politics. The sharper and livelier it is the less capable it is of comprehending social evils. The classical period of political intelligence is the French Revolution. Far from seeing the source of social defects in the state, the heroes of the French Revolution see in social defects the source of political misfortunes.[3]

Thus although the theory of the merely political revolution held that it was open to everyone to emancipate himself by becoming a bourgeois, by definition not everyone could do so and the inevitable result was the exploitation of one group in society by another.

The most important characteristic of the next revolution was

[1] *Early Texts*, p. 125.   [2] Ibid. p. 103.   [3] Ibid. p. 214.

that it would be social and not merely political: it would not only proclaim abstract rights that in fact only a few could enjoy, but achieve a general emancipation by penetrating to the real life of man – his socio-economic life. This would be the first revolution to involve the whole of society:

> All previous historical movements were movements of minorities, or in the interest of minorities. The proletarian movement is the self-conscious, independent movement of the immense majority, in the interests of the immense majority. The proletariat, the lowest stratum of our present society, cannot stir, cannot raise itself up, without the whole superincumbent strata of official society being exploded into the air.[1]

Thus the radicalism of the revolution depended on the class that was carrying it out: the proletariat could represent the interests of society as a whole, a society in which class antagonisms were sharpened and simplified to an extent that permitted their abolition. Marx returned to this distinction between the political and the social in his discussion of the Paris Commune which he claimed was 'the political form of social emancipation'.[2]

Marx was at pains to point out that he did not conceive of revolution as a mechanical result of the conflict of economic forces; it was something that had also to be accomplished by human beings:

> Of all the instruments of production, the greatest productive force is the revolutionary class itself. The organisation of the revolutionary elements as a class presupposes the existence of all the productive forces that could be engendered in the womb of the old society.[3]

But the revolution was not, in Marx's eyes, merely a task for the proletariat to perform: it was also a means of their own education. In making the revolution the proletariat changed themselves, for the revolution required a massive transformation of its own agents. In the *German Ideology* Marx said:

> Both for the production on a mass scale of this Communist consciousness, and for the success of the cause itself, the alteration of men on a mass scale is necessary, an alteration which can

[1] *MESW* I 44.   [2] Ibid. 522.   [3] *The Poverty of Philosophy*, p. 196.

only take place in a practical movement, in a revolution; this revolution is necessary, therefore, not only because the ruling class cannot be overthrown in any other way, but also because the class overthrowing it can only in a revolution succeed in ridding itself of all the muck of ages and become fitted to found society anew.[1]

The name that Marx gives to this activity that embodies objective and subjective elements – the unity of theory and practice – is 'revolutionary *praxis*'. He sums this up by saying: 'In revolutionary activity, the changing of oneself coincides with the changing of circumstances.'[2] It followed from this that a certain degree of class-consciousness was necessary before a successful revolution could be expected: the proletariat would have had to become a class 'for itself'.

Because he was no prophet, Marx did not go into great detail concerning the exact nature and circumstances of the revolution he believed to be imminent. He did, however, say something about when he thought there might be a revolution, where it would break out, and whether it would be violent or not.

Concerning the conditions necessary to produce a successful revolution, Marx was more or less sanguine according to the historical situation in which he found himself. Marx's expectations were at their height during the 1848 revolutions, and faded gradually thereafter except for a brief renascence during the Paris Commune of 1871. In 1846, in his quarrel with Weitling, Marx was reported to have said: 'There can be no talk at the present moment about the inauguration of communism; the bourgeoisie must first take over the rudder.'[3] On the eve of the 1848 revolutions, Marx declared in the *Communist Manifesto*: 'The bourgeois revolution in Germany will be but the prelude to an immediately following proletarian revolution'.[4] Even in March 1850 after the failure of the revolution, Marx, in his *Address to the Communist League*, still advocates this idea of 'permanent revolution': after the attainment of the aims of the petty-bourgeoisie, it was the task of the workers to make the revolution permanent 'until all the more or less possessing classes have been forced from power and state power has been taken over by the proletariat'.[5] And the

[1] *The German Ideology*, p. 87. [2] Ibid. p. 234.
[3] Hess, *Briefwechsel*, p. 151. [4] *MESW* i 65. [5] Ibid. 110.

Address ends with the words: 'the battle cry of the proletarian party must be: Permanent Revolution!' It is difficult to reconcile this optimistic approach with the idea of the gradual development of political systems dependent on the economic basis of society, an idea with which Marx's last *Address*, in September 1850, was much more in line: 'we tell the workers: You have to endure and go through 15, 20, 50 years of civil war in order to change the circumstances, in order to make yourselves fit for power.'[1]

During 1850 Marx had become convinced of the importance of economic factors in determining the possibilities of revolution. His economic studies during that year led him to the conclusion that a successful revolution could only be the result of a severe economic crisis: 'a new revolution is possible only in consequence of a new crisis. It is, however, just as certain as this crisis.'[2] Marx was so convinced of this that he was prepared to dissolve the Communist League when it appeared to be falling into the hands of men like Willich who believed in attempting a revolution whatever the economic situation. Throughout the early 1850s he expected the crisis that would provoke a revolution. Later, he took a more long-term view of the economic causes of revolution. In the *Grundrisse* the impression is given that capitalism has a very long way to go before it exhausts its capacities to exploit the enormous possibilities of automated machinery; on the other hand the Drafts of the *Civil War in France* and Marx's remarks on Bakunin indicate that Marx conceived of the possibility of a successful proletarian revolution in countries where the majority of the population were peasants.

Linked to this problem was the question of where the revolution would break out first. Marx's materialist view of history would seem to indicate the most advanced industrial countries as those most ripe for revolution. Yet he realised that European revolutions were becoming more dependent on the general world situation. In a letter to Engels in 1859 he mentioned the opening up of California, Australia and the Far East and continued: 'Revolution is imminent on the Continent and will also immediately assume a socialist character. Can it avoid being crushed in this small corner, because the movement of bourgeois society is in the ascendant over much larger areas of the earth?'[3] But Marx also thought that in some underdeveloped countries (for example

[1] *MEW* viii 598.   [2] *MESW* i 231.   [3] *MEW* xxix 359 f.

Germany) a bourgeois revolution could spark off a subsequent proletarian revolution. Later in his life he came to believe that Russia might prove the starting-point of the revolution which 'begins this time in the East, hitherto the invulnerable bulwark and reinforcement of the counter-revolution'.[1] Of Russia he said a year before his death: 'If the Russian revolution becomes the signal for a proletarian revolution in the West, so that both complete each other, then the present Russian system of community ownership of land could serve as the starting point for a communist development'.[2]

Marx was certainly well aware of the importance of colonial exploitation for the coming revolution. After describing the influence of English industry on India, he outlined the prospects that this afforded for a world-wide revolution: 'Bourgeois industry and commerce create these material conditions of a new world in the same way as geological revolutions have created the surface of the earth. When a great social revolution shall have mastered the results of the bourgeois epoch, the market of the world and the modern powers of production, and subjected them to the common control of the most advanced peoples, then only will human progress cease to resemble that hideous pagan idol, who would not drink the nectar but from the skulls of the slain.'[3]

One of the reasons why Marx did not think that the revolution would automatically occur in the most advanced countries was that he thought that in some of these countries communism could come about by peaceful means. In 1872 he spoke of his belief in the possibility of a peaceful revolution in America, England and Holland. He took the same line in 1879 when he wrote: 'A historical development can only remain "peaceful" so long as it is not opposed by the violence of those who wield power in society at that time. If in England or the United States, for example, the working class were to gain a majority in Parliament or Congress, then it could by legal means set aside the laws and structures that stood in its way.'[4] In this situation, Marx continued, any violence would come from the other side. However, in 1871 he blamed the Commune for not being willing to start a civil war, and declared at the Congress of the International in the same year: 'we must make clear to the governments, we know that you are the armed power that is directed against the proletariat; we will proceed

[1] *MESW* xxxiv 296. [2] *MESW* i 24. [3] Ibid. 358. [4] *MEW* xxxiv 498.

against you by peaceful means where that is possible and with arms when it is necessary'.[1] But however much Marx may have thought that sometimes force was the midwife of revolution, he never (except briefly in 1848 and under Tsarist conditions in Russia) approved of the use of revolutionary terror. He strongly criticised the use of terror by the Jacobins in the French Revolution; its use was for him a sign of the weakness and immaturity of that revolution which had to try to impose by sheer force what was not yet inherent in society. Marx wrote: 'In moments of particular self-consciousness political life tries to repress its presuppositions, civil society and its elements, and to constitute itself as the real, harmonious life of man. However, this is only possible through violent opposition to its own conditions, by declaring the revolution to be permanent . . .'[2] Thus a revolution, if the socio-economic conditions are not appropriate, inevitably leads to a reign of terror during which the revolutionary powers attempt to reorganise society from above.

Physical force, however, as opposed to terror, was to Marx a perfectly acceptable revolutionary weapon provided that the economic, social and political conditions were such as to make its use successful. In Marx's view the form of government that would be set up following a successful revolution was a dictatorship of the proletariat, and the most detailed information in its programme is contained in the tentative ten points listed at the end of the second section of the *Communist Manifesto*. This expression was seldom used by Marx and never in documents for publication. In a letter to his friend Weydemeyer Marx claims as one of his contributions to socialist theory that it demonstrates that 'the class struggle necessarily leads to the dictatorship of the proletariat; that this dictatorship itself is only a transitional stage towards the abolition of all classes'.[3] And in the *Critique of the Gotha Programme* Marx wrote that when capitalist society was being transformed into communist society, there would be 'a political transition period during which the state can be nothing but the revolutionary dictatorship of the proletariat'.[4] It should also be noted that the word 'dictatorship' did not have quite the same connotation for Marx that it does for us. He associated it principally with the Roman office of *dictatura* where all power was legally concentrated in the hands of a single man during a limited

[1] *MESW* xvii 652.   [2] *Early Texts*, p. 96.   [3] *MESC* p. 86.   [4] *MESW* ii 33.

period in a time of crisis. Although Marx seldom discusses the measures that such a government would enact, the fullest account is the ten-point programme outlined in the *Communist Manifesto*, which is in many respects a fairly moderate programme.

It was also Marx's view that a successful revolution – at least in the long run – was impossible if confined to one country. In *The Class Struggles in France* Marx criticised the leaders of the proletariat for thinking that 'they would be able to consummate a proletarian revolution within the national walls of France, side by side with the remaining bourgeois nations'.[1] But equally the degree of working-class organisation necessary to produce an international revolution could only be achieved by building up working-class parties within existing nations. Marx was strongly in favour of the unification of Germany and Italy and of the resurgence of Polish nationalism.

B. Texts

Political revolution dissolves civil life into its component parts, without revolutionising and submitting to criticism these parts themselves. Its attitude to civil society, to the world of need, to work, private interests, private law is that they are the foundation of its existence, its own presupposition that needs no further proof, and thus its natural basis. Finally, man as a member of civil society counts for true man, for man as distinct from the citizen, because he is man in his sensuous, individual, immediate existence, while political man is only the abstract fictional man, man as an allegorical or moral person. This man as he actually is, is only recognised in the form of the egoistic individual, and the true man only in the form of the abstract citizen.

On the Jewish Question (1843); *Early Texts*, p. 107.

Every revolution is social in so far as it destroys the old society. Every revolution is political in so far as it destroys the old power. . . .

A political revolution with a social soul is as rational as a social revolution with a political soul is paraphrastic or nonsensical. Revolution in general – the overthrow of the existing power and

[1] *MESW* I 148.

dissolution of previous relationships – is a political act. Socialism cannot be realised without a revolution. But when its organising activity begins, when its peculiar aims, its soul comes forward, then socialism casts aside its political cloak.
Critical Notes on 'The King of Prussia and Social Reform' (1844);
Early Texts, p. 221.

In all revolutions up till now the mode of activity always remained unscathed and it was a question of a different distribution of this activity, a new distribution of labour to other persons, whilst communist revolution is directed against the preceding *mode* of activity, does away with *labour*, and abolishes the rule of all classes with the classes themselves, because it is carried through by the class which no longer counts as a class in society, is not recognised as a class, and is in itself the expression of the disso- lution of all classes, nationalities, etc., within present society; and both for the production on a mass scale of this communist consciousness, and for the success of the cause itself, the alteration of men on a mass scale is necessary, an alteration which can only take place in a practical movement, a *revolution*; this revolution is necessary, therefore, not only because the *ruling* class cannot be overthrown in any other way, but also because the class *overthrowing* it can only in a revolution succeed in ridding itself of all the muck of ages and become fitted to found society anew.
The German Ideology (1845–6) p. 87.

The coincidence of the changing of circumstances and of human activity or self-changing can be conceived and rationally under- stood only as *revolutionary practice*.
The German Ideology (1845–6) p. 600.

Just as the *economists* are the scientific representatives of the bourgeois class, so the *Socialists* and the *Communists* are the theoreticians of the proletarian class. So long as the proletariat is not yet sufficiently developed to constitute itself as a class, and consequently so long as the struggle itself of the proletariat with the bourgeoisie has not yet assumed a political character, and the productive forces are not yet sufficiently developed in the bosom of the bourgeoisie itself to enable us to catch a glimpse of the material conditions necessary for the emancipation of the proletariat and for the formation of a new society, these theoreticians are merely utopians who, to meet the wants of the oppressed classes, improvise systems and go in search of a regenerating science. But in the measure that history moves forward, and with it the struggle of the proletariat assumes clearer outlines, they no longer need to seek science in their minds; they have only to take note of what is happening before their eyes and to become its mouthpiece. So long as they look for science and merely make systems, so long as they are at the beginning of the struggle, they see in poverty nothing but poverty, without seeing in it the revolutionary, subversive side, which will overthrow the old society. From this moment, science, which is a product of the historical movement, has associated itself consciously with it, has ceased to be doctrinaire and has become revolutionary.

The Poverty of Philosophy (1847) pp. 140 ff.

This sum of productive forces, capital funds and social forms of intercourse, which every individual and generation finds in existence as something given, is the real basis of what the philosophers have conceived as 'substance' and 'essence of man', and what they have deified and attacked: a real basis which is not in the least disturbed, in its effect and influence on the development of men, by the fact that these philosophers revolt against it as 'self-consciousness' and the 'Unique'. These conditions of life, which different generations find in existence, decide also whether or not the periodically recurring revolutionary convulsion will be strong enough to overthrow the basis of the entire existing system. And if these material elements of a complete revolution are not present (namely, on the one hand the existing productive forces, on the other the formation of a revolutionary mass, which revolts not only against separate conditions of society up till then, but against the very 'production of life' till then, the 'total activity' on which it was based), then, as far as practical development is concerned, it is absolutely immaterial whether the *idea* of this revolution has been expressed a hundred times already, as the history of communism proves.

The German Ideology (1845–6) p. 51.

All the preceding classes that got the upper hand, sought to fortify their already acquired status by subjecting society at large to their conditions of appropriation. The proletarians cannot become masters of the productive forces of society, except by abolishing their own previous mode of appropriation, and thereby also every other previous mode of appropriation. They have nothing of their own to secure and to fortify; their mission is to destroy all previous securities for, and insurances of, individual property.

All previous historical movements were movements of minorities, or in the interests of minorities. The proletarian movement is the self-conscious, independent movement of the immense majority, in the interests of the immense majority. The proletariat, the lowest stratum of our present society, cannot stir, cannot raise itself up, without the whole superincumbent strata of official society being exploded into the air.

The Communist Manifesto (1848); *MESW* i 44.

It is self-evident that the conspirators do not limit themselves by systematically organising the revolutionary proletariat. Their task consists precisely in anticipating the process of revolutionary development, to bring it artificially to a crisis, to improvise a revolution without the conditions of a revolution. For them, the one and only condition for a revolution is that their plot be sufficiently organised. They are alchemists of revolution and share the mental disarray, the narrowness of mind and the prejudices of the alchemists of former times. They throw themselves into inventions which will bring about revolutionary miracles: incendiary bombs, infernal machines with magic reactions, riots whose effects are the more stupefiant as their basis is less rational.

Review of A. Chenu, *The Conspirators* (Paris, 1850);
MEW vii 267.

While the democratic petty bourgeois wish to bring the revolution to a conclusion as quickly as possible, and with the achievement, at most, of the above demands, it is our interest and our task to make the revolution permanent, until all more or less possessing classes have been forced out of their position of dominance, until the proletariat has conquered state power, and the association of proletarians, not only in one country but in all the dominant countries of the world, has advanced so far that competition among the proletarians of these countries has ceased and that at least the decisive productive forces are concentrated in the hands of the proletarians.

Address of the Central Committee to the Communist League (1850); *MESW* I 110.

Men make their own history, but they do not make it just as they please; they do not make it under circumstances chosen by themselves, but under circumstances directly encountered, given and transmitted from the past. The tradition of all the dead generations weighs like a nightmare on the brain of the living. And just when they seem engaged in revolutionising themselves and things, in creating something that has never yet existed, precisely in such periods of revolutionary crisis they anxiously conjure up the spirits of the past to their service and borrow from them names, battle cries and costumes in order to present the new scene of world history in this time-honoured disguise and this borrowed language.

The Eighteenth Brumaire of Louis Bonaparte (1852); *MESW* I 247.

Bourgeois industry and commerce create these material conditions of a new world in the same way as geological revolutions have created the surface of the earth. When a great social revolution shall have mastered the results of the bourgeois epoch, the market of the world and the modern powers of production, and subjected them to the common control of the most advanced peoples then only will human progress cease to resemble that hideous pagan idol, who would not drink the nectar but from the skulls of the slain.

The Results of British Rule in India (1853); *MESW* I 358.

This antagonism between modern industry and science on the one hand, modern misery and dissolution on the other hand; this antagonism between the productive powers, and the social relations of our epoch is a fact, palpable, overwhelming, and not to be controverted. Some parties may wail over it; others may wish to get rid of modern arts, in order to get rid of modern conflicts. Or they may imagine that so signal a progress in industry wants to be completed by as signal a regress in politics. On our part, we do not mistake the shape of the shrewd spirit that continues to mark all these contradictions. We know that to work well the

new-fangled forces of society, they only want to be mastered by
new-fangled men – and such are the working men. They are as
much the invention of modern time as machinery itself. In the
signs that bewilder the middle class, the aristocracy and the poor
prophets of regression, we do recognise our brave friend, Robin
Goodfellow, the old mole that can work in the earth so fast, that
worthy pioneer – the Revolution. The English working men are
the first-born sons of modern industry. They will then, certainly,
not be the last in aiding the social revolution produced by that
industry, a revolution, which means the emancipation of their
own class all over the world, which is as universal as capital-rule
and wages-slavery. I know the heroic struggles the English
working class have gone through since the middle of the last
century – struggles less glorious, because they are shrouded in
obscurity, and burked by the middle-class historian. To revenge
the misdeeds of the ruling class, there existed in the Middle Ages,
in Germany, a secret tribunal, called the *Vehmgericht*. If a red
cross was seen marked on a house, people knew that its owner
was doomed by the *Vehm*. All the houses of Europe are now
marked with the mysterious red cross. History is the judge – its
executioner, the proletarian.

> *Speech on the Anniversary of the People's Paper* (1856);
> *MESW* ɪ 360.

At a certain stage of their development, the material productive
forces of society come in conflict with the existing relations of
production, or – what is but a legal expression for the same
thing – with the property relations within which they have been
at work hitherto. From forms of development of the productive
forces these relations turn into their fetters. Then begins an epoch
of social revolution. With the change of the economic foundation
the entire immense superstructure is more or less rapidly transformed. In considering such transformations a distinction should
always be made between the material transformation of the
economic conditions of production, which can be determined with
the precision of natural science, and the legal, political, religious,
aesthetic or philosophic – in short, ideological forms in which men
become conscious of this conflict and fight it out.

> *Preface to a Critique of Political Economy* (1859);
> *MESW* ɪ 363.

Thus a total economic revolution is taking place. On the one hand, this process creates first of all the real conditions of the domination of capital over work, perfects them and gives them an adequate form; on the other hand it brings to birth, within the productive forces of labour and the conditions of production and circulation developed at the expense of the workers, the real conditions of a new mode of production, abolishing the antagonistic form of the capitalist mode of production and thus creating the material basis of a new social life, a new type of society.

Results of the Immediate Process of Production (1865)

We are aware of the importance that must be accorded to the institutions, customs and traditions of different countries; and we do not deny that there are countries like America, England (and, if I knew your institutions better, I would add Holland) where the workers can achieve their aims by peaceful means. However true that may be, we ought also to recognise that, in most of the countries on the Continent, it is force that must be the lever of our revolutions; it is to force that it will be necessary to appeal for a time in order to establish the reign of labour.

Speech at Amsterdam (1872); *MEW* xviii 160.

The working class know that they have to pass through different phases of class-struggle. They know that the superseding of the economical conditions of the slavery of labour by the conditions of free and associated labour can only be the progressive work of time, that this economical transformation requires not only a change of distribution but a new organisation of production, or rather the delivery (setting free) of the social forms of production in present organised labour from the trammels of slavery, from their present class character (engendered by present industry), and their harmonious national and international co-ordination. They know that this work of regeneration will again and again be relented and impeded by the resistance of vested interests and class egotisms. They know that the present 'spontaneous action of the natural laws of capital and landed property' can only be superseded by 'the spontaneous action of the laws of the social economy of free and associated labour' by a long process of development of new conditions, as was the 'spontaneous action of the economic laws of slavery' and the 'spontaneous action of the economical laws of serfdom'. But they know at the same time that great strides may be made at once through the communal form of political organisation and that the time has come to begin that movement for themselves and mankind.

Drafts for *The Civil War in France* (1871)

Where the mass of the peasants are still owners of private property, where they even form a more or less important majority of the population, as they do in the states of the Western European continent, where they have not yet disappeared and been replaced by agricultural wage labourers, as in England; in these cases the following situation arises: either the peasantry hinders every workers' revolution and causes it to fail, as it has done in France up till now; or the proletariat (for the landowning peasant does not belong to the proletariat and even when his own position causes him to belong to it, he does not *think* he belongs to it) must as a government inaugurate measures which directly improve the situation of the peasant and which thus win him for the revolution; measures which in essence facilitate the transition from private to collective property in land so that the peasant himself is converted for economic reasons; the proletariat must not, however, come into open collision with peasantry by, for example, proclaiming the abolition of inheritance or the abolition of property; this latter is only possible where the capitalist landlord has expropriated the peasant and the real worker of the land is just as much a proletarian wage labourer as the city worker, and thus has directly the same interests.

Marx on Bakunin (1875); *MEW* xviii 630 ff.

Bakunin: Once the proletariat is the ruling class, over whom will it rule?

Marx: This means, that as long as the other classes, and in particular the capitalist class, still exist, as long as the proletariat is still struggling with it (because, with the proletariat's conquest of governmental power its enemies and the old organisation of society have not yet disappeared), it must use coercive means, hence governmental means; it is still a class and the economic conditions on which the class struggle and the existence of classes depend, have not yet disappeared and must be removed by force, or transformed and their process of transformation speeded up by force.

Marx on Bakunin (1875); *MEW* xviii 630.

Schoolboy's asininity! A radical social revolution is tied to certain historical conditions of economic development; these are its prerequisites. It is therefore only possible where, with capitalist production, the industrial proletariat occupies at least a significant position among the mass of the people. And so in order to have any chance whatever of victory, it must at least be able to do as much immediately for the peasants, *mutatis mutandis*, as the French bourgeoisie did in its revolution for the then existing French peasants. A fine idea, that the rule of labour includes the suppression of rural labour!

But there the innermost thought of Mr Bakunin comes to light. He does not understand a thing about social revolution, only the political phrases about it; its economic conditions do not exist for him. Now since all hitherto existing economic forms, developed or undeveloped, include the servitude of the worker (be it in the form of the wage worker, peasant, etc.) he believes that in all of them a *radical revolution* is equally possible. But even more! He wants the European social revolution, founded on the economic basis of capitalist production, to take place at the level of the Russian or Slav agricultural and pastoral people. *Will*, not economic conditions, is the foundation of his social revolution.

Marx on Bakunin (1875); *MEW* xviii 633f.

FURTHER READING

S. Avineri, *The Social and Political Thought of Karl Marx* (Cambridge, 1968).

S. Bloom, *The World of Nations* (New York, 1941) chap. 8.

H. Draper, 'Marx and the Dictatorship of the Proletariat', *Études de Marxologie*, vi (1962).

H. Draper, 'The Principle of Self-emancipation in Marx and Engels', *The Socialist Register,* 1971.

J. Sanderson, *An Interpretation of the Political Ideas of Marx and Engels* (London, 1969) chap. 5.

R. Tucker, *The Marxian Revolutionary Idea* (London, 1970) chap. 1.

E. Voegelin, 'Formation of the Marxian Revolutionary Idea', *Review of Politics* (1950).

CHAPTER EIGHT

Future Communist Society

A. COMMENTARY

IT is important to emphasise at the outset that Marx was no 'prophet' and said very little about the shape of the communist society that he envisaged. This is not surprising: like his master, Hegel, he was extremely chary of predicting the future and often castigated more 'utopian' socialists for their idealistic forecasts.[1] For if all ideas were a product of contemporary social reality, then a detailed projection of these ideas into a distant future was bound to result in idealism – ideas that were completely imaginary since lacking an empirical reference. Marx would have agreed completely with Hegel's remark that 'it is just as silly to suppose that any philosophy goes beyond its contemporary world, as that an individual can jump beyond his time'.[2]

Nevertheless, the broad outlines of Marx's picture are clear enough. One of the phrases that usually comes to mind is that of the 'withering away' of the state. This is, in fact, an expression of Engels who was much readier than Marx to draw parallels between the natural and social sciences. Marx talked more of the 'transcendence' (a term with philosophical, Hegelian overtones) or 'abolition' of the state.[3] In all of Marx's discussions of this subject it is important to remember that at the time of his writing the state did much less than it does now: there were virtually no social services provided, industry was all in private hands, and state organisation of education was only just beginning, so there was proportionately less to 'wither'. Marx's ideas on this subject were

---

[1] See the section in the *Communist Manifesto, MESW* i 61 ff.

[2] G. Hegel, *Werke* (Berlin, 1832 ff.) viii 18.

[3] The Hegelian aspects are most worked out in S. Avineri's *The Social and Political Thought of Karl Marx* (Cambridge, 1968). For a criticism, see the article by M. Evans in *Political Studies* (1970).

undoubtedly influenced by Saint-Simon, who much earlier had proclaimed the transition from the 'government of people to the administration of things'.[1] A central passage on this transition is to be found in the *Communist Manifesto*:

> When, in the course of development, class distinctions have disappeared, and all production has been concentrated in the hands of a vast association of the whole nation, the public power will lose its political character. Political power, properly so called, is merely the organised power of one class for oppressing another.[2]

One of the things implied by the purification of the 'political' facets of public power was the abolition of its 'bureaucratic' element. This theme, too, may have had its origin in Saint-Simon's constant polemics against the unproductive class of rulers. The problem of bureaucracy was one that had exercised Marx since his earliest days as a political journalist: in his 1843 manuscript he strongly criticised Hegel's view of the bureaucracy as a mediating element between the state and civil society[3] and saw the solution to the problem at least adumbrated by the Commune. Of course, there would still be public power in a future communist society, but 'when class rule will have disappeared there will no longer be any state in the present political sense of the word'.[4]

Thus for Marx the abolition of a state based on class distinction involved the abolition of an independent state apparatus in which an irresponsible executive and judiciary ensured the invulnerability of the bureaucracy. What the Commune meant for Marx was the destruction of 'the centralised state power, with its ubiquitous organs of the standing army, police, bureaucracy, clergy and judicature'.[5] Marx twice uses the word 'association' to describe the subsequent society, once in the *Communist Manifesto* where he says that in place of the old bourgeois society there will be an 'association in which the free development of each is the condition for the free development of all'.[6] And in the *Holy Family* he said that the working class would set up 'an association which excludes class division and which will have no political power properly speaking'.[7]

---

[1] Cf. F. Manuel, *The New World of Henri Saint-Simon* (Cambridge, 1956.)
[2] *MESW* i 54.   [3] Cf. *Early Texts*, pp. 68 ff.   [4] *MEW*, xviii 634.
[5] *MESW* i 516.   [6] Ibid. 54.   [7] *The Holy Family*, p. 57.

In the *Communist Manifesto* and Marx's critique of Bakunin's *Statism and Anarchy* the political structure of the dictatorship of the proletariat certainly seems to be very centralised, and in the *Address to the Communist League* of March 1850 Marx urges the communists to 'strive not only for a single and indivisible German republic, but also within this republic for the most determined centralisation of power within the hands of the state authority. . . . As in France in 1793 so today in Germany it is the task of the really revolutionary party to carry through the strictest central-isation.'[1] Of course this applies to the period immediately preceding the revolution, though it is evident that a large measure of centralisation is necessary to carry out the sort of measures that Marx suggests as a programme for the dictatorship of the proletariat, the stage of incomplete communism referred to in the *Paris Manuscripts* and the *Critique of the Gotha Programme*. The disappearance of the state as such is reserved for the time when 'all the springs of co-operative wealth flow more abundantly',[2] and the exercise of 'political' power is no longer necessitated by economic pressure. A slightly different picture is presented by the *Civil War in France* where the Commune is praised for heralding a rather more decentralised government; though it is always open to question how much Marx really agreed with the measures taken by the Commune and how much he felt obliged to refrain from criticism when writing an obituary.

So the question arises: what function will the public power have to perform in this 'association'? Marx does say, in the *Civil War in France*, that the central government will have left to it 'few but important functions'.[3] What exactly these functions will be was never made precise by Marx, for he considered that the question 'what social functions, analogous to the functions now fulfilled by the state, will remain in a communist society' could 'only be answered scientifically'.[4] Forces, it seems, would not be needed by communist governments, certainly not exterior force, for the revolution would be nothing if not international; and not even inside the state, for punishment would be 'the judgement of the criminal upon himself'.

Of course, these questions, like those concerning Marx's views on marriage and the family, the abolition of money,[5] and the

[1] *MESW* I 115.   [2] Ibid. II 24.   [3] Ibid. I 520.   [4] Ibid. II 32.
[5] See particularly the final section of *Capital*, vol. II.

distribution of the social product according to need, depend ultimately on his conception of the sort of human nature that would be prevalent in the future communist society. For if many of the anti-social tendencies now manifested by men were capable of ultimate eradication, then naturally the organisation of a communist society could well be very different from any readily imaginable at present. To what extent, then, did Marx think that human drives could be modified by the social situation? He devoted considerable space to a discussion of the question in *The German Ideology*. Here Marx distinguished between constant desires 'which exist under all circumstances, only their form and direction being changed by different social circumstances', and relative desires 'which owe their origin merely to a particular form of society, to particular conditions of production and exchange'. In a communist society, the former would merely be changed and given the opportunity to develop normally, whereas the latter would be destroyed by being deprived of the conditions of their existence. Marx continued: 'which desires would be merely altered under a communist organisation and which would be dissolved, can only be decided in a practical way, through the changing of real, practical desires, and not through historical comparisons with earlier historical circumstances'. He goes on to mention several desires (among them the desire to eat) as examples of fixed desires, and continues: 'neither do the communists envisage abolishing the fixity of desires and needs . . . they only aim to organise production and exchange in such a way as to make possible the normal satisfaction of all desires, that is, a satisfaction limited only by the desires themselves'.[1] Those changes in the social nature of man and the regulation of desires can be made possible, according to Marx, by man's recovery of what he, in his earlier writings, referred to as man's essence. This essence is communal creativity, the fact that man controls the process of his self-creation and his relationship to nature, all of which is part of Marx's concept of work. In the future communist society everyone will be a worker: 'with labour emancipated every man becomes a working man, and productive labour ceases to be a class attribute'.[2] How fundamental this notion was to Marx can be gauged by the fact that he thought its general acceptance would

[1] *The German Ideology*, pp. 282 ff. (the translation is my own).
[2] *MESW*, I 522.

lead to the solution of humanity's eternal problem, war. In the *Civil War in France* he spoke of the society 'whose international rule would be peace, because its natural ruler would be everywhere the same – labour!'[1]

In spite of his refusal to write 'recipes for the cook-shops of the future',[2] Marx's general outline of the economic organisation of communist society is clear. The employment of the industrial reserve army and the ability to exploit the manifold talents latent in most individuals would make communist society much richer. Production would be communal, no longer mediated through money, but evaluated according to its quality; the use of time would be planned so that each individual could enjoy the maximum of free time to develop into a 'universal individual'. Unlike the utopian socialists before him, Marx saw this society as a necessary product of historical movement. Passages in the *Grundrisse* show that in many ways the introduction of machinery and automation was the key factor in this movement.

B. TEXTS

Communism is the positive abolition of private property and thus of human self-alienation and therefore the real reappropriation of the human essence by and for man. This is communism as the complete and conscious return of man conserving all the riches of previous development for man himself as a social, i.e. human being. Communism as completed naturalism is humanism and as completed humanism is naturalism. It is the genuine solution of the antagonism between man and nature and between man and man. It is the true solution of the struggle between existence and essence, between objectification and self-affirmation, between freedom and necessity, between individual and species. It is the solution to the riddle of history and knows itself to be this solution.

1844 Manuscripts; Early Texts, p. 148.

Atheism as the supersession of God is the emergence of theoretical humanism, and communism as the supersession of private property

[1] *MESW*, i 490.   [2] *Capital*, i 17.

is the indication of real human life as man's property, which is also the emergence of practical humanism. In other words, atheism is humanism mediated with itself through the supersession of religion, and communism is humanism mediated with itself through the supersession of private property.

1844 Manuscripts; Early Texts, p. 173.

Socialism is the positive self-consciousness of man no longer mediated through the negation of religion, just as real life is the positive reality of man no longer mediated through communism as the negation of private property. Communism represents the positive in the form of the negation of the negation and thus a phase in human emancipation and rehabilitation, both real and necessary at this juncture of human development. Communism is the necessary form and dynamic principle of the immediate future, but communism is not as such the goal of human development, the form of human society.

1844 Manuscripts; Early Texts, p. 156.

In communist society, where nobody has one exclusive sphere of activity but each can become accomplished in any branch he wishes, society regulates the general production and thus makes it possible for me to do one thing today and another tomorrow, to hunt in the morning, fish in the afternoon, rear cattle in the evening, criticise after dinner, just as I have a mind, without ever becoming hunter, fisherman, shepherd or critic. This fixation of social activity, this consolidation of what we ourselves produce into an objective power above us, growing out of our control, thwarting our expectations, bringing to naught our calculations, is one of the chief factors in historical development up till now.

The German Ideology (1845–6) p. 45.

Communism is for us not a *state of affairs* which is to be established, an *ideal* to which reality will have to adjust itself. We call communism the *real* movement which abolishes the present state of things. The conditions of this movement result from the premises now in existence.

The German Ideology (1845–6) p. 48.

It is just as empirically established that, by the overthrow of the existing state of society by the communist revolution . . . and the abolition of private property which is identical with it, this power, which so baffles the German theoreticians, will be dissolved; and that then the liberation of each single individual will be accomplished in the measure in which history becomes transformed into world history . . . . It is clear that the real intellectual wealth of the individual depends entirely on the wealth of his real connections. Only then will the separate individuals be liberated from the various national and local barriers, be brought into practical connection with the material and intellectual production of the whole world and be put in a position to acquire the capacity to enjoy this all-sided production of the whole earth (the creations of man). *All-round* dependence, this natural form of the *world-historical* co-operation of individuals, will be transformed by this communist revolution into the control and conscious mastery of these powers, which, born of the action of men on one another, have till now overawed and governed men as powers completely alien to them.

The German Ideology (1845–6) pp. 49 ff.

Stirner imagines that the so-called organisers of labour wanted to organise the entire activity of each individual, and yet it is precisely among them that a difference is drawn between directly productive labour, which has to be organised, and labour which is not directly productive. In regard to the latter, however, it was not their view, as he imagines, that each should do the work of Raphael, but that anyone in whom there is a potential Raphael should be able to develop without hindrance . . . . The exclusive concentration of artistic talent in particular individuals, and its suppression in the broad mass which is bound up with this, is a consequence of division of labour. If, even in certain social conditions, everyone was an excellent painter, that would not at all exclude the possibility of each of them being also an original painter, so that here too the difference between 'human' and 'unique' labour amounts to sheer nonsense. In any case, with a communist organisation of society, there disappears the subordination of the artist to local and national narrowness, which arises entirely from division of labour, and also the subordination of the artist to some definite art, thanks to which he is exclusively a painter, sculptor, etc., the very name of his activity adequately expressing the narrowness of his professional development and his dependence on division of labour. In a communist society there are no painters but at most people who engage in painting among other activities.

The German Ideology (1845–6) pp. 441 f.

These measures will of course be different in different countries.

Nevertheless in the most advanced countries, the following will be pretty generally applicable.

1. Abolition of property in land and application of all rents of land to public purposes.

2. A heavy progressive or graduated income tax.

3. Abolition of all right of inheritance.

4. Confiscation of the property of all emigrants and rebels.

5. Centralisation of credit in the hands of the State, by means of a national bank with State capital and an exclusive monopoly.

6. Centralisation of the means of communication and transport in the hands of the State.

7. Extension of factories and instruments of production owned by the State; the bringing into cultivation of waste-lands, and the improvement of the soil generally in accordance with a common plan.

8. Equal liability of all to labour. Establishment of industrial armies, especially for agriculture.

9. Combination of agriculture with manufacturing industries; gradual abolition of the distinction between town and country, by a more equable distribution of the population over the country.

10. Free education for all children in public schools. Abolition of children's factory labour in its present form. Combination of education with industrial production, etc., etc.

When, in the course of development, class distinctions have disappeared, and all production has been concentrated in the hands of a vast association of the whole nation, the public power will lose its political character. Political power, properly so called, is merely the organised power of one class for oppressing another. If the proletariat during its contest with the bourgeoisie is compelled, by the force of circumstances, to organise itself as a class, if, by means of a revolution, it makes itself the ruling class, and, as such, sweeps away by force the old conditions of production, then it will, along with these conditions, have swept away the conditions for the existence of class antagonisms and of classes generally, and will thereby have abolished its own supremacy as a class.

In place of the old bourgeois society, with its classes and class antagonisms, we shall have an association, in which the free development of each is the condition for the free development of all.
Manifesto of the Communist Party (1848); *MESW* 1 53 f.

If we suppose communal production, the determination of time remains, of course, essential. The less time society requires in order to produce wheat, cattle, etc., the more time it gains for other forms of production, material or intellectual. As with a single individual, the universality of its development, its enjoyment and its activity depends on saving time. In the final analysis, all forms of economics can be reduced to an economics of time. Likewise, society must divide up its time purposefully in order to achieve a production suited to its general needs; just as the individual has to divide his time in order to acquire, in suitable proportions, the knowledge he needs or to fulfil the various requirements of his activity.

On the basis of community production, the first economic law thus remains the economy of time, and the methodical distribution of working time between the various branches of production; and this law becomes indeed of much greater importance. But all this differs basically from the measurement of exchange values (labour and the products of labour) by labour time. The work of individuals participating in the same branch of activity, and the different kinds of labour are not only quantitatively but also qualitatively different. What is the precondition of a merely quantitative difference between things? The fact that their quality is the same. Thus units of labour can be measured quantitatively only if they are of equal and identical quality.
Grundrisse (1857–8) pp. 75 f.

If we conceive society as being not capitalistic but communistic, there will be no money-capital at all in the first place, nor the disguises cloaking the transactions arising on account of it. The question then comes down to the need of society to calculate beforehand how much labour, means of production, and means of subsistence it can invest, without detriment, in such lines of business as for instance the building of railways, which do not furnish any means of production or subsistence, nor produce any useful effect for a long time, a year or more, while they extract labour, means of production and means of subsistence from the total annual production. In capitalist society however where social reason always asserts itself only *post festum* great disturbances may and must constantly occur.

Capital, vol. ii (1869) pp. 318f.

The Commune intended to abolish that class-property which makes the labour of the many the wealth of the few. It aimed at the expropriation of the expropriators. It wanted to make individual property a truth by transforming the means of production, land and capital, now chiefly the means of enslaving and exploiting labour, into mere instruments of free and associated labour. – But this is Communism, 'impossible' Communism! Why, those members of the ruling classes who are intelligent enough to perceive the impossibility of continuing the present system – and they are many – have become the obtrusive and full-mouthed apostles of co-operative production. If co-operative production is not to remain a sham and a snare; if it is to supersede the Capitalist system; if united co-operative societies are to regulate national production upon a common plan, thus taking it under their own control, and putting an end to the constant anarchy and periodical convulsions which are the fatality of Capitalist production – what else, gentlemen, would it be but Communism, 'possible' Communism?

The Civil War in France (1871); *MESW* i 523.

Marx: Asinine! This is democratic verbiage, political drivel! An election is a political form, both in the smallest Russian commune and in the Artel. The character of the election does not depend on this description, but on the economic basis, the economic interrelations of the electors, and as soon as the functions have ceased to be political, then there exists (1) no governmental function; (2) the distribution of general functions has become a business matter which does not afford any room for domination; (3) the election has none of its present political character.

Bakunin: Universal suffrage by the whole people of representatives and rulers of the State – this is the last word of the Marxists as well as of the democratic school. They are lies behind which lurks the despotism of a governing minority, lies all the more dangerous in that this minority appears as the expression of the so-called people's will.

Marx: Under collective property, the so-called will of the people disappears in order to make way for the real will of the co-operative.

Bakunin: Result: rule of the great majority of the people by a privileged minority. But, the Marxists say, this minority will consist of workers. Yes, indeed, but of ex-workers, who, once they become only representatives or rulers of the people, cease to be workers.

Marx: No more than a manufacturer today ceases to be a capitalist when he becomes a member of the municipal council.

Bakunin: And from the heights of the State they begin to look down upon the whole common world of the workers. From that time on they represent not the people but themselves and their own claims to govern the people. Those who can doubt this know nothing at all about human nature.

Marx: If Mr Bakunin were in the know, if only with the position of a manager in a workers' co-operative, he would send all his nightmares about authority to the devil. He should have asked himself: what form can administrative functions assume on the basis of that workers' state, if it pleases him to call it thus?

Marx on Bakunin (1875); *MEW* XVIII 635.

What we have to deal with here is a communist society, not as it has *developed* on its own foundations, but, on the contrary, just as it *emerges* from capitalist society; which is thus in every respect, economically, morally and intellectually, still stamped with the birth marks of the old society from whose womb it emerges. Accordingly, the individual producer receives back from society – after the deductions have been made – exactly what he gives to it. What he has given to it is his individual quantum of labour. For example, the social working day consists of the sum of the individual hours of work; the individual labour time of the individual producer is the part of the social working day contributed by him, his share in it. He receives a certificate from society that he has furnished such and such an amount of labour (after deducting his labour for the common funds), and with this certificate he draws from the social stock of means of consumption as much as costs the same amount of labour. The same amount of labour which he has given to society in one form he receives back in another.

Here obviously the same principle prevails as that which regulates the exchange of commodities, as far as this is exchange of equal values. Content and form are changed, because under the altered circumstances no one can give anything except his labour, and because, on the other hand, nothing can pass to the ownership of individuals except individual means of consumption. But, as far as the distribution of the latter among the individual producers is concerned, the same principle prevails as in the exchange of commodity equivalents: a given amount of labour in one form is exchanged for an equal amount of labour in another form.

Hence, *equal right* here is still in principle – *bourgeois right*, although principle and practice are no longer at loggerheads, while the exchange of equivalents in commodity exchange only exists *on the average* and not in the individual case.

In spite of this advance, this *equal right* is still constantly stigmatised by a bourgeois limitation. The right of the producers is *proportional* to the labour they supply; the equality consists in the fact that measurement is made with an *equal standard*, labour.

But one man is superior to another physically or mentally and so supplies more labour in the same time, or can labour for a longer time; and labour, to serve as a measure, must be defined by its duration or intensity, otherwise it ceases to be a standard of measurement. This *equal* right is an unequal right for unequal labour. It recognises no class differences, because everyone is only a worker like everyone else; but it tacitly recognises unequal individual endowment and thus productive capacity as natural privileges. *It is, therefore, a right of inequality, in its content, like every right*. Right by its very nature can consist only in the application of an equal standard; but unequal individuals (and they would not be different individuals if they were not unequal) are measurable only by an equal standard in so far as they are brought under an equal point of view, are taken from one *definite* side only, for instance, in the present case, are regarded *only as workers* and nothing more is seen in them, everything else being ignored. Further, one worker is married, another not; one has more children than another, and so on and so forth. Thus, with an equal performance of labour, and hence an equal share in the social consumption fund, one will in fact receive more than another, one will be richer than another, and so on. To avoid all these defects, right instead of being equal would have to be unequal.

But these defects are inevitable in the first phase of communist society as it is when it has just emerged after prolonged birth pangs from capitalist society. Right can never be higher than the economic structure of society and its cultural development conditioned thereby.

In a higher phase of communist society, after the enslaving subordination of the individual to the division of labour, and therewith also the antithesis between mental and physical labour, has vanished; after labour has become not only a means of life but life's prime want; after the productive forces have also increased with the all-round development of the individual, and all the springs of co-operative wealth flow more abundantly – only then can the narrow horizon of bourgeois right be crossed in its entirety and society inscribe on its banners: From each according to his ability, to each according to his needs!

Critique of the Gotha Programme (1875); *MESW* II 23f.

Further Reading

R. Adamiak, 'The "Withering Away" of the State: A Reconsideration', *Journal of Politics* (Feb, 1970).

S. Bloom, 'The "Withering Away" of the State', *Journal of the History of Ideas* (1946).

I. Fetscher, 'Marx, Engels and Future Society', *Survey* (1961).

A. Harris, 'Utopian Elements in Marx's Thought', *Ethics* (Jan 1950).

D. McLellan, 'Marx's View of the Unalienated Society', *Review of Politics* (1969).

H. Mayer, 'Marx on Bakunin: A Neglected Text', *Cahiers de l'ISEA* (1959).

J. Sanderson, *An Interpretation of the Political Ideas of Marx and Engels* (London, 1969) chap. 6.

Chronological Table

Date	Writings	Personal	Historical
1818		Birth of Marx	
1832			Great Reform Bill
1834			Zollverein in Germany
1835		Study at University of Bonn	
1836		Study at University of Berlin	
1837	*Letter to his Father*		Victoria's reign begins
1838	Begins doctoral thesis	Death of father	Rise of Chartism
1841	Ends doctoral thesis	Receives doctor's degree	
1842	Articles for *Rheinische Zeitung*	Editor of *Rheinische Zeitung*	
1843	*Critique of Hegel's Philosophy of Right* *On the Jewish Question*	Marries Jenny von Westphalen; moves to Paris	
1844	*Critique of Hegel's Philosophy of Right: Introduction* *Economic and Philosophic Manuscripts* *Critical Notes on 'The King of Prussia and Social Reform'* *The Holy Family*	Editor of *Deutsch-Französische Jahrbücher*; birth of Jenny	
1845	*Theses on Feuerbach*	Moves to Belgium; birth of Laura	
1846	*The German Ideology* *Letter to Annenkov*	Sets up Correspondence Committee; birth of Edgar	Repeal of Corn Laws
1847	*The Poverty of Philosophy*	Joins Communist League	
1848	*The Communist Manifesto*	Moves to Germany to edit *Neue Rheinische Zeitung*	Year of Revolutions; Californian Gold Rush

1849	*Wage-Labour and Capital*	Birth of Guido; settles in London	
1850	*Address of the Central Committee to the Communist League*	Death of Guido; moves to Dean Street	Ten Hours Act
	The Class Struggles in France		
1851– 62	Articles for *New York Daily Tribune*	Birth of Franziska and Frederick Demuth	Great Exhibition
1852	*The Eighteenth Brumaire of Louis Bonaparte*	Death of Franziska	Second Empire in France begins
1854		Birth of Eleanor; death of Edgar	Crimean War
1855		Moves to Grafton Terrace	
1856			
1857	*General Introduction*		Indian Mutiny
1858	*Outlines of a Critique of Political Economy (Grundrisse)*		
1859	*Preface to a Critique of Political Economy*		Darwin's *Origin of Species*, Mill's *On Liberty*
	Critique of Political Economy		
1860	*Herr Vogt*	Visit to Lassalle in Germany	Kingdom of Italy established
1861			Serfdom abolished in Russia
1862	*Theories of Surplus Value*		Bismarck Minister-President in Germany
1863		Death of mother	
1864	*Capital*, vol. II (until 1877)	Moves to Maitland Park Road	First International founded
	Capital, vol. III		
	Inaugural Address of First International		
1865	*Value, Price and Profit*		
1866			Austro–Prussian War

Continued

Date	Writings	Personal	Historical
1867	*Capital*, vol. I		Dominion of Canada established
1868			First Gladstone Ministry
1869		Engels moves to London	Social Democratic Party founded in Germany
1870	*Two Addresses on Franco–Prussian War*		Franco–Prussian War
1871	*The Civil War in France*		Paris Commune, German Empire
1875	*Critique of the Gotha Programme*		
1876	*Comments on Bakunin's Statism and Anarchy*		
1877			Russo–Turkish War
1879	*Circular Letter*		
1880			Gladstone's Second Ministry
1881	*Letter to Vera Sassoulitch*	Death of Jenny Marx	
1882	Preface to second Russian edition of *Communist Manifesto*		
1883		Death of Marx	Nietzsche's *Thus Spake Zarathustra*

Select General Bibliography

TEXTS

K. Marx, *Selected Essays*, ed. H. Stenning (London and New York, 1926, reprinted 1968).
A collection of seven essays from the early Marx, most of them minor.

K. Marx, F. Engels, *Selected Works* (Moscow, 1935, several reprints).
The 'classical' anthology. None of the early writings are included and less than half the material is by Marx. Nevertheless provides complete and faithful translations of many of Marx's works.

K. Marx, *Capital, The Communist Manifesto and Other Writings*, ed. M. Eastman (New York, 1932).
Concentrates on *Capital* to the complete exclusion of early writings.

K. Marx, F. Engels, *Basic Writings on Politics and Philosophy*, ed. L. Feuer (New York, 1959).
Concentrates on Marx's historical writings, with a useful selection of letters and essays at the end.

K. Marx, *Selected Writings in Sociology and Social Philosophy*, ed. T. Bottomore and M. Rubel (London, 1956).
In many ways the best anthology, drawing on all Marx's writings whether available in English or not.

K. Marx, *Early Writings*, ed. T. Bottomore (London, 1963).
Contains the essays in the *Deutsch-Französische Jahrbücher* and the complete text of the *Paris Manuscripts*.

Writings of the Young Marx on Philosophy and Society, ed. L. Easton and K. Guddat (New York, 1967).
A comprehensive collection of Marx's writings from 1841 to 1847. Contains extracts from *The Holy Family* and *The German Ideology*.

The Essential Writings of Karl Marx, ed. D. Caute (London and New York, 1967).
Small excerpts with emphasis on the philosophical and revolutionary aspects of Marx.

Marxist Social Thought, ed. R. Freedman (New York, 1968).
Fairly comprehensive on the sociological aspects of Marx's later works. Little reference to economics or to Marx's early writings.

K. Marx, *The Early Texts*, ed. D. McLellan (Oxford, 1971).
A comprehensive selection of writings up to and including 1844, with letters.
The Portable Marx, ed. E. Kamenka (New York, 1971).
A selection containing longer extracts and some newly translated material.

COMMENTARIES

H. Acton, *The Illusion of the Epoch* (London, 1955).
A critique of Marxism–Leninism as a philosophical creed.
H. Acton, *What Marx Really Said* (London, 1967).
A useful short discussion of Marx's work focusing on historical materialism.
H. Adams, *Karl Marx in his Earlier Writings*, 2nd ed. (London, 1965).
The first examination in English of Marx's early writings up to the *Holy Family*. Slightly dated.
L. Althusser, *For Marx* (London, 1970).
A controversial interpretation of . Marx using structuralist and Freudian concepts. Supports the idea of a radical break between the young and the old Marx.
L. Althusser, *On Reading Capital* (London, 1970).
An attempt to analyse *Capital* in a scientific manner and give an account of the philosophy underlying it.
S. Avineri, *The Social and Political Thought of Karl Marx* (Cambridge, 1968).
An important and interesting book which emphasises the continuity of Marx's thought from its earliest formulations and the influence of Hegel.
S. Avineri (ed.), *Marx's Socialism* (New York, 1971).
A useful series of articles on controversial aspects of Marx's ideas.
I. Berlin, *Karl Marx*, 3rd ed. (London, 1963).
A very readable short biography of Marx.
S. Bloom, *The World of Nations*, 2nd ed. (New York, 1967).
An exposition of Marx's views on the position of nation states in the contemporary world and his attitude to the various nation states of his time.
W. Blumenberg, *Karl Marx* (London, 1972).
An admirable short biography mainly using Marx's own words.
M. Bober, *Karl Marx's Interpretation of History*, 2nd ed. (New York, 1965).
The oldest and fullest discussion of 'historical materialism' in English.

T. Bottomore (ed.), *Karl Marx* (New York, 1971).
A collection of commentaries on Marx, with an introduction, in the 'Makers of Modern Social Science' series.

T. Bottomore, *The Sociological Theory of Marxism* (London 1972).
Contains an analysis of Marx's theories on classes, the state, revolution, etc.

E. Carr, *Karl Marx: A Study in Fanaticism* (London, 1934).
A well-written critical biography of medium length.

H. Collins and C. Abramsky, *Karl Marx and the British Labour Movement* (London, 1965).
A very well-documented study of the role of Marx in the First International with special reference to Britain.

B. Delfgaauw, *The Young Marx* (London, 1967).
A short account of the ideas of the young Marx and their relevance today.

R. Dunayevskaya, *Marxism and Freedom* (New York, 1958).
Contains sections on the philosophical aspects of the *1844 Manuscripts* and *Capital*.

L. Dupré, *The Philosophical Foundations of Marxism* (New York, 1966).
A straightforward discussion of the development of Marx's thought up to the *Communist Manifesto*, with some preliminary chapters on Hegel.

I. Fetscher, *Marx and Marxism* (New York, 1971).
Contains articles on the continuity in Marx's thought, bureaucracy, future communist society, etc.

E. Fischer, *Marx in his Own Words* (London, 1970).
A slight, but faithful, run-through of Marx's main ideas.

E. Fromm, *Marx's Concept of Man* (New York, 1961).
Contains portions of the translation of the *Paris Manuscripts* by Bottomore with an introduction which emphasises the humanist, and even spiritualist, elements in Marx.

A. Gamble and P. Walton, *From Alienation to Surplus Value* (London, 1972).
Concentrates on labour and surplus value as unifying themes in Marx's thought.

R. Garaudy, *Karl Marx: The Evolution of his Thought* (London, 1967).
A reliable and readable account by (at the time of writing) an orthodox Communist.

A. James Gregor, *A Survey of Marxism* (New York, 1967).
The first few chapters discuss the philosophical aspects of Marx.

S. Hook, *Towards the Understanding of Karl Marx* (New York, 1933).
Still a good introduction to the more systematic parts of Marx's thought.

S. Hook, *From Hegel to Marx*, 2nd ed. (Ann Arbor, 1962).

A study of the relationship of Marx to Hegel and the Young Hegelians.

Z. Jordan, *The Evolution of Dialectical Materialism* (London, 1967).
The early chapters contain an account of naturalism and materialism in Marx.

E. Kamenka, *The Ethical Foundations of Marxism* (London, 1962).
A description and critique of Marx's ethics from an analytical philosophical position.

E. Kamenka, *Marxist Ethics* (London, 1969).
A brief analysis of the Marxian ethical tradition.

E. Kamenka, *Marx* (London, 1971).
Examines the main philosophical themes in Marx's thought.

G. Lichtheim, *Marxism: A Historical and Critical Study* (London, 1961).
An excellent study of the development of Marxist doctrines from their origins up to 1917.

G. Lichtheim, *From Marx to Hegel* (New York, 1971).
Contains a series of essays on the Hegelian-Marxist tradition up to the present day.

K. Löwith, *From Hegel to Nietzsche* (London, 1967).
A wide-ranging account of nineteenth-century German philosophy: Marx is considered – among many others – in the Hegelian tradition.

D. McLellan, *The Young Hegelians and Karl Marx* (London, 1969).
An examination of the social and political thought of the Young Hegelians and its influence on the genesis of Marx's thought.

D. McLellan, *Marx before Marxism* (New York, 1970).
A detailed account of the development of Marx's thought up to and including the writing of the *Paris Manuscripts*.

D. McLellan, *Marx's Grundrisse* (New York, 1971).
A translation of excerpts with an introduction emphasising the importance of the *Grundrisse* in Marx's thought as a whole.

J. Maguire, *Marx's Paris Writings: An Analysis* (Dublin, 1972).
A well-informed and thorough commentary on the *Paris Manuscripts*.

E. Mandel, *The Genesis of Marx's Economic Thought* (New York, 1971).
An excellent analysis of the development of Marx's economic thought up to and including the *Grundrisse*.

F. Mehring, *Karl Marx* (London, 1934).
The classical biography of Marx; somewhat out-of-date and slightly hagiographical.

I. Maszaros, *Marx's Theory of Alienation* (London, 1970).
Obscurely written and awkwardly constructed, but pulls together research in a useful overview.

B. Ollman, *Alienation: Marx's Critique of Man in Capitalist Society* (Cambridge, 1971).
An original and well-documented study of alienation in Marx, paying

close attention to the way Marx uses his concepts.

R. Payne, *Marx: A Biography* (London, 1968).
A lot of information on Marx's private life, though the author's understanding of Marx's ideas is extremely deficient.

J. Plamenatz, *German Marxism and Russian Communism* (London, 1954).
Contains one of the 'classical' discussions of historical materialism as outlined in Marx's *Preface*.

J. Plamenatz, *Man and Society*, vol. II (London, 1963).
A clear, critical analysis of the main social and political themes in Marx.

J. Sanderson, *An Interpretation of the Political Ideas of Marx and Engels* (London, 1969).
A short book which aims to pull together the main texts of Marx and Engels on historical materialism, the state, revolution and the future communist society.

A. Schmidt, *The Concept of Nature in Marx* (London, 1971).
An important and well-documented consideration of the nature of Marx's materialism.

R. Tucker, *Philosophy and Myth in Karl Marx* (Cambridge, 1961).
A highly original – though in places also highly dubious – interpretation of Marx's thought as a continuity based on certain eschatological assumptions.

R. Tucker, *The Marxian Revolutionary Idea* (London, 1970).
A series of essays dealing with the state and revolution in Marx.

D. Turner, *On the Philosophy of Marx* (Dublin, 1968).
A slight book, written mainly for philosophers.

V. Venable, *Human Nature: The Marxian View* (London, 1946).
One of the best statements of the Marxist view of man.

B. Wolfe, *Marxism: 100 Years in the Life of a Doctrine* (London, 1967).
A study of the evolution of Marxist doctrines with sections on Marx's political ideas in 1848 and 1871.

I. Zeitlin, *Marxism: A Re-examination* (New York, 1967).
A short book which minimises the Hegelian element in Marx and presents in a favourable light the sociological elements in Marx's thought.

Index

235